The Library of Liberal Arts

OSKAR PIEST, *General Editor*

[NUMBER EIGHTY-TWO]

BOCCACCIO ON POETRY

BOCCACCIO ON POETRY

Being the Preface and the Fourteenth and Fifteenth
Books of Boccaccio's *Genealogia Deorum Gentilium*
in an English Version with Introductory Essay
and Commentary

BY

CHARLES G. OSGOOD

THE LIBERAL ARTS PRESS

NEW YORK

Published at 153 West 72nd Street, New York 23, N. Y.

Printed in the United States of America

PREFATORY NOTE TO THE SECOND EDITION

At eighty-five a man has no more right to tamper with the work of his fifties than with the work of another man. Indeed, this book was the work of another man, younger by a generation than I, and, among all my issue of lesser years, my favorite. I may, therefore, be allowed happy satisfaction that its life is being prolonged by this new edition. And I am content that it should survive without correction or change.

CHARLES G. OSGOOD

Princeton, September 15, 1956

PREFACE

I have undertaken in these pages to make more accessible and, I hope, more intelligible the Fourteenth and Fifteenth Books of Boccaccio's *Genealogia Deorum Gentilium*. They have been so often described in histories of literature and related works, that one need not again assert their importance in the history of humanism. But no one has yet fully measured their strong determinant influence upon the poetry, criticism, and scholarship of later times.

Partly for the historic worth of these books, partly because the ideas which they contain may not be wholly unsalutary in this latter day, and partly because they lead to intimacy with that very engaging person, the author, this version has seemed worth the making. It had its origin more than twenty years ago in a suggestion of the late Professor Cook.

The translation is based upon Hecker's text as published in his *Boccaccio-Funde,* Brunswick, 1902, from an autograph which embodies Boccaccio's latest known revisions of his text.[1] The so-called Vulgate text, which is the text of all other manuscripts and editions, is earlier. The significant differences, however, are not many nor great.

I have not attempted a closely literal rendering. It has often been necessary to disregard the limits of Boccaccio's sentences, or to resort to something like paraphrase, in order to convey more of the meaning as well as the quality of the original.

I am happy to express my thanks for most useful criticism to my friends, Dean Frederick M. Padelford, Professor David Magie, and Professor Charles S. Baldwin. Dean Padelford read the Introduction with care, Professor Magie reviewed many details of my rendering, and Professor Baldwin gave expert advice on the parts dealing with rhetoric.

If material in the Introduction and Notes sometimes seems obvious to more seasoned scholars, I can only repeat Boccaccio's excuse on page 136, and add my wish that the book may be a useful means of orientation to younger students. It will realize an even happier end, if it should impart to anyone the irresistible enthusiasm for the Ancients of this charming Florentine. In any event, as he himself says: " Si minus bene dixero, saltem ad melius dicendum prudentiorem alterum excitabo."

Princeton, December 28, 1929.

---

[1] Hecker, pp. 107, 134.

LIST OF ABBREVIATED TITLES MORE OFTEN CITED IN INTRODUCTION AND NOTES

Am. Vis.   Boccaccio, *Amorosa Visione* in *Opere Volgare,* ed. Moutier, Florence, 1833, vol. 14.

C.D.   Augustine, *De Civitate Dei* in Migne, *Patrologia Latina,* vol. 41.

Com.   Boccaccio, *Il Comento di Giovanni Boccaccio sopra la Commedia,* ed. D. Guerri, Bari, 1918. Cited by Lezione, volume, and page of Boccaccio, *Opere Volgari* in *Scrittori d'Italia* 84-6.

De Cas.   Boccaccio, *De Casibus Virorum Illustrium.* Consulted in Betussi's Italian version, Venice, 1545; Florence, 1596, 1598.

De Mont.   Boccaccio, *De Montibus, Sylvis, Fontibus, Lacubus, Fluminibus . . . Liber.* in vol. with *De Genealogia Deorum,* Basel, 1532, pp. 402-504.

De Rem.   Petrarch, *De Remediis utriusque Fortunae* in the Basel ed., 1581, of Petrarch's *Works,* pp. 1-222.

De Vit. Sol.   Petrarch, *De Vita Solitaria,* in Basel ed., pp. 226-92.

D.I.   Lactantius, *Divinae Institutiones,* in Migne, *Patrologia Latina,* vol. 6.

Etym.   Isidore of Seville, *Etymologiae,* in Migne, *Patrologia Latina,* vol. 82.

Fam.   Petrarch, *Lettere di Francesco Petrarca delle Cose Familiari* (*Litterae de Rebus Familiaribus*) in 24 Books, ed. G. Fracassetti, Florence, 1863. Cited by Book, number, volume, page.

Hauvette   Hauvette, H., *Boccace: Etude Biographique et Litteraire,* Paris, 1914.

Hecker	Hecker, O., *Boccaccio-Funde,* Brunswick, 1902.
Hortis	Hortis, A., *Studi sulle Opere Latine del Boccaccio.* Trieste, 1879.
Inv.	Petrarch, *Invectivae contra Medicum,* in Basel ed., 1581, of Petrarch's *Works,* pp. 1087-1117. Cited by Book and page.
Lett.	Boccaccio, *Le Lettere Edite e Inedite di Messer Giovanni Boccaccio,* ed. F. Corazzini, Florence, 1877.
Life	Boccaccio, *Vita di Dante,* ed. D. Guerri, Bari, 1918. Cited by section, volume, and page of Boccaccio, *Opere Volgari* in *Scrittori d'Italia,* 84.
Robinson and Rolfe	Robinson, J. H., and Rolfe, H. W., *Petrarch the First Modern Scholar,* etc., New York and London, 1899.
Schöningh	Schöningh, D., *Die Göttergenealogien des Boccaccio,* Posen, 1900.
S.D., S.H., etc.	Vincent of Beauvais, *Speculum Doctrinale, Speculum Historiale, Speculum Morale.*
Sen.	Petrarch, *Lettere Senile (Litterae Seniles)* in 17 Books, ed. in 2 vols. by G. Fracassetti, Florence, 1869. Cited by Book, number, volume, page.
Var.	Petrarch, *Lettere Varie (Litterae Variae)* in one Book, in vol. 5 of *Lettere,* ed. Fracassetti.
Zenatti	Zenatti, O., *Dante e Firenze,* Florence, 1902, containing on pp. 206-237 an abridged modern Italian version of Books 14 and 15, with many notes.

CONTENTS

[ix]

CONTENTS

INTRODUCTION

IF AT this moment Boccaccio were to inquire concerning his reputation, he would no doubt be disappointed. Fame is his, in measure such as he craved, but not in kind. To be generally famous as the author of the *Decameron,* a mere teller of tales, a "vulgar" poet, a novelist, when he had dreamed of so different a reputation, would seem to him the very irony of fame. One hears him protest: "It is my peculiar boast and glory—meum est hoc decus, mea est gloria—to cultivate Greek Poetry among the Tuscans." Clearly it was his passionate hope to survive as the scholar-humanist, rather than as the literary artist.

There are, then, two Boccaccios—poet and scholar—one famous, the other obscure. It is easy to dwell upon an imagined antinomy between poet and scholar, but in Boccaccio at least, if not in general, such antinomy is quite fictitious. One cannot remind oneself too often that Boccaccio's scholarship and his art were but projections of the same powers of his mind, and that his humanistic Latin prose works come unmistakably from the hand of a poet. To conceive them otherwise is to miss their meaning. The author of the *Decameron* and of the *Genealogy of the Gods* is one and the same man, employing in these achievements the same energies and enthusiasms.

The *Genealogy* is a huge encyclopaedic repository of classical mythology in fifteen books. Both in form and in plan it is a book of its times. It embodies the Aristotelian-Catholic idea of the cycle of learning, with pagan precedents such as the works of Pliny and Varro. More contracted times required more contracted epitomes; Augustine's *De Ordine,* Isidore's *Etymologiae,* Rabanus' *De*

Universo, and many others, offered a whole conspectus of learning in small compass. As learning revived such works expanded. The twelfth century produces the *Metalogicus* and *Policraticus* of John of Salisbury, to be followed in time by the stupendous achievements of Albertus, Aquinas, and the four vast *specula* of Vincent of Beauvais and his imitator.

Boccaccio designed his book as a speculum of ancient myth. The design was exquisitely appropriate. It is easy for us to forget that a cultivated man of his time could learn from his reading of Latin classics almost as much about classic myth as most of us know today. Vergil, Ovid, Horace, Statius, Seneca, Claudian, such commentators as Servius on Vergil and Lactantius on Statius, Cicero on the Nature of the Gods, Pliny, the Fathers, Apuleius, Macrobius, Fulgentius, Boethius—all these authors were accessible, and contain most of the legends of mythology; but accessible as these writers were to the student, the tales were too scattered and confused for general knowledge and use. Boccaccio makes the first attempt on a large scale to assemble, arrange, incorporate, and explain the vast accumulation of legend, and reduce it, after the manner of his times, to convenient encyclopaedic form.[1]

It was the work of a generous and patriotic poet. Warm enthusiasms and deep convictions quicken it throughout. Whether or no Boccaccio undertook the project at the request of King Hugo, as he avers in his Preface, his labor was never perfunctory. From the age of thirty or thereabouts to the end of his life he had the task by him. His endeavors were doubtless interrupted for long periods, or slackened under the very weight of the labor. But he was clearly in love with the work, and even when not closely engaged upon it, was ever alert for material, whether in

---

[1] For earlier projects of the sort by Barlaam, Paul of Perugia, and Theodontius, see 15.6 and nn.

his reading, in chat with scholar, or traveller, or connoisseur, or in observation of ruins and localities as he journeyed about. Even near the end of his life he was loth to part with it as a finished work. Revision and additions kept on. He writes to Pietro di Monteforte in high indignation that a friend, Count Hugo of San Severino, to whom he had lent the work not yet ready for publication, should have allowed it to be copied.[2]

[2] It is impossible to say when Boccaccio began the book. During his first years in Naples, in his twenties, he was deeply interested in the subject, as appears by his works then composed, and by his references to Paolo Perugino at 15.6. Some time between 1340 and 1350 he actually set to work. In 1371 he wrote his indignant letter blaming the borrower for allowing the unfinished book to be copied. Thus he had the task by him for about thirty years. There is some reason to think that Donino first saw Boccaccio and discussed the proposed study with him at Forlì or Naples late in 1347 (Pref., p. 3; Hauvette, p. 419). In 1350 Bechino Bellincioni met Boccaccio at Ravenna (15.13), and roused to new efforts his flagging industry. The work is dedicated and. throughout addressed to King Hugo of Cyprus, who abdicated November 24, 1358, and died in 1359, and Boccaccio makes nowhere any allusion to his death or abdication. But the text contains various citations of Leontius and Homer which could not have been made before 1360 (see 15.7 n. 10). Books 1-13, then, may have been set down in a first version by 1360 or soon after, and this version may also have contained the germ of Boccaccio's apology for poetry and for himself. A revision of the whole, and the development of Books 14 and 15 may have taken place at Certaldo after Boccaccio's return from Naples and Venice in 1363. These are Hauvette's conjectures on the basis of a careful examination of the revisions in the autograph. They are, however, but conjectures. The two books contain certain passages later than 1363. In 14.10 and 15.6 the allusions to Petrarch's *De Remediis* make at least these passages as late as 1366, and by that time Boccaccio must have heard of Hugo's death. Why does he continue to speak to, and of, him as if he were still alive? Hauvette thinks it quite uncharacteristic of him to have done so for the sake of mere aesthetic unity; but I cannot escape the impression that the proud tone of the latter half of 15.13 would not be what it is if Hugo were thought of as still alive. As the fact of dedication to Hugo was closely inwoven with the texture of his work throughout, Boccaccio seems resolved to sustain it to the end—even to the point of protesting its genuineness a little too much to be convincing. He may have intended to add some obituary reference to Hugo, and the unfulfilled

His love for the work no doubt grew in part out of his delight in the very material which he was handling. But in part it derived from his purpose in having assumed so oppressive a task. This purpose was definite and serious if not wholly single. In the Preface to his geographical dictionary, *De Montibus,* etc., he says that he has prepared this book especially for students of poetry and history, particularly of the works of pagan writers, to help in explaining geographical allusions. He must have been well aware that very similar would be one of the commonest uses of the *Genealogy of the Gods.*

But the book must prove useful to poets as well as to readers of poetry. Boccaccio, true to his critical tradition, insists upon learning as indispensable to the poet, and he was quite aware that he was making material of first importance available for future poets.[3] At any rate for two or three subsequent centuries the book dispensed much of the material for poetic adornment most in fashion in the Renaissance. Many a poet and man of letters in cultivated Europe saved himself a deal of trouble by Boccaccio's very readable encyclopaedia, and incidentally achieved renown for wide reading of the Ancients which he did not wholly deserve.[4] Altogether Boccaccio very likely conceived all his

intention may have increased his annoyance when the copy escaped in 1371. Hecker's attempt to date a passage in 15.6 (see n.15) in 1371 appears untenable (p. 274, n.4), and his dating of the latest revision in 1373 is unconvincing.

[3] Such was, in part, Milton's purpose in compiling his *History of Britain*: "I have therefore determined to bestow the telling over even of these reputed tales; be it for nothing else but in favor of our English poets and rhetoricians, who by their art will know how to use them judiciously" (Book I, near beginning, *Prose Works* ed. Bohn, 5.165). See also Shelley, p. 157.

[4] Other books of the sort were compiled to meet the demand, notably Giraldi's *De Deis Gentium . . . Historia,* 1548; and Conti's (Natalis Comes) *Mythologiae . . . Libri X,* 1551. See Frank L. Schoell, *Les Mythologistes Italiens de la Renaissance et la Poésie Elisabéthaine,* in *Revue de Litt. Comp.,* 1924, 1-25, esp. pp. 4, 5. On the continued popularity of the *Genealogy* see pp. xliv-xlvi.

humanistic works—*De Claris Mulieribus, De Casibus Virorum Illustrium,* the *Genealogy, De Montibus, etc.,* as constituting an encyclopaedic set of works useful to poets and students, and therefore an agent for the increase of poetry. Of these the *Genealogy* was the greatest.

But another intention—possibly more occasional, though none the less sincere—informs the book. This is the justification and defence of ancient classical literature. It is this purpose of the author which particularly concerns us, since it involves his convictions on the very nature of poetry itself.

It was not enough merely to rehearse the ancient myths, nor to arrange them genealogically in as articulate a system as the discrepant accounts would permit. As mere tales, however ingenious or strange, they have no lasting claim on our attention, no power or right to survive. But the poetic literature of the Ancients is charged with immutable truth that deserves, nay, insures immortality; and Boccaccio undertakes to discover this truth by the aid of many commentators and authorities, ancient and modern, at his disposal. Where they fail to inform or satisfy him, he relies upon his own poetic insight. Thus he reveals the glory and vitality of ancient poetry.

These various intentions Boccaccio summarizes in declaring the "usefulness, both public and private" in which the book's chief value lies: "Some men have thought that the learned poet merely invents shallow tales, and is therefore not only useless, but a positive harm. This is because they read discursively and, of course, derive no profit from the story. Now this work of mine removes the veil from these inventions, shows that poets were really men of wisdom, and renders their compositions full of profit and pleasure to the reader. So if poets who seemed to have perished from want of appreciation are now brought back to life, as it were, and to a high place in the state, while their usefulness to the individual, which was ignored because it was unrecognized, is now revealed by this work of mine, they thus rouse the reader's mind to higher feelings. Furthermore, I hope that men will rise up as they have done in the past who will devote themselves to the study of poetry. As they peruse the memorials and remains of the Ancients, they cannot fail to derive much help from this work of mine, which will prove valuable to them if not to others." [5]

Boccaccio speaks, then, at once as poet, critic, and scholar. Nor does he from time to time exchange one function for another, but all three powers of his mind are coactive throughout his discussion, if indeed they are not really one and single.

To enter into his ideas it is necessary always to bear in mind the basic equation that to him the highest poetry was ancient poetry, the poetry of Rome and Greece, and that the essential matter of ancient poetry was myth. Thus he regards poetry, classical antiquity, and mythology, as pretty much one and the same thing, a deep and abounding source of civilization and spiritual energy; and his task is to defend, explain, and revive this regenerating power. The obvious approach, then, to Boccaccio's defence of poetry and the classics in the two books here rendered is by way of his treatment of his material, that is, poetic fable, in the preceding thirteen.

It is easy for modern critical scholarship, from its impregnable if sometimes cheerless heights, to patronize Boccaccio's way of proceeding; [6] but such complaisance stands in its own light, and estops its perception of his real values. At all events his methods were the methods of his

---

[5] 15.1; cf. 3, Pr.: "I would show that the ancient poets, though wanting an orthodox idea of God, were highly illustrious men, and, for their wonderful skill, well worthy of reverence."

[6] For example, Voigt, *Wiederbelebung des Class. Alt.* 3rd ed., 1.169.

day—or a little better—which is perhaps the most that can be said of any methods. Nor do they want power of edification at any time, even for scholars and professional critics. His interpretations of the myths are essentially allegorical, of course, but even so are instructive, at least in exhibiting all the varieties and resources of mediaeval theory and practice in the use of ancient fable.

The allegorical interpretation of Greek myth is, to be sure, almost as ancient as any record of a given myth itself. Already evident in Homer and Aeschylus, it flourishes in Plato, is a favorite practice of Stoics and neo-Platonists, and a poetic resource of Vergil, Ovid, and others of highest importance to Boccaccio's criticism.[7] Such interpretation is prone to extravagance, especially in the later writers whom he employed, both pagan and Christian—Apuleius, Macrobius, Augustine, Lactantius, Martianus, Cassiodorus, and Fulgentius, a writer at times too fanciful, recondite, and unreliable even for Boccaccio.[8]

To Boccaccio every myth is alive, quick to stir anew a poetic imagination as it had often done before. "One must bear in mind," he says, "that these myths contain more than one single meaning. They may indeed be called 'polyseme,'[9] that is, of multifold sense."

Three traditional systems or schemes of interpretation Boccaccio either describes or at least has in mind. In reality they amount perhaps but to different arrangements of the same ideas; and if Boccaccio, in his artistic freedom, adheres rigorously and consistently to no one of them, his interpretations may all find their places somewhere in these

[7] Schöningh, p. 14.

[8] He is prolix and inept at 4.24; incorrect at 4.30; 10.10, end; 11.7 (where Boccaccio omits Fulgentius' explanation, "as he goes soaring off into the sublime"); 13.58. For his debt to contemporary or very recent poets and scholars, see 15.6 and nn.

[9] 1.3. He caught the word from Servius, on *Aen.* 1.1, or Dante, To Can Grande, *Ep.* 10.7.

schemes. Furthermore, as they embody the mediaeval conclusions on the subject of classic myth, they will bear rehearsing.

1. He proceeds to set forth the familiar fourfold mediaeval system of interpretation:[10] "The first meaning is the superficial, which is called literal. The others are deeper, and are called allegorical. To make the matter easier, I will give an example. According to the poetic fiction, Perseus, son of Jupiter, killed the Gorgon, and flew away victorious into the air. Now, this may be understood superficially in its literal or historical sense. In the moral sense it shows a wise man's triumph over vice and his attainment of virtue. Allegorically it figures the pious man who scorns worldly delight and lifts his mind to heavenly things. It admits also an anagogical sense, since it symbolizes Christ's victory over the Prince of this World, and his Ascension. But all these secondary meanings, by whatever name, are essentially allegorical. For 'allegory' is from ἄλλο, Latin *alienum,* and is so called being alien from the literal or historical sense. But it is not my intention to unfold all these meanings for each myth when I find one quite enough."[11] In fact he very rarely employs this fourfold system.[12] Such rigor would heavily impede his freedom and pleasure in studying the old poets. His favorite interpretations, therefore, are "moral," and in the narrower sense "allegorical."

2. Boccaccio recognizes also a second system, though in effect it agrees with the fourfold method just described. Augustine quotes Varro as distinguishing three aspects of ancient religion or theology—the mythical; the physical; the civil: that is, the mythology of the poets, the mythology

[10] cf., among others, the fine exposition of it in Dante, *Convivio* 2.1.
[11] 1.3.
[12] Minerva, 2.3; Briareus, 4.18; Prometheus, 4.44 (see below, pp. xxivff.) ; Cupid and Psyche, 4.22, are rare instances of anagogy. See 15.8.

of the philosophers, and the mythology of popular worship and superstition.[13] To the second, or the mythology of the philosophers, Boccaccio would assign all myths embodying the facts of physical nature or moral truth, whether treated by philosophers or poets, that is, all myths or myth-handling at all edifying and worthy of a place in his treatise.

3. A more explicit arrangement, which perhaps amounts to the same thing as Varro's, but which proves of greatest use in understanding the poet's use of Greek myth in any age, is described by Augustine in the *City of God* 18.14.[14] The gods are after all in reality (a) eminent men deified by legend; or (b) they are deified forces of nature and human life, "elements of this world which the true God made;" or (c) they are "creatures who were ordained as principalities and powers according to the will of the Creator," that is, the angels, both good, and fallen.

Boccaccio's actual practice derives from these three theories of interpretation. A given legend, then, may be

(a) only the result of history glorified by the poets in honor of a great or ambitious man. Such is its literal or historical sense, Varro's mythical "theology," or, more technically, euhemeristic myth. Or

(b) the story in a competent poet's hands may express allegorically the mysterious forces of nature, or of human life—the moral use, or "allegorical" in the narrower sense, corresponding to the physical theology of Varro. Or

(c) the story may conform to Christian truth, or adumbrate it in anagogical fashion. The gods may really be but the angels and emissaries of God imperfectly understood without revelation, and even some myths gropingly shadow forth the Christian mysteries. Obviously the Platonic tradition lies behind this view.

A passage from the first chapter of the Eleventh Book

[13] Pref., p. 6; 15.8 and n.   [14] See below 14.8 and n. 12.

will perhaps furnish the best and briefest exhibition of Boccaccio's procedure. On the authority of Cicero he has distinguished three Joves, of which Jove III is the great Jove, he of Crete. He then assembles the details of the legend, chiefly on the authority of Lactantius and the authors cited by Lactantius. Vergil, Pliny, Eusebius, Servius, and Petrarch all contribute something. "You see then, O illustrious King, how the man [Jove III] went to work to win long-lived fame, empty glory, and divinity for himself—with what ingenuity and luck, and what help from the wiles of our Old Enemy [Satan]." And erring mortals are prone enough to such perversion; there, for example, are those poor Lystrians in the Bible, who euhemeristically took Barnabas for Jove and Paul for Mercury.

So much for the literal, historical, euhemeristic import of the legend.

But once they had transformed this superman, Jove III, into Jupiter of Olympus, the poet-theologians confused him with the true God, since Jupiter had long been a name for God, and Olympus a name for Heaven. Hence they naturally alleged that he was father of gods and king of Heaven. Thus the popular conception of God became corrupted with the legends of adulteries, betrayals, and iniquities of historic superman. "But the really enlightened men of that time, as often as they were aware of the true God, instead of this Jove, though they inaccurately use the name Jove, actually mean the natural process or operation of the forces of nature (*naturae naturatae*), which is, of course, the work of God."

The wiser of them did not accept polytheism, but "regarded those divine powers attributed to various gods merely as agencies of the one true God, considering that God, like mortals, acts through agents. All this Apuleius shows very clearly in his book *De Dogmate Platonis*.[15] But

---

[15] The theory of Apuleius is set forth also by Augustine in *C.D.* 9.23

we believe more truly as does the Psalmist who says: 'God spake and it was done' (33; Vulg. 32.9). *Yet we do not deny that God employs ministers, some of justice, such as demons, some of grace as angels, some of opportunities and vicissitudes, as the celestial bodies."*

This last interpretation, though Boccaccio makes little use of it, may detain us for a moment.[16] Its final clause identifies the gods of mythology with planetary influences, and points the alliance between the old paganism and astrology, which, though repudiated by earlier Christians, was accepted by Dante, Boccaccio, and their times.[17] But the astrological use of this theory mingles with the finer conception that the gods were actually the spiritual ministers of the true God—"some of justice, such as demons, some of grace, as angels"—but imperfectly apprehended by the Ancients as gods, for want of divine revelation. Thus to conceive the old mythology, not as mere make-believe, but as describing, however dimly, the operations of the Celestial Hierarchy, gives it dignity, reality, and a certain perennial truth. Dante seems naturally to have preferred this finer conception, and it may well account for the lively energy which fills all his use of classic myth in the *Divine Comedy.*[18]

(cf. 7.28) with Scriptural authority, and with some measure of approval.

[16] See below, p. 65.

[17] See Theodore Wedel, *The Mediaeval Attitude toward Astrology,* Yale Studies in English LX. Professor Wedel finds the pagan origins of astrological theory in Aristotle (cf. *Meteores* 1.2; *De Gen. et Corr.* 2.10). All transformations of things perishable may be traced to the motion of imperishable things, i.e., the fixed stars, and these derive their motion from the Prime Mover, God. The two texts were accessible through twelfth century versions from the Arabic. The Stoics had carried on the tradition; cf. Cicero, *De Divinatione.*

[18] Dr. Edward Moore, *Studies in Dante* 1.163-4, ascribes its origin in Dante's mind to Augustine, *C.D.* 7.28; but the *De Deo Socratis* of Apuleius, or the *De Dogmate Platonis* are more explicit, and were accessible to Dante. The stock Scriptural authority is Ps. 146.4,5

Then, there is the reverse aspect or corollary—"some of justice, such as demons." It is usually expounded and elaborated as a distinct theory—that the gods are but the fallen angels in disguise, ranging through the world to the undoing of mankind and the upbuilding of their Lord Lucifer's infernal kingdom. Especially did they practice deceit through the oracles;[19] and since the oracles have ceased, these fallen angels continue to pervert man through his lusts and passions. The early Christian apologists, in their attack on paganism, swung this interpretation of pagan myth with deadly effect.[20] Though Boccaccio mentions it, he naturally finds it not well suited to his purpose.[21]

These, then, are the various ancient and mediaeval theories concerning mythology, and Boccaccio resorts to them with the purpose of saving this precious lore to posterity;[22] for is it not poetry, and therefore essentially true? Does it not contain historical truth, truth concerning the physical universe, astrological truth, moral truth, nay, religious and theological truth? It is his office, therefore, as poet-scholar-critic, to discern and reveal this truth.[23]

One is tempted in passing to observe a paradoxical contrast between the mediaeval treatment of mythology and

(Vulg.) : "Qui numerat multitudinem stellarum, et omnibus eis nomina vocat. Magnus Dominus noster; et magna virtus ejus; et sapientiae ejus non est numerus."

[19] The theory leaned heavily upon the interpretation of δαίμων as "demon" instead of "divinity," and upon such texts as I Cor. 10.19,20; Ps. 96.5 (Vulg. 95) : "Quoniam omnes dii gentium demonia." Boccaccio quotes this text at *Com.* 2,12.141.

[20] See Tertullian, *Apol.* 22; 25-7; *Ad Nat.* 2; Augustine, *C.D.* 8.24; Lactantius, *D.I.* 1.8-15; 4.27; Minucius Felix, *Octavius* 26; Arnobius, *Adv. Gent.* 1.23; Commodian, *Adv. Gent. Deos* 16; etc. Milton makes gorgeous use of it in his *Nativity Ode,* and in *Par. Lost* 1.356-521; *Par. Reg.* 2.174-191.

[21] See below, p. 128. He refers to it at 4.20; 6.6; 9, Proem; 11.1.

[22] See O. Gruppe, *Geschichte der klass. Mythologie . . . wahrend des Mittelalters, etc.,* suppl. to Roscher's *Ausführliches Lexikon.*

[23] See Hortis, pp. 211ff. for a review of mediaeval spokesmen for the classics before Boccaccio.

[xxii]

that of the Renaissance. The Middle Ages, with what one scholar calls their "encyclopaedic grasp of the Universe,"[24] found a significant place for mythology, as for all else, in their scheme of things. They assume a reality in the old myths, an essential truth variously reflected, but truth and reality nevertheless. The Renaissance, with its advance in classical scholarship, knew more and more about mythology, but took it less seriously. With increase of knowledge the conviction of reality declines, at least in artistic use, and the old myths tend to become mere playthings, material of applied ornament and superficial decoration. Such they are in all but the greatest poetry of the Renaissance, and at times even there.

Of the various interpretations which Boccaccio describes, he employs far oftenest the euhemeristic, the naturalistic, and the moral, and of these, perhaps the last two.[25] His

[24] G. L. Kittredge, *Chaucer and his Poetry*, p. 7.

[25] All three are popularly exploited by Carlyle, Ruskin, Hawthorne, and other moderns; and one or other underlies more or less consciously most modern verse on mythological subjects. In his *Life of Dante* 21,12.37-8, Boccaccio traces the evolution of the various theories. The earliest origin of myth was a sense of the true God stirred by wonder at the forces of Nature; this wonder inspired liturgy, then poetry. Then, as the effects of the various planets and elements were manifest, each tended to become a god; hence, polytheism. Further corruption is the work of supermen who planted and fostered the legend of the deity of their houses with the help of poets. "Yet if we would but reasonably consider the matter with all our wits, I think we could easily see that the ancient poets have really followed, as far as is possible for the human mind, in the steps of the Holy Spirit, who as we see in Holy Writ, revealed to future generations his deepest secrets through many mouths, causing them to speak in veiled language what he purposed to show unveiled, through works in due time." Hence (chap. 9), commingled with their fictions, the poets convey much divine truth. Indeed poetry and theology deal with the same subject, and theology is, as it were, God's poetry. See 15.8 and quotation from Augustine in n. 2. In 8.1 Boccaccio suggests that the planets may have been named from the gods according as their influences corresponded to the characteristics of the several gods, or of men and women euhemeristically deified. But at 11.1, end, he inti-

treatment of the legend of Prometheus, one of his most elaborate, is withal a fair illustration of his methods.[26]

Historically, Prometheus must have been some distinguished teacher. So Pliny regards him, as do Eusebius, Augustine, Lactantius, Servius, and others. Lactantius guesses that he was the first to make mud images, and Pliny that he was the first to strike fire from a rock. Hence the legends of his creating men from mud and stealing fire from heaven. Boccaccio consults also Ovid, Horace, Claudian, Fulgentius, and Theodontius; and at second-hand cites Varro, Sappho, Hesiod, and Aeschylus, "a Pythagorean poet," who tells the story "in a rather long poem"![27]

Prometheus, then, was the eldest son of Iapetus, but forsook his inheritance in his youthful enthusiasm for study among the Chaldeans. At length he retired to the summit of the Caucasus to meditate and investigate the stars and the secrets of nature. In time he descended to teach the rude Assyrians astrology and meteorology until they became highly enlightened and civilized. Such, Boccaccio finds, is the literal, historical basis of the story.

Mystically, however, he sees in Prometheus as the creator of man, adumbrations of (1) God Omnipotent; or (2) of Nature producing each after its kind; or (3) of the natural man, perfect in Eden until the Fall. Then arises the second Prometheus, the learned man raising his fellows to civilization in morals, knowledge, and virtue—"so that some are mere children of nature, but others are newly created of doctrine." The fire which he stole from the wheel of the sun's chariot is but the gleam of heavenly truth proceeding from God's bosom, to light every man that cometh into the world. The wheel symbolizes its eternity, without be-

mates that the man Jove or Jupiter was named from the planet whose characteristics he exemplified.

[26] 4.44.

[27] Hortis does not know whence he heard of Aeschylus. Macrobius quotes Aeschylus more than once, but not as a "Pythagorean."

ginning or end; and his furtive method hints that truth is not to be found in crowded cities, but only by meditation in silent solitudes. The tale of the gods' resentment and of the chaining to the Caucasus is but a concession of the poets to the vulgar notion, that the intense labor necessary to success in a laudable purpose is really a punishment inflicted by an angry God. As a matter of fact Prometheus visited Caucasus *before* he gave fire to men. Mercury, the gods' interpreter, led him thither and bound him, as the inspiring teacher lures one into solitary study and contemplation. The fetters are but self-imposed devotion to study, and the lacerations of the eagle but the pains of high meditation, healed at length by the joy of discovery.

Such lucubrations, usually less elaborate, accompany perhaps half of the myths recorded in the first thirteen books of the *Genealogy*. And if, as they must, they seem to us irresponsible, yet they gave large room and free play to Boccaccio's poetic imagination, which was highly necessary to the accomplishment of his humanistic purpose.

Yet the spirit of criticism was awake in him, and at times very keen. He is suspicious of extravagance in such authorities as Fulgentius and Leontius. He strives his utmost, by use of genealogies, chronologies, theories of origin, and the like, to assemble in orderly relation the facts and fictions of mythology. Nor does he proceed as one who would impose upon this matter an arbitrary scheme, but rather believes that the order is inherent in the matter itself, and that he must discover it and conform to it in the exhibition of his subject.[28]

Demogorgon, therefore, with the help of Theodontius and Lactantius, he finds to be the grand progenitor of all the gods. Then Cicero shows that there were three Joves, instead of one, each paternally responsible for a line of

[28] See 15.2; 15.12 and n.1.

gods and demigods. He also distinguishes three Mercuries, four Apollos, four or more named Hercules. These last no doubt were historical strong men called Hercules generically, after the great original strong son of Alcmena. So at any rate imply Rabanus and Varro.[29] Here Boccaccio almost anticipates the modern mythologist's practice of distinguishing local cults; for he adds that these different men of one name explain why we hear of a Tyrinthian Hercules, an Argive Hercules, a Theban, a Libyan, and such.

Etymology is a favorite solvent of myth with Boccaccio. His strenuous use of it shows pretty clearly both the extent and the limitations of his knowledge of Greek.[30] Some etymologies he learned from Leontius, some from such cited authorities as Cicero, Lactantius, Macrobius, Servius, Fulgentius, Isidore, Rabanus, "Albericus," and Paul. "Some say Melantho means 'whiteness' . . . . I know not where they find the notion; but I *do* know that Greek *melan* means Latin *nigrum*."[31] Usually, however, he is content to quote his etymologies, with the mildest disagreement, if any. He accepts Fulgentius' notion that Orpheus was called the son of Apollo (wisdom) and Calliope (Greek for "sweet sound") because his own name Orpheus means *aurea phone,* "the sweet voice of eloquence." Yet it is a "far-fetched" fancy of Fulgentius that Pegasus is from Greek *pege,* all because Pegasus tapped a spring by the stroke of his hoof![32]

If such amusing vagaries abound in the *Genealogy,* they are redeemed by the enthusiastic curiosity that enlivens

---

[29] 13.1.   [30] See 15.7.

[31] 7.10; he knows also that *leucos* means "white" (7.20).

[32] 10.27. Hercules, says Leontius, is from *hera,* "earth" and *cleos,* "glory"; or it may derive from *heros* and *cleos*; Paul brings it from *eri* (Latin *lis*) and *cleos,* Rabanus from *heruncleos,* "fame of strong men." "Heracles" is the more correct form, but "Hercules" is acceptable from long Latin custom (13.1).

them. This same curiosity, moreover, assumes a measure of grandeur in Boccaccio's yearnings for a fuller knowledge of his subject, particularly of Greek. No passage in the *Genealogy* is so eloquent as that in which, with modest pride, he relates his part in the translation of Homer by Leontius, and the introduction of Greek as a liberal study into Florence. Besides Homer there were few Greek authors of whom Boccaccio could have had even such knowledge as he could gain from a Latin translation.[33]

It is clear that certain instincts of the great scholar were strong in Boccaccio. His faith in the essential consistency of ancient myth, his desire for order, his occasional suspicion of documentary statement, all stir in him genuine concern over discrepant accounts and the desire either to reconcile them or to determine which speaks with the best authority. These discrepancies are most often matters of chronology or identity. Jerome's version of Eusebius' *Chronicon* is his usual criterion in dates, preferable to pagan Cicero or Ovid.[34] When Eusebius' dates disagree, he blames Eusebius' sources,[35] or resorts to the device of plural Joves or Circes. He questions Vincent of Beauvais' statement that the French kings are descended from Hector, yet "all things are possible with God."[36] He is annoyed with a version of the Io-Isis myth which he got from Barlaam through Leontius, so full of contradictions that it has lost all verisimilitude.[37] The family affairs of

[33] See Hortis, pp. 367-88, who mentions Homer, Plato, Aristotle, Euclid, Josephus, and Ptolemy as the only Greek authors whose works Boccaccio could have read in Latin versions. In a long list of Greeks of whom he knew indirectly, Hortis omits Sappho (see above, p. xxiv; *Lett.*, p. 193). Boccaccio seems to have used Leontius' version of Homer rather than the original Greek, in which he could never have attained to much facility. A citation of *Il.* 21.74-96 in *G.D.* 6.31, compared with Leontius' version quoted in Baldelli's *Life of Boccaccio*, p. 264 n., is a case in point. See 15.7 n. 10.

[34] 5.3; 7.22.   [36] 6.24.
[35] 5.25.   [37] 4.46.

Apollo II as reported by Theodontius and Leontius are so confused that "I know not what account to prefer. The manuscripts have met such destruction at the hands of time and of rascally scribes that we have lost the means of ascertaining the truth. Lies are suffered to range far and wide, and one writes what he pleases about the ancient world."[38]

The task of arbitration he sometimes takes lightly: "From these citations it is my business to settle by conjecture upon a date for Bacchus. Without mentioning my reasons, then, I will take the earliest of those mentioned, or at any rate the next after, as that of his birth and exploits. But I leave such problems to those who are more curious about them, and pass on to the legend proper."[39] And on the troublesome question of the date and identity of Io-Isis: "The inquiry for the truth in this matter may be left to experts."[40] On another point: "Let God discern the truth of this; I cannot understand these intricacies, let alone untangle them."[41] Clearly his scholarship in the narrower sense was unpretentious; nor did its power of generalization become choked with details.

We of the modern literal habit can more easily spy out its faults than its virtues. We miss in Boccaccio the scrupulous responsibility which we demand of one another. But his real responsibility as a scholar lay in his passion for Italy and in his yearning for a revival in her of the energies of antiquity.

Thus his scholarship is not merely literary, let alone grammatical. With the grand ruins and associations of Roman antiquity about him on every hand, he naturally insists that the true poet-scholar shall study also "the monuments and relics of the ancients."[42] One is not surprised to come upon an elaborate lament in Petrarchan

[38] 5.16.
[39] 5.25; 7.22.
[40] 4.46.

[41] 7.24; cf. 2.55; 63; 5.1.
[42] 14.7 and n.

manner over the imaginary ruins of the temple of Juno in Samos,[43] or to hear him lay stress upon the temples and accoutrements of primitive worship from which poetry sprang.[44] He feels too a lively interest in ancient painting and sculpture, which may in some measure have been stirred by the rising vigor of Italian art.

It is clear, then, that Boccaccio's artistic sense and his scholarship are not at odds, but reinforce each other, or indeed operate as one. He is keenly sensitive to the beauty of every myth he touches, and his delight in them all permeates and quickens his whole work. Many of his tales provoke no interpretation or comment. He is quite content with mere narration, partly, it may be, to leave room for the reader's poetizing imagination, partly, perhaps, because the tale justifies itself in the telling.[45] In his best manner he thus fashions the story of Atalanta, of Oedipus, of Orpheus and Eurydice, of Cupid and Psyche—all with the essential quality of the *Decameron*.[46]

So tedious, if cursory a review of Boccaccio's learning and scholarship could hardly excuse itself, were his lucubrations and his theories of interpretation not so integral a part of his conception of literature and poetry. As we saw in the beginning, classical antiquity, mythology, and poetry are to him essentially one. Therefore to explore and defend antiquity or mythology is to explore and defend the art of poetry.[47]

Boccaccio's apology in the two concluding books of his great work is a defence of poetry. Furthermore, it embodies a defence of the Liberal Arts; it particularly defends

[43] 9, proem; cf. 8.17; 10.5,13.   [44] 14.8.

[45] See 15.12 and n. 15. M. Hauvette's statement, however, is extreme: "En realité une seule chose l'interesse: l'art de raconter des histoires" (p. 274).

[46] 10.57; 2.70; 5.12; 22; see pp. 50, 51.

[47] 14.3.

[xxix]

the study of ancient literature; it assembles and makes articulate, as had never before been done, the critical ideas that had prevailed for a thousand years and more. Thus articulate, these ideas awaited but the recovery of Aristotle's *Poetics* in the fifteenth century, to unite with it and form the substance of literary theory for the Renaissance.

Boccaccio's defence has the superior value which must attach to a discussion of poetry by a poet, not by a mere professional critic. It is thus of a kind with the essays of Horace, Tasso, Ronsard, DuBellay, Sidney, Spenser, Jonson, Boileau, Dryden, Pope, Wordsworth, Coleridge, and Shelley. Like most of these it is polemic, or at least was provoked by stupid and prejudiced mishandling of the subject.[48]

The author is both explicit and diverting in his arraignment of the enemies of poetry. Beneath the incidental, contemporary details, picturesque as these were bound to be from the hand that wrought the *Decameron,* he has discerned with an unerring eye certain counter-forces, instincts, notions, that are perennially resistant to liberal culture and enlightenment.

The first class of these enemies, familiar enough at any time, is the wealthy fast set, whose life consists in eating and drinking, in wine, woman, and song. Poetry and things of the mind bore them. Boccaccio well knew their kind, especially in Naples. His way with them is brief. They are mere cattle, incapable of ideas, therefore not formidable, and best left to their own beastly devices.[49]

The second group,[50] if more respectable, is quite as dull. To scholarship and discipline they prefer smatterings and phrases picked up from diluted compendia and textbooks, or crumbs of cant and catch-phrases dropped by genuine scholars. Their scant knowledge is at second-hand. The

---

[48] Boccaccio defends poetry also in *De Cas.* 3.14; *Com.* 3; 5.
[49] 14.2.　　　　　　　　　[50] 14.3.

Liberal Arts, law, history, ethics, they scorn in comparison
with theology. With this supreme mistress of knowledge,
what need of any other? Hence their disparagement of
all else, including poetry. Poetry they especially vilify without ever having read it. But they are so incompetent, so
undisciplined in thought and expression, so ignorant, that
it is not worth the trouble to discuss the matter with them.

In Italy the study of scholastic theology was not, as in
the North, an especial concern of the university, but rather
the business of the conventual school.[51] In its secure isola-
tion from the liberalizing discipline of the university, it
tended, not only to minimize the importance of the Liberal
Arts and literature—much more, of the new humanism—
but actually to fear them as inimical to its interests.

Yet not all of the *theologi,* the teachers in the monas-
teries, were so insignificant as these. Some were learned
and able enough to rehearse to their pupils the traditional
arguments against poetry and humanism. Such might have
been the monastic teachers of Petrarch's brother Gherardo,[52] and "our theologians" mentioned by Petrarch in his
Invective[53]—narrow indeed, yet with some elementary
schooling in the Liberal Arts, versed in the more obvious
of the Christian texts.

More dangerous is the third group of Philistines;[54] for
these are men of mind, who enjoy a measure of cultivation, and who bring to the case a fixed and clear conviction
which they are fully able to urge. They are the lawyers
of the day who follow the profession for money. They
are ready to commend poetry, both the creation and the
study of it, as a pretty accomplishment, an intellectual
cosmetic. But to their mind the real test of culture, nay, of
ability and character, is the power to get money. A poet or
a serious student of poetry, a scholar—proves his in-

[51] 14.3 nn.
[52] *Fam.* 10.4; 17.1.
[53] 3, p. 1101.
[54] 14.4.

[xxxi]

capacity by his very career. He may indeed be gifted in a sort, but can he make this business of literature pay? That is the test. His modest and threadbare showing in the world is against him.

Again Boccaccio knows the kind—had in fact been of their very household. Had he not braved the wrath of his father, a successful banker, who condemned him first to business, and then to canon law, as easy roads to affluence?[55] Had he not wasted nearly a dozen years of his youth between them in preparation for a money-getting career? It was a time like ours, of quick and sensational fortunes. Boccaccio had heard the supreme importance of wealth dinned into his ears from childhood. He admits everybody's susceptibility to it, and confesses the force of this hard-headed disparagement of poetry.

The modern defender of humanism might argue that liberal humanistic culture actually does pay—wins more money for the man who gets it than the man without it can gather. Boccaccio stops at no such compromise, but carries the case at once to higher ground. He contrasts the wealth of mind and spirit with mere gold. The interests of poetry are high and eternal; those of money-getting are sordid and shifting and ephemeral. Poetry is an art; business a mere technique. The ages ring with the poet's praise; the seeker of wealth is forgotten.

But far the most formidable group is the fourth—more cultivated, more able, more subtle than the rest—men who call forth Boccaccio's extreme effort. At first they seem hardly distinguishable from the second group of antagonists. Both are of theological cast, both are superficial in scholarship, both affect authority in high matters, both collect a large and ignorant following by claptrap. But this fourth group is more in, and of, the world than the second. Of all the enemies of poetry these are the most

[55] 15.10.

erudite. As pupils in the schools they were both aggressive and obsequious, courting the attention and favor of their masters. They have gone forth into the world with more regard for the selfish uses of learning than for learning itself. By this and every other means they gain influence, meddle with politics and society, assume authority, and cover their ignorance with loud vilification. Some are privately licentious.[56] While they are noisy and truculent in one direction, they are subservient in another. They set high store on worldly title and decoration. Yet they have no appreciation of higher arts. In the new humanistic culture they detect, by blind if unerring instinct, their natural and mortal enemy. They know enough to muster all the cant arguments of the ages against this enemy. Their number, energy, ignorance, and insensibility exasperate Boccaccio. He knows them well and wisely belabors them with their own truncheons as the only weapon they can feel.

It is easy to identify this group with the friars;[57] its resemblance to the friars of the *Decameron,* of Chaucer, of Langland, and many another, is obvious.[58] No doubt the friars were the dominant and loudest element in this group, and perhaps Boccaccio has them chiefly in mind when he wields his bludgeon. But the cant objections to poetry which he repels have arisen from widely various quarters by no means restricted to the friars. Petrarch heard them from a physician,[59] from "our theologians,"[60] from his brave and self-effacing, if not highly enlightened brother Gherardo, from Gherardo's monastic teacher,[61] from a

---

[56] 14.16,18.

[57] Hortis, pp. 181-3; Zenatti, p. 225, n.1, who both cite John of Salisbury's chapters on hypocrites, two centuries earlier.

[58] The mendicants were in high favor at Joanna's court at Naples. Petrarch describes one Roberto, confessor to King Andrew, as ambitious, arrogant, self-righteous, and truculent (*Fam.* 5.3).

[59] *Inv.,* p. 1101. cf. *Inv.* I, p. 1092; Robinson and Rolfe, pp. 211ff.

[60] *Inv.,* p. 1102.   [61] *Fam.* 10.4; 16.2.

certain "Sicilian dialectician,"[62] from the rhetorician, Benvenuto da Imola,[63] possibly from people of Averroist, or generally sceptical tendency.[64] Distinct among the rest is the narrow but likable old man who at a university exercise made rather a scene over the matter in Boccaccio's hearing.[65]

Clearly Boccaccio recognizes the wide variation of minds arrayed against him. For, while he waxes loud and coarse at those who are susceptible only of such offence, yet he also urges the case of poetry in sweeter and subtler terms, which impart his deepest and most impassioned convictions to such as he may hope to carry with him.[66]

But, particulars aside, Boccaccio's opponents were hidebound conservatives recognizable in any generation—the poor whom we have with us always. Some are honest but narrow-minded; some are hypocrites of low order, who shriek incoherent abuse at any new idea which unsettles their selfish interests; some are fanatics; some are formalists, academic or ecclesiastical, practised in the art of self-exploitation, deceiving the crowd with their specious attainments, usurping the places of better men, incapable of genuine humanism.

Sincere or insincere, these men were to be justified in their instinctive sense of an enemy in the humanistic study of the Ancients by the ultimate paganizing of almost the entire ecclesiastical structure. Indeed Boccaccio seems himself to have felt misgivings on this point.[67] But these are

---

[62] *Inv.*, p. 1092.   [63] *Sen.* 15.11.

[64] cf. *Inv.*, I, p. 1092; Robinson and Rolfe, pp. 211ff.

[65] P. 73. Possibly the enemies of "poetry" were exasperated by the rising tide of humanistic enthusiasm, for which Petrarch, like Pope in his day, holds himself responsible (*Fam.* 13.7; cf. *Sen.* 5.3, Robinson and Rolfe, p. 198).

[66] Boccaccio's rudeness may easily seem exaggerated to the modern taste (cf. Hauvette, p. 101), but such methods were quite within the rules of mediaeval polemics, and may have seemed a matter of course to a contemporary.   [67] 15.9, end.

quite outweighed by his heartfelt belief that the truth in whatever form of expression, once understood, can do naught but reinforce the Faith. To him the truth in the great Ancients is authentic by all the deeper intuitions of his eager, generous mind. Thus fortified, he throws himself with fine enthusiasm into the defence of the study of the classics, that is, the defence of poetry.

A summary of Boccaccio's ideas concerning poetry properly begins with his definition. Poetry is *"fervor quidam exquisite inveniendi, atque dicendi, seu scribendi quod inveneris"*—"fervid and exquisite invention, with fervid expression in speech or writing, of that which the mind has invented."[68]

This is a practising poet's definition, not that of a speculative critic. It inclines rather to the act and experience of creation than to a description of a finished poem. Boccaccio agrees with his fellow poets in recognizing two necessary processes by which a great work of art comes into the world—first, "inspiration" or emotional excitement, then deliberate critical afterthought or revision—"nature" plus "art," to use more recent terms. "This fervor," he adds, "impels the soul to a longing for utterance; it brings forth strange and unheard of creations of the mind; it arranges these meditations in a fixed order, adorns the whole composition with an unusual interweaving of words and thoughts, and thus it veils truth in a fair and fitting garment of fiction."

Poetry, then, is an art, not a mere craft or technique.[69] Poetry differs from rhetoric in its rhythm and metre; its style is more exalted, its meaning far more subtle, its invention more free and spontaneous.[70] Poetry differs from history in departing from the chronological order of events to gain more artistic effect; but particularly is it dis-

68 P. 39
69 P. 25.
70 Pp. 41, 61, and nn.

tinguished by its moral or secondary intention, for it may so alter historical fact by suppression or elevation as better to veil and convey the poet's ideas of truth in whatever field.

As for philosophy, while poetry and philosophy win towards one goal, the truth, they seek it by different ways —the philosopher by the slower pace of reason, the poet by contemplation. The philosopher is literal, scornful of embellishment; the poet "writes in metre, with an artist's most scrupulous care, and in a style distinguished by exquisite charm."[71] A philosopher is a propagator, consorting to that end with his fellow men; a poet dwells apart. And if philosophy is the keener investigator, and poetry in this respect, is, as it were, ancillary to her, yet poetry more carefully protects the truth beneath her subtle veil.[72]

But above all the poet is the creator who fashions a new world of nature and of man in all their phases and activities, and so manipulates the illusion of this new world as to capture and control the minds of his hearers.[73]

But not all poetry is good. Poets and poetry there are also that corrupt the soul and pervert readers to vicious thought and action. Such poets Plato would have banished from the State, and only such; such it was that Boethius condemned. Ovid's *Art of Love* is a case in point, and the "comic" poets.[74]

Good poetry and great is the product of more than mere technique; it is a high creative art, the gift of heaven to only a few rare souls. But we are not to suppose that even the "fervor," the divine afflatus, is enough

[71] P. 79.   [73] Pp. 39, 50, 63, 79, 80.
[72] P. 83.

[74] Whoever they may be. Boccaccio caught the term ultimately from Augustine: see p. 70; 14.19 n. 25. At 14.16 he specifies Catullus and Propertius, apparently on hearsay from Petrarch, as well as Ovid; and he mentions Ovid again at 14.19, but excepts Plautus and Terence. Macrobius, whom Boccaccio seems to have in mind on this point, mentions Apuleius and Petronius.

for great poetry without instruments of learning—thorough schooling in the Liberal Arts, in science, both moral and natural, in history, in literature, archaeology, and geography;[75] in short, the full cycle of knowledge as the mediaeval mind comprehended it.

Finally the poet's learning is not mere erudition, nor is it a mere assembling of raw materials for his work. It furnishes him thoughts and objects for long, careful, and high contemplation, from which genius derives its impulse to creation and its fertile ideas.[76]

Small wonder then if poets have always seemed to the rest of men a little strange and egregious—if they have avoided the crowd and its acclaim, to meditate and sing in solitude. They are withal the true aristocrats, and find their natural kinship among men of highest genius in whatever field, even of war and state.

But the glory of poetry appears not only in its nature, its rarity, and the quality of its creators, but in its very ancient origin. For, while authorities cannot agree whether the Hebrews, the Babylonians, or the Greeks invented the

[75] Pp. 21, 40; cf. above, p. xiv.

[76] So Spenser:

> Rapt with the rage of mine own ravisht thought,
> Through contemplation of those goodly sights,
> And glorious images in heaven wrought,
> Whose wondrous beauty breathing sweet delights,
> Do kindle love in high conceipted sprights:
> I faine to tell the things that I behold.

(H.H.B. 1-6; cf. F.Q. 6, Pr. 1.)

So Milton's Cherub Contemplation on his "fiery-wheeled throne," Pens. 53; and the thoughts "that voluntary move harmonious numbers," Par. Lost 3.37. Wordsworth, to prove his fitness for his art, would find within himself

> that first great gift, the vital soul,
> The General Truths, which are themselves a sort
> Of Elements and Agents, Under-powers,
> Subordinate helpers of the living mind.

And lastly, the sense of "external things, forms, images" (Prel. 1.150-5).

art, two facts are clear: poetry is a primitive art; and its origin is religious. It arose from primitive wonder at the forces of nature, which to the unsophisticated man implied a God. To placate or honor him men consecrated temples and devised a ritual, and this worship required exalted and uncommon language—metrical and polished discourse. This demand brought forth the first poets, who, working under divine stimulus created the first poetry, in which they veiled the mystery. And this is what Aristotle means by calling the first poets theologians; for such they were.[77] Yet Moses, composing much of the Pentateuch in heroic verse, and the holy Prophets, are distinguished by inspiration through the Holy Ghost from secular poets, whose inspiration is rather through sheer energy of genius. Wherefore these were called *vates*.[78]

Lastly, poetry is distinguished by its effects and functions. Poetry is essentially a veil of fiction which clothes the naked truth. Such it is in the holy Prophets and the Apocalypse; such it is in secular masterpieces.[79] This fair investure, far from defeating or impairing the truth, much enhances its power among men. It thus finds protection from weaklings who only misunderstand it, pervert and abuse it. Besides, truth made common and obvious suffers desecration through ordinary utterance into cant and platitude. It grows cheap and weak. But the outward poetic veil, while it gives mere sensuous pleasure to the unskilful, only allures and challenges the worthier intellect, which accordingly exercises itself by every effort and at length wins the priceless guerdon of truth itself.

This allegorical theory of poetry, deriving from the Ancients, and sustained from early mediaeval times by a naturally strong inclination to symbolism and allegory,

[77] 15.8. [78] 14.8 and n. 23.
[79] 14.7 and n. 8; but Boccaccio often reiterates the thought: See Index, *s.v.* Poetry, a veil.

supports the allegorical quality of literature and art from Prudentius to Spenser.[80] Nor is it confined only to formal allegory such as the *Divine Comedy,* but suspects and seeks ulterior meaning in all art and poetry worthy of the name.

Yet is it a stumbling-block and foolishness to modern critics and historians, who remark its esoteric and aristocratic complexion. For such there is no room in these democratic days. Yet who that, like Boccaccio, has taken active part in the propagation of poetry at any time can believe that poetry belongs to everybody; and not rather only to such as are qualified in mind and heart to comprehend it—to pierce the veil?[81] Such is his opinion. But he is not without serious concern for novices and tenderer minds, and excuses his prolixity on the ground that a fuller account appeals to the less educated and the young.[82]

His great humanistic undertakings draw much of their energy from his conviction that the appreciation of poetry is something which can be imparted to others by instruction. Did not Petrarch teach King Robert to enjoy it in his old age?[83] The study of poetry, however, has been grievously neglected as compared with that of philosophy, law,

---

[80] Spenser's treatment of classic myth shows its kinship by derivation from mediaeval conceptions in various ways. His habit of poetizing the gods by etymology is like the practice of Macrobius, Fulgentius, Isidore, and Boccaccio, among others. His use of genealogy of the gods, his allegorizing of myths, his euhemeristic tendency in allying the gods with his characters in a quasi-historical fashion, either through genealogy or otherwise, are all traditional. Occasionally he hints other mediaeval theories, such as the demonological; see *F.Q.* 3.8.8.

[81] So Petrarch, *Fam.* 13.7: "Although the delights of poetry are most exquisite, they can be fully understood only by the rarest geniuses, who are careless of wealth, and possess a marked contempt for the things of this world, and who are by nature especially endowed with a peculiar elevation and freedom of soul" (Robinson and Rolfe, p. 166).

[82] 15.12, end.　　　　　[83] 14.21.

medicine, theology, and the arts both liberal and technical.[84] Like the poet, the student of poetry needs learning and erudition, and these Boccaccio has done his part to supply. But even these are not enough. "You must read, you must persevere, you must sit up nights, you must inquire, and exert to the utmost every power of your mind. If one way does not lead to the desired meaning, take another; if obstacles arise, still another, until, if your strength holds out, you will find that clear which at first looked dark."[85] Above all you must experience a kind of conversion before the qualities of poetry will reveal themselves unto you.

Then will you be capable of its twofold Horatian power, to delight and to teach: to delight with its music and its beauty of language, and with a delight that is not effeminate nor unworthy as some allege; to teach not by precept alone, but, by the very charm of its beauty and its music, to refine your emotions and make you susceptible unawares to impulses toward noble and upright action.[86]

It will readily appear that Boccaccio offers his reader no new ideas. Even a well read man of the fourteenth century could hardly have thought his apology very original. The considerations of his defence of poetry are such as had been accessible and current during all or part of the millennium before him. Petrarch, Isidore—and through him Suetonius and Varro—Gregory, Macrobius, Lactantius, Augustine, Jerome, and Horace were Boccaccio's chief instructors. But he is also indebted in some measure, not always easy to define, to Dante, Rabanus, the pseudo-Dionysius, Fulgentius, Boethius, Apuleius, Quintilian, Vergil with Servius' commentary, Cicero, and perhaps indirectly to the *Poetics* of Aristotle.[87] Virtually every ob-

---

[84] 15.6, end.

[85] P. 62.   [86] Pp. 50, 78, 104.

[87] More specific designation of his various debts may be found in the Notes.

jection of his opponents had been revived from the Christian apologists, Augustine, Lactantius, and Jerome; and most of Boccaccio's replies derive from these men. He has furthermore made very good use of contemporary scholars, to whom he pays generous acknowledgment.[88]

But single and peculiar among those who helped Boccaccio is Petrarch. In his works he assembled the stock objections to poetry rehearsed by Boccaccio: that poets are liars;[89] that they are useless and unintelligible;[90] that they are unsociable and poor;[91] immoral and irreligious;[92] condemned by Plato,[93] Boethius,[94] Jerome.[95]

To meet these objections he either compiled from various sources the replies already in common use, or devised refutations which Boccaccio used after him.[96]

If Boccaccio owes his chief debt for his ideas to Petrarch, yet in all fairness the credit for assembling these ideas may belong to Albertino Mussato.[97]

[88] 15.6.

[89] *Inv.* 1, p. 1092.

[90] *Inv.* 3, p. 1105.

[91] *Inv.* 4, p. 1110ff; *De Rem.* 2.9.

[92] *Inv.* 3, p. 1101.

[93] *Inv.* 3, p. 1104.

[94] *Inv.* 1, p. 1091; 3, p. 1103.

[95] *Sen.* 1.5; *Frac.* 1.44,5.

[96] Such are: the origin and antiquity of poetry (*Fam.* 10.4); the reconciliation of paganism with Christianity (*De Sui Ipsius et Aliorum Ignorantia*); the moral distinction between good and bad poetry (*Sen.* 15.11: 2.438-40); the replies to the alleged objections of Plato, Jerome, and Boethius (see nn. on 14.18-20); that poetry is a veil which invests the truth to enhance its beauty and power, and to save it from desecration (see 14.7 n. 8); cf. Hortis, p. 219.

[97] His collected works were published at Venice in 1636. I have not been able to see them, but I give here a résumé of the history of his defence from Antonio Zardo's *Albertino Mussato,* Padua, 1884, pp. 302-10. A brother Giovannino of Mantua of the preaching order had at Christmas given a public discourse on theology. He had disparaged all the other arts but poetry. Mussato laughed at those who taught the other arts, alleging that poetry had been excepted as a part of theology. Giovannino explained that it was an oversight on his part, whereupon Mussato wrote a letter, now lost, in defence of poetry as a divine art. Many of its lines are embodied in his *Epp.* 4, 7. He argues: that poetry is the primitive art, arising out of theology;

What mark of distinction, then, what glow of original-
ity, raises Boccaccio's performance as a critic to high
significance?

If Petrarch was the more original, more enterprising,
yet Boccaccio was the more generous, the more catholic of
the two. As Zenatti observes, Petrarch wrote in effect to
defend only his own performance in Latin verse, Boccaccio to defend all poetry. Boccaccio, to be sure, is content with certain traditions, definitions, conceptions, for-
mulae; and the limitations in his more literal use of the
words "poet" and "poetry" are obvious. Critics love to
point them out.[98] They seem, however, to forget that
Boccaccio himself was primarily a poet, and that, however he may at moments lapse into literalism, his experi-

that it is divine because it deals with gods and things celestial, because
those who follow it are *vates,* because it comes from God, because
it merits highest admiration and brings delight, because Moses used
it to praise God and bring his people out of slavery, because it agrees
with Holy Writ, because it lives in eternal splendor, because it reveals
the Christian faith. To this Giovannino replied that poetry had been
called theology only because the first poets were the first philosophers,
but their teaching was false; that poets give divine honors to mere
men and things; that poets are *vates* from *vieo,* weave, but philosophers, priests, and prophets are *vates* from *vi mentis;* that poetry
comes not from God but men; that it is delightful only for its wonders and ornaments; that if Moses did compose verse, other verse is
not divine; that Holy Writ employs figure to veil the truth, but poetry
only for pleasure; that the first poets, Orpheus and such, lived long
after Moses. Mussato replied in his *Ep.* 18 that to call Ocean god is
but symbolic like the use of water in baptism; that if poets call men
gods, we call them saints; that if poets are allegorical, so are Christians when they represent Christ as a lamb; that other arts or sciences
are either *theoretica* or *practica,* while poetry is both, since, like the
parables it hides truth under a veil, but is *practica* in its technique;
that Orpheus and Musaeus were not the first poets, but that poetry
is as old as any of the other arts; that if Isaiah, Ezechiel, and others
could be Christians without Christ, so also could Vergil and Statius,
whose verses agree with the prophets.

[98] e.g., Hortis, p. 209: "Il poeta difeso dal Boccaccio è il poeta
filosofo e teologo, o, come disse uno scrittore moderno [Burckhardt,
Renaissance in Italy, pp. 206-7, § 3, cap. 4], il poeta filologo."

ences, enthusiasms, intuitions, as a creative artist are bound to assert themselves, and subtly to qualify all that he has to say on the subject of mythology and poetry.[99]

Above all theories and minor motives which actuated Boccaccio is his conception of poetry as an agency of regeneration in the State. He saw about him an Italy deplorably given over to war, rapine, intrigue, greed, selfish ambition. Yet he saw her giving birth to men—notably Dante and Petrarch—as great as those who had glorified the name of Rome. How, then, could her gifts be turned to her regeneration? By the moral and intellectual forces of poetry. For these would grow by what they fed upon. Poets would stir in statesmen a higher notion of fame; statesmen in turn would encourage poets; and the power of poetry thus increasing would permeate the imaginations and conduct of the whole state.[100]

The propagation of poetry, then, was the object not only of the Fourteenth and Fifteenth Books, but of the whole of the *Genealogia,* and, indeed, of all Boccaccio's encyclopaedic works in Latin. No one could have been better fitted for the task. With the keen instinct of the journalist—and there is a journalistic element in his work —he seizes an occasion of controversy, knowing that contest most certainly engages the human attention. To refute his opponents, then, is after all an occasional and minor object.[101] To get his book read was paramount. To this end his style is fluent, voluble, often diffuse, bad as Latin, excellent for its purpose, lively, saturated with the writer's charm.[102] And he succeeded. Not in regenerating

[99] His opinion, for example—or his expression of it—on the matter of the *volgare eloquio* in preference to Latin is more flexible than Petrarch's.

[100] Letter to Pizzinghe, *Lett.* 192-8. Salutato clearly discerned these purposes (*Ep.* 1.226,7).

[101] See 14, 7 n. 1; 15.1 and n. 11.

[102] See his consideration of this matter, pp. 110, 135-6.

Italy, of course, but, as often happens, in something greater. He produced a book which was a powerful implement of literary cultivation for two or three hundred years. The large number of manuscripts and editions, especially in the sixteenth century, is only one sign of its popularity. As a mere handbook of mythology and interpretation of myth its traces are everywhere recurrent in the literature of the Renaissance.[103] In English alone they appear in Chaucer,[104] Spenser,[105] Jonson,[106] Greene,[107] Milton,[108] perhaps Dryden;[109] and the figure of Demogorgon as employed by Shelley in his *Prometheus Unbound* is in the tradition that derives from the opening chapter of Boccaccio's work. It is not unlikely that Shelley may have picked up an old copy in Italy. They were numerous in some editions, and are still easy to find.[110]

[103] Hortis (pp. 919-23) describes twenty-seven manuscripts of the *Genealogia;* on pp. 769-85 he lists and describes ten printed editions between 1472, or earlier, and 1532. French versions appeared in 1498 and 1531; Betussi's Italian version was printed and reprinted at least twelve times: 1547, 1553, 1554, 1564, 1569, 1574, 1581, 1585, 1588, 1606, 1627, 1644. All of these editions of Betussi are in the Princeton University Library except that of 1627. The edition of 1553 is not mentioned by Hortis. Other editions of the *Genealogia* in Latin, French, or Italian, unverified and sometimes suspected by Hortis, are mentioned, pp. 891-5, and various abridgments, pp. 220-7.

[104] Professor Albert W. Liddle informs me that the legend of Ariadne in *L.G.W.* shows definite traces of indebtedness to *G.D.* 10.48; 11.29-30; Bellona, at *Anelida and Arcite* 5 apparently derives from *G.D.* 5.48. In many other instances the relation is possible but not finally demonstrable.

[105] *F.Q.* 1.1.37; 5.22; 4.2.47.

[106] *Alchemist* 1.1; 2.1.

[107] *Friar Bacon,* Oxf. 1905, 2.64; add *Selimus,* ed. Grosart, Lond. 1898, 1317-21; R. Barnfield, *Poems* (Arber), 1882, 7.69.

[108] Osgood, *Classical Myth. in Milton,* p. 27.

[109] *Essay on Satire* in *Essays of Dryden,* ed. Ker, 2.36-7 and n.

[110] For other sporadic references see E. Koeppel, *Laurents de Premierfait und John Lydgates Bearbeitungen von Boccaccios De Casibus Vir. Illustr.,* München, 1885, p. 60 and nn.; G. Douglas, *Aeneid,* Pr. 201-5; Peter Martyr, *De Orbe Novol.* 347-8; 2.298. Several of the references here and in n. 107 I owe to my friend Professor Robert R.

But as a propagator of ideas concerning the art of poetry the book was quite as effective. These ideas reappear early in the next century in the letters of Salutato, in reply to the stock objections,[111] and thenceforward are current and recurrent in the flood of critical essays that abound for two hundred and fifty years.[112]

No better example of their persistence is needed than Sidney's *Defence of Poesy,* based upon Italian tradition, particularly Minturno. In it we hear again of the ancient religious origin of poetry, of the *vates,* of the metrical and poetic quality of Holy Writ, especially the Pentateuch, the Psalms, the Prophets, the parables, and the Apocalypse.

Cawley. Bacon's allegories of the myths in his *Wisdom of the Ancients* owe nothing in detail to Boccaccio's interpretations, though the manner and the theory are the same. Cowley proposes (*Davideis* 41-2):

> T' unbind the Charms that in slight Fables lie,
> And teach that Truth is truest Poesie.

Even Wordsworth echoes the favorite mediaeval theory concerning myths (*Excursion* 6.545-7):

> Fictions in form, but in their substance truths,
> Tremendous truths! familiar to the men
> Of long-past times, nor obsolete in ours.

[111] *Epistolario* 3.221-31; 287-94: in rejoinder to a Carmelite monk of San Miniato, and to Carlo Malatesta.

[112] Thus Vicenzo Gravina, *Della Ragion Poetica* 1.7, shows the usefulness of poetry as a veil of fiction for truth; in 1.8 he asserts on the same authority as Boccaccio, the primitive origin of poetry in religion; in 1.11 the usefulness of fable, etc. The allegorical theory is rehearsed and objections met in Hawes, *Pastime of Pleasure* 701-819; cf. Berdan, *Early Tudor Poetry* 76-8. Minturno, in *L'Arte Poetica,* Rag. 3 (ed. 1725, p. 167), rehearses the religious origin of melic poetry. The same ideas echo as late as Dryden (*On Satire,* ed. Ker, 2.45,6) and even as John Toland; Fracastoro, in his *Naugerius,* distinguishes the poet as primarily an inventor, but learned and practised in style and embellishments; and seems reminiscent of Boccaccio when he touches upon mythology as poetry, upon the "unhistorical" story of Aeneas, upon Plato's objections; cf. R. Kelso, *Girolamo Fracastoro, Naugerius, etc.,* pp. 66, 69, 70, 72. Cf. Harington's *Apologie,* 1591, in G. Smith, *Elizabethan Critical Essays,* 2.202-3. The story of the influence of the *Genealogy* upon later criticism is yet to be written.

Sidney insists upon the moral values of poetry, admits that
some poetry is vicious, and uses this distinction to refute
the belief that Plato banished the poets. Like Boccaccio he
meets the objections that poetry is a waste of time, a
mother of lies, a breeder of license. As Boccaccio elevates
poetry by comparison with rhetoric, history, and philosophy, Sidney to the same end cites history and philosophy,
though his points of comparison, under the influence
of the recovered *Poetics* of Aristotle, naturally differ
somewhat. Both critics insist upon the supreme function
of the poet to create—Boccaccio, perhaps, less than Sidney,
who had the advantage of Aristotle's help. Both, after
Horace, urge the twofold function of poetry to teach and
to delight. In Boccaccio is distinctly implied the subtle,
unconscious edification through the beauty of poetry,
which Sidney argues at length. It is not necessary to suppose that Sidney borrowed these notions directly from
Boccaccio, though verbal echoes indicate first-hand acquaintance; they may have been more than once removed.[113]
But the translation and frequent reprinting of the *Gene-*
alogy in the sixteenth century prove that it was still widely
read. Common sources were also accessible. The discovery
of the *Poetics* wrought a fundamental change in all critical
ideas. But instead of superseding the old ideas, it only ef-
fected in them necessary adaptation for the time being, and
the fact remains that they had the power to survive.[114]

[113] See F. N. Scott, *M.L.N.* 6.193ff.; Elizabeth Woodbridge,
P.M.L.A. 13.333ff.

[114] Spenser's lost treatise on *The Poet* probably had quite as much
in common with Boccaccio as Sidney's essay. At any rate, the *Faery*
Queen is almost as literal an embodiment of Boccaccio's ideas as is
the *Divine Comedy*. Note for example the language of *F.Q.* 2, Pr. 4, 5:

> . . . in this antique ymage thy great auncestry.
> The which O pardon me thus to enfold
> In covert vele, and wrap in shadowes light,
> That feeble eyes your glory may behold,
> Which ells could not endure those beames bright.

See above, p. xxxviii and n. 79.

But Boccaccio's essay must not be weighed as a mere document in the history of criticism and scholarship. To look upon it only as such is to miss the very quality which made it a document, the power that gave it momentum in the minds of men. Into it passed a winsome personality, which permeated and quickened the old tradition. For all his polemics, he is no fanatic, trying to subvert the old culture by a new. Rather is his the greater way, to revive the old by infusing it with the energies of a new humanization. Therefore his defence of poetry and the classics is not, as often implied, a manifestation of his lower powers, a reflection of the lesser Boccaccio, with his creative imagination laid asleep. Into it he poured his entire self—his thirst for knowledge and his tireless industry; his skill in narrative and his lively imagination; his half-conscious drollery, his delight in beauty, his persuasive humanism, his moral sense, his love of Italy; his eagerness to share his enthusiasms with others; his sympathies, his warm and loyal adorations, and his irresistible charm.[115]

Obsolete as his critical ideas may be in their literal sense, they show, under his handling, a constant tendency to transcend it and escape into larger implications, to become perennial. Boccaccio's book is a composite of elements which in the last five hundred years—for whatever reason—has dissolved. Scholarship has perforce become a specialty, and with increasing specialism scholars suffer increasing occupational deformity. Criticism too has warped and shrunk in an opposite direction towards impressionism, more or less ephemeral and journalized. Even poets now are specialists, in matter, manner, and form. I fancy this disintegration of function would have appalled

[115] Grâce au zèle infatigable avec lequel il étudia, interrogea les grands maîtres de l'antiquité, cherchant à leur arracher le secret de leur harmonie, de leur équilibre et de leur élégance expressive, il ne cessa pas, jusqu'à sa maturité, d'affiner et d'enricher ses qualités personnelles.—Hauvette, p. 313.

Boccaccio, in whom, if I may repeat, artist, scholar, and critic were all one and united in action. The feebler scholar, he who is not essentially artist and critic, the feebler artist who is not scholar and critic, the feebler critic who is not artist and scholar.

As a student of literature he pays all heed to the necessity of concrete knowledge. One cannot know enough, he would say, his utmost scholarship cannot suffice to understand the full truth and value of poetry. But it is by no means wholly a matter of concrete knowledge. Give range too to the individual mind; let the warm imagination brood and hover until it provokes a meaning—*the* meaning—from the work of art, confirmable but unattainable by mere scientific scholarship. Withal the whole process must be subject to both stimulus and guidance of a God-given artistic sense that knows what is right and true as the artist knows it.[116]

It would be vain to wish back the encyclopaedic days of Boccaccio, with all the limitations that made their success possible. It would be vain to try to imitate him. But there

---

[116] The thought is essentially in Petrarch. In *Sen.* 4.5, citing Augustine's *Confessions* in reference to the books of Moses, he says: "E veramente la materia di cui trattiamo capace di spiegazioni molte e diverse, le quali, se giuste sieno e al senso letterale ben rispondenti, rifutar non si debbono, quantunque per avventura mai non venissero in capo a que' poeti," etc. Doubtless he felt as did Boccaccio that the meaning of a myth was an accretion from the ages through which the tradition had passed, from the unconscious force of genius in the inventor, from many mysterious sources, and such varied store of meaning authorized the freedom of the interpreter's imagination, and made room for it. Plutarch, *De Is. et Osir.* 58 is an early instance; a recent one comes from a reviewer in the London *Times Literary Supplement*, August 17, 1922, p. 531: "Great poetry is more than what the poet means; and true poets know this. Only the other day the writer of this review was talking to a poet about the meaning of one of his poems, and, in reply to a suggested interpretation, got the answer, 'No: I didn't think of that. But keep to it. No doubt the poem means it though I didn't'!. . . The poet was speaking in simple sincerity, realizing, more than some commentators do, the richness and range of his art."

is something infectious and edifying to the student of these latter days in his fervor, his tense curiosity, his mustering and deploying of all his extraordinary powers in the humanizing of literature as a means of new life to his people.

SELECTED BIBLIOGRAPHY

Boccaccio, Giovanni, *Genealogia deorum gentilium libri,* edited by V. Romano. 2 vols. Bari, 1951.

——, *Teseida,* edited by A. Roncaglia. Bari, 1941.
(Contains Boccaccio's notes to his poem.)

Seznec, Jean. *The Survival of the Pagan Gods.* New York, 1953.
(Contains material on the tradition to which Boccaccio's poetic theory belongs and on its influence.)

Wilkins, E. H. *A History of Italian Literature.* Cambridge, Mass., 1954.

——, The University of Chicago Manuscript of the *Genealogia deorum gentilium* of Boccaccio. Chicago, 1927.

THE GENEALOGY OF THE GENTILE GODS

THE GENEALOGY OF THE GENTILE GODS

Cyprus

PREFACE[1]

IF I HAVE understood aright, O famous King,[2] the words
of your distinguished soldier, Donino of Parma, you particularly wish to have compiled a Genealogy of the Gentile
Gods and of the heroes who, according to ancient mythology, sprang from them. At the same time you desire
an explanation of the meaning which various eminent men
have perceived beneath the surface of these myths. Furthermore, from your exalted position, you have chosen
me, as one supposed to enjoy deep and wide erudition in
such matters, to be the author of this vast work. I will not
dwell upon my wonder at your desire, for it becomes not
a humble person to scrutinize the motives of a King; and
I refrain from uttering my misgivings at your choice of
me, for in showing my insufficiency to the task I might
seem by subterfuge to try to escape that office which
you impose. But before I express my opinion of this task,
I should like, most Serene King, to relate at least a part
of the conversation between your eminent soldier Donino
and me, in which he imparted to me the commands of
your Highness; so that, as you read it over, you may see
your opinion of me set over against my temerity in obey-
ing your Majesty.

He began with an eloquent description of your Majesty's
studies in sacred subjects, of your wonderful acts as King,
and a long and witty account of your eminent and distinguished titles. At last he endeavored with no little pains

to bring me to your opinion by citing many reasons, some of which, I admit, seemed valid. When he paused, I answered at some length as follows:

BOCCACCIO. "My eloquent soldier, perhaps you, or your King, who, by the grace of God, will soon be ours too, have supposed that this infatuate wish of the Ancients to be considered descendants of gods prevailed in only a small corner of the earth, that, being so absurd, it lasted but a short time, and that it can as easily be reduced to a description as any modern subject. But—always by indulgence—may I say that the fact is quite different. For the tinder of this foolishness blazed up not only on the Cyclades[3] and other Aegean islands, but in Achaia, Illyria, and Thrace, especially during the days of the Greek Republic. It further infected the shores of the Black Sea, the Hellespont, the coast of Maeonia, Icaria, Pamphylia, Cilicia, Phoenicia, Syria, and Egypt. Even Cyprus, the fair adornment of our King, was not immune. It lapped all the shore of Lybia, the Syrtes, Numidia, the coast of the Atlantic, the western ocean and even the far-remote gardens of the Hesperides. Not content with Mediterranean shores, it penetrated to nations far inland. Together with the peoples of the coast all those along the sourceless Nile[4] fell into this error, the pest-ridden sands of Lybia and the solitudes of most ancient Thebes. So too the upper Egyptians, the people of torrid Garamantia, the hot and hairy Ethiopians, the perfumed Arabs, the rich Persians, the people of the Ganges and handsome blacks of India, the Babylonians, they who dwell upon the lofty heights of Caucasus, and its rough slopes toward the torrid south as well as the icy north; the peoples by the Caspian Sea, at Tanais and Rhodope in its eternal snow; the grim Hyrcani, and the gross barbarians of Scythia. When finally it had tainted the waves of the eastern ocean and the islands of the Red Sea, it turned at last to us in

[4]

Italy, so that Rome, Mistress of the World, was also wrapped in this cloud. Not to mention all the regions into which this ignorant belief managed to penetrate, there was, as you can see, only a small corner[5] of the earth to the northwest which, unlike the others, was not dignified by any heaven-descended family, though, like the rest, it was infected with unspeakable cruelty.

"All this belongs not to our age. Abraham was yet a youth[6] when such ideas began to creep among the Sicyoni, and insinuate themselves into the minds of ignorant men. In the heroic period they grew in fervor, attained at length their greatest splendor and vogue, and persisted as late as the fall of Troy; for I remember reading that in the Trojan war there fell certain sons of the gods,[7] and that Hecuba was changed to a dog and Polydorus to a twig. That indeed is very remote—many centuries ago. In short this foolish faith[8] without doubt flourished everywhere, and great tomes were written to commemorate for posterity the divine nobility of the Ancients. I always supposed the number of men ambitious for such fame was not small, but Paul[9] of Perugia, a serious man, a very learned and eager investigator of such matters, has repeatedly said in my hearing what he had learned from Barlaam the Calabrian, a scholar of the first rank in Greek literature—that, during the florescence of that fatuity, there was never a man of distinction, political or otherwise, who did not try to prove his descent from one or another of the ancient gods. What then, am I to do, or you, in view of an error so widespread, so ancient, so persistent, recorded in so many documents, and propagated at large among so many men? Do you think I can possibly carry out the King's wishes? Doubtless—if mountains offer easy passage and trackless deserts an open and travelled road; if rivers are fordable and seas tranquil; if Aeolus from his cave sends me in my course strong

and favorable winds; or, better still, if a man might have
on his feet the golden sandals of Argeiphontes,[10] to fly
whithersoever he pleased for the asking. Hardly then
could he cover such extent of land and sea, though his life
were never so long, and he did nothing else. Nay, further,
let us suppose that a man could visit all these places in a
moment, and by God's grace could understand the characters and idiom of various peoples and find entire libraries ready and waiting, who would there be in all the
world—not to mention myself—strong enough, keen
enough, and with good enough memory, first to observe
what is relevant, then to understand it, retain it, note it
down, and finally reduce it to order? You added a further
request, that I explain the meaning which wise men had
hidden under this cover of absurd tales, on the ground that
his renowned Majesty thought it a stupid notion for men
learned in nearly every doctrine to spend time and labor
merely telling stories which are untrue and have only a
literal meaning.

"Well, I will not deny it—the royal discernment which
you report has won me, and given me a very definite subject, since, as you were saying, his genius is really divine;
and it has impelled me to grant his wish, if only my powers
are adequate. Such interpretations are harder than you
think; they are properly the business of a theologian, for
Varro,[11] in treating of many matters both divine and
human, holds that such subjects as this constitute a sort of
theology which may be called 'mythical,' or as others
would say—more accurately, perhaps—'physical.' In view
of such an opinion, and of the large element of absurd un-
truth in mythology, there is the more need of skill in sep-
arating true from false.

"Wherefore, my learned warrior, a man's powers must
be weighed and his abilities carefully considered, if fit and
commensurate burdens are to be laid upon them. Atlas was

able to uphold the heaven on his head, and Alcides was
equal to relieving him of the weary load—divine men both
and both invincibly strong. But me? What am I but a little
fellow, weak, slow-witted, forgetful. And here you are trying to pile on my shoulders not heaven alone, which was
enough for those old heroes, but earth too, and the seas,
nay, the very gods with all their notable train! Why, it's
nothing but a proposal to crush and destroy me. But great
as was the King's conception of this work, if any human
being was really equal to it, it is that distinguished man
Francis Petrarch,[12] at whose feet I have long been a
listener. He is really a man of godlike genius, unfailing
memory, and wonderful eloquence, thoroughly familiar
with the history of the various nations, and learned in the
meaning of myths; one, moreover, who understands every
secret in the bosom of sacred Philosophy."

Here I paused. After a bit he went on, serene of feature
and urbane of speech.

DONINO.   "I suppose that what you say is truer than I
realize, and I can see the difficulties. But, my
dear Giovanni, do you think, pray, that our King is without circumspection? Why, he is a ruler with his eyes open,
well-disposed, and of laudable, royal good nature! Far be
it from him wittingly to oppress you or anyone else; rather
it has long been his habit to lighten the people's burdens;
and in precisely that intention must his commands be understood and accepted.

"I can well believe that those nations you mention are
inaccessible, and that such records as they possess are
wholly unknown to the Latins. But whatever has passed
by way of Greek literature among the Latins, or whatever can be found in Latin writers themselves, who in
early times won no little distinction and glory in literature,
let it all be brought to light, and, if all of it is not available, then King Hugo asks for at least so much as your

endeavors can procure. Therefore please undertake this task without misgiving, and with lively hope in God. Do as well as you can, for no one asks of you the impossible. It has not been my good fortune to meet that noble man, Petrarch, nor has he visited Cyprus, though his fame is universal. I suppose God wills that a man so busy with affairs of utmost importance should be spared this work, and that I should suggest this honorable task to you, a young man,[13] that from it your reputation[14] may soon rise higher and shine even in Cyprus."

BOCCACCIO. "I see, my valiant soldier," I replied. "You suppose this book can be compiled from Greek and Latin sources, without recourse to the recondite books of the barbarians. Dear me, Donino, do you not see for yourself that by such a concession you take back the greatest part of the work? But grant that, as the Roman rulers long since divided the empire into an eastern and western half, we distinguish two bodies of this monster— the one, barbarian, and the other Greek and Latin. Let us, then, suppose that books in Greek and Latin such as you yourself mention, have really existed. Next consider, please, how many enemies these books have had during the passing centuries. Not to cite particular instances, you will admit that a great many collections have perished by fire and flood. Even had the Alexandrian library,[15] which Philadelphus long since collected with utmost care, been the only one lost, the loss would have been appalling, since it contained, according to the Ancients, any book you might want. Furthermore as Christ's most glorious name[16] grew in power, and the pure and radiant light of Truth drove away the shades of the deadly Gentile error; as the glory of the Greeks declined, and the messengers of Christ cried out against the doomed religion and drove it to extermination, there is no question that these zealots destroyed ere they died many books replete with material on this subject, while they were showing by true and pious preaching that instead of many gods and their offspring there was but one God the Father and His only-begotten Son. You will admit that avarice,[17] whose force is very great, has been another enemy of learning. They who are skilled in the study of poetry certainly get no money by it; and the avaricious man values nothing that does not get money; hence he not only neglects anything that gets no money but despises and rejects it. Now as nearly all men are in the race for wealth with both feet, books dealing with our subject have fallen into disuse, and straightway quickly perished. With other forces of destruction was joined the hatred of princes who conspired against books as against their enemies. The number which perished thus, not merely on mythology, but on various arts, could not easily be computed. But if all these enemies had relented, they would never have escaped the silent and adamantine tooth of fleeting time, which slowly eats away not books alone, but hardest rocks, and even steel. It has, alas, reduced much of Greek and Latin literature to dust. And yet, though these and many other losses have occurred, including that of books which would be particularly useful to a task like mine, I cannot deny that much is left. But there is no one book that I know of which contains all this matter about which you are so very curious. The names and tribes of gods and their progenitors are scattered hither and yon all over the world. Here a book and there another has something to say on the subject. But pray who is there that would wish, for no useful result, or at least very little, to hunt them all up, read, and finally gather a few notes? More than this I should not say."

Steadfastly and gravely he looked at me; then he said:

DONINO. "I had not overlooked your probable objections to my moderate request. But they will not cut off my every escape. I will not deny the truth of what you say; and yet I repeat, do what you can! It is only the bit you *can* gather here and there that the King is asking for. You surely cannot refuse him that, can you? But alas, I am afraid that unworthy indolence[18] invents such reasons. You are trying to get out of some hard work. There is nothing worse than an idle young man. If work must be done—and we are all born to it—to whom can you devote your labors more wisely than to this best of kings? Arise, then, shake off this inertia, and gird up your good wits for the task. Thus you will at once obey the King, and make for yourself a path to high renown. You will surely arrive, if you are careful, at the point whither I am urging you. You know how courage and hard work win in everything; you know how fortune favors the brave, and above all else how God never fails those who trust in Him. Come, then, with so much in your favor, turn the books over, nay, inside out; seize your pen, and in the same act serve the King and make your name reverberate to remotest time."

Then I:

BOCCACCIO. "I am vanquished—more by the charm of your plea than by the force of your reason. You urge, drive, yes, force me to comply, willing or unwilling."

And thus, O most merciful King, to address you in person, after contending, your Donino and I, for some time, at last, whether equal to this task or not, I am perforce won to your view—how fitly you shall see. At your behest, then, I leave behind the mountain snails and barren soil of Certaldo,[19] and, raw seaman that I am, embark in my frail little craft[20] on a stormy sea all involved with reefs, little knowing whether my voyage will be worth the trouble. For I may trace every shore and traverse every mountain grove; I may, if need be, explore dyke and den afoot, descend even to hell, or, like another Daedalus, go winging to the ether. Everywhere, to your heart's desire,

I will find and gather, like fragments of a mighty wreck strewn on some vast shore, the relics of the Gentile gods. These relics, scattered through almost infinite volumes, shrunk with age, half consumed, well-nigh a blank, I will bring into such single genealogical order as I can, to gratify your wish.

And yet I shudder to embark on so huge a task; why, if another Prometheus should appear, or the very one who, as poets tell, upon a time made men from clay, I hardly think they would be equal to the task, let alone me. Therefore, illustrious King, to prevent future surprise and disappointment on your part, I would warn you now not to expect, even after great outlay of time and midnight oil, that a work of this sort will have a body of perfect proportion.[21] It will alas, be maimed—not, I hope, in too many members—and for reasons aforesaid distorted, shrunken, and warped. Furthermore, O excellent Prince, to arrange the members in any order, I must proceed to tear the hidden significations from their tough sheathing, and I promise to do so, though not to the last detail of the authors' original intentions. Who in our day can penetrate the hearts of the Ancients?[22] Who can bring to light and life again minds long since removed in death? Who can elicit their meaning? A divine task that—not human! The Ancients departed in the way of all flesh, leaving behind them their literature and their famous names for posterity to interpret according to their own judgment. But as many minds, so many opinions. What wonder? There are the words of Holy Writ, clear, definite, charged with unalterable truth, though often thinly veiled[23] in figurative language. Yet they are frequently distorted into as many meanings as there are readers. This makes me approach my own task with less misgiving. Where I do not perform it well, at least I shall arouse a wiser man to do it better.

It is, therefore, my plan of interpretation first to write what I learn from the Ancients, and when they fail me, or I find them inexplicit, to set down my own opinion. This I shall do with perfect freedom[24] of mind, so that men who are ignorant and fastidiously despise the poets whom they do not understand, may see that the poets, though not Catholics, were so gifted with intelligence that no product of human genius was ever more skilfully enveloped in fiction, nor more beautifully adorned with exquisite language,[25] than theirs. Whence it is clear that they were richly imbued with secular wisdom not often found in their jealous accusers. And these interpretations will enable you to see not only the art of the ancient poets, and the consanguinity and relations of the false gods, but certain natural truths, hidden with an art that will surprise you, together with deeds and moral civilization of the Ancients that are not a matter of every-day information. Furthermore, as the work will prove to be far more extensive than you suppose, I think it will be convenient both for purposes of reference and of memory to divide it into several parts or books. Before each book I plan to set a tree;[26] at the root sits the father[27] of the line, and on the branches, in genealogical order, all his progeny, so that you may have an index of what you are looking for in the book that follows. These Books you will find divided into chapters with proper and fuller rubrics corresponding to the mere name which you have already noted on the tree.

I shall conclude with two books, in the first of which I shall reply to certain objections that have been raised against poetry and poets. In the second—and last of all—I shall endeavor to remove such criticisms as may possibly be levelled at me. But for fear you may think it my fault, I must not fail to explain that it is the Ancients who are to blame, not I, if you often meet in reading my work with statements that are so wide of the truth, so discrepant, that you could never suppose them the utterances of philosophers, no, not even the inventions of rustics; other inconsistencies you will observe in their chronology. All these discrepancies and more I do not purpose to reconcile or correct, unless they naturally submit to some order. I shall be satisfied merely to write down what I find and leave learned disputation to the philosophers.

Finally, it has long been a wise and fitting custom, as Plato advises,[28] in entering upon even the least of ventures, to invoke God's help, and set out in His name. Without it any initiation, Torquatus tells us, is fundamentally unsound. I can quite realize this labor to which I am committed—this vast system of gentile gods and their progeny, torn limb from limb and scattered among the rough and desert places of antiquity and the thorns of hate, wasted away, sunk almost to ashes; and here am I setting forth to collect these fragments, hither and yon, and fit them together, like another Aesculapius restoring Hippolytus. If I trust my own strength I should stagger under this overload. Wherefore to the most merciful Father, the one true God, Maker and Ruler of all things, in whom we mortals have our being, I humbly pray that He favor and aid this vast, ambitious work of mine. May He shine upon my way, a fixed and radiant star, and rule the helm of my little boat as she plows an untried sea. May He at right seasons spread her sails to the wind, that I may follow a course redounding to the splendor, laud, honor, and eternal glory of His name; but to all detractors confusion, ignominy, disgrace, and eternal damnation!

dialectic

pagan pitted against Christian

O Odyssey

BOOK XIV

Here begins the Fourteenth Book of the Genealogy of the Gentile Gods; *wherein the Author, in Reply to their Objections, inveighs against the Enemies of the Name of Poetry.*

PROEM

WITH stumbling pace, yet led of the divine light, I have now made my way[1] through the habitations of Orcus, dark and far from heaven, and past the seat of guilty souls. Tireless has been my voyage, and wide its circuit; I have visited the rocky shores of the farthest sea, and islands that lie scattered under many a sun; I have even sounded[2] with exploring glance the lowest depths of Ocean—the sea-green palaces of Neptune, the old Proteus, the choric bands of nymphs, the chambers of their abode; even the monsters of that deep have I beheld and the hordes of fishes, and have looked also upon the fountains of rivers. Thence came I to famous cities, and shaded groves, to trackless forests, high mountains, steep gorges, and caves hidden away in the rocks. Nay, I have traversed seas of vast extent and passed through desert places whose very name would make one shudder. Then, soaring in imagination as on the wings of Daedalus, I have been borne aloft to heaven, there to gaze upon the golden throne[3] of Jove, the golden house of the Sun, the courts of the gods, the temples exceeding splendid with gems and gleaming gold; and the consistory of those on high, adorable, refulgent; I have considered, too, the everlasting splendors of the stars, their turnings and their returnings, and their motions wonderfully ordered. On all hands, O merciful King, I have according to my promise collected such fragments of the ancient wreck as God willed, and wrought them into a kind of whole, as best I could. I have traced the line of the gods even from Demogorgon[4]—he whom the Ancients in their error, for sake of a beginning, called the first god— through his descendants in order down to Aeolus, the youngest son of Jove the Third,[5] nay, to Athamas, son of Aeolus, and Learchus and Melicertes, sons of Athamas. This have I done with all diligence, that your wish might be fulfilled. And, to disappoint you in no particular, I have added an explanation to each myth, either such as I have found among the Ancients, or have approved in my own judgment; which with God's help you will perceive presently.

Now that all is done, and I have, as it were, reached the home or haven which I sought from the beginning, the desire of rest has been growing stronger within me, urging me to leap ashore[6] from the bow, offer due thanks to God for his gift of a safe return, fix the laurel on my triumphant little boat, and at last depart to my long-sought leisure.

But God hath inspired a far more worthy purpose in me. We are taught by the wise that from the past we may infer the future. Even the greatest ships, especially when ill provided, have often been harassed with hostile winds, sometimes to their destruction. What then can one expect for my little shallop if she be abandoned in mid-ocean without pilot or moorings? Wherefore it is no small task that still awaits me. Her bow must be lashed to the shore and steadied with stout anchors, and she must further be covered with all protection at our command, lest she be burned by fiery thunderbolts in a storm, or swamped with hail and rain, or dashed to pieces by the wind, perhaps the shrieking North, or the stormy South, the mad East or the Southwest, or other winds blowing in wild disorder, or be ground to pieces upon rock or sand, or swallowed up by the weltering waves, and so perish, after I have strained every nerve to bring her to her journey's end through many tides and clashing rocks and currents and a thousand other perils. But indeed I shall consider the venture at an end only when I shall have beaten off with valid reasons certain objections,[7] such as have long been urged by her enemies against the art and works of poetry, or are likely to be urged.

For my part, I know, and well remember, how many and how foolish have been the words of the ignorant as long as they had no opponent. Hence I am fully aware what they, out of envy,[8] will say against poets, and against me, as they read this work. Wherefore unto this last of my labors, which I shall conclude with the two following books, may our Heavenly Father grant his help, who is of all things the Alpha and Omega, the Beginning and the End.

I. THE AUTHOR ADDRESSES THE KING

I HAVE resolved, O illustrious King,[1] that, with Christ's help, this work shall reach the sacred hands of your Highness before it finds its way elsewhere, in order that it may first submit itself to the judgment of him who commanded it, and do him reverence according to its worth. After you have graciously received and reviewed it, and with your high intelligence examined various parts in detail, you will wonder, I think, that what your Majesty asked for has expanded into a bulk so great; though, for lack of books, I personally regard it as in many places quite incomplete. Perhaps as you read, you will wonder to see the meaning that was lately hidden under a rough shell brought forth now into the light—as if one were to see fresh water gushing from a globe of fire—and you will even praise yourself with a kind of mild satisfaction, that you have long been of the right opinion about poets, not, like the

invidious, taking them for mere story-tellers, but rather *poets*
for men of great learning, endowed with a sort of divine
intelligence and skill. Of course, I am not wholly sure what
your estimate of the work as a whole will be after a careful review; yet, it is my private opinion that, in pure justice, you will render a fair and unbiased judgment of both
body and members; and I am equally sure that, while, in
your royal kindness, you object to whatever is at all inept,
you will commend whatever you find praiseworthy. This is
of great—nay of utmost—moment to me, and in this very
hope I am happy and content! But, after your own perusal,
when you offer this work to your friends, and it goes forth,
by your permission, into the world, it will, I fear, not be
weighed in so just a scale by everybody. This is nothing
new under the sun—everyone thinks as he likes. Besides
there is a sort of gnawing malice, a disease, a death-in-life,
which has so usurped men's hearts since the beginning of
the world that, when this fever rages, almost no one can
get fair judgment. Thus many will rise up against my
work, yelping like mad dogs, and wherever they find it
weak, they will seize it with their impious jaws and tear it
to pieces. These and their cant objections, which, as I just
said, I can readily forecast, I am forced to oppugn with
timely reply, that this laborious achievement be not
easily dissipated, and, under attack of their fiery darts,
perish in sparks and ashes. But I beseech you, most noble
King, for whom I have labored now so long, to support me
in this conflict with your noble spirit, and by so doing
make sure that the enemies of my work vanish like smoke
into thin air.

II. A BRIEF ARRAIGNMENT OF THE IGNORANT

AROUND my book, as usual at the sight of a new work,
will gather a crowd of the incompetent. The learned will
also attend, and, after a careful inspection, doubtless some
of them who are revered for their righteousness, and pos-

sess both fairness of mind and scholarship, will, by your
example, praise whatever is commendable and, in all reverence, criticise whatever is not. To such I am constrained to
express my kindest and most respectful acknowledgment,
and to commend the fairness of their opinion. But a far
more numerous crowd will gather about in a ring, and pry
curiously into the chinks of a work none too articulate,[1] or
into other possible defects. They hunger more to consume
than to approve. With these is my quarrel, with these must
I fight; and these I must overcome with the aid of better
reasons than I have cited thus far. Yet not against the whole
crowd at once shall I go forth, for it would readily sur-
round and put me down. But I will engage isolated groups,
that my hand may grow used to the conflict and by degrees wear out the enemy. First, then, I take the weakest.

There are, among others in this crowd, certain madmen[2] so garrulous and detestably arrogant that they pre-
sume to shout abroad their condemnation of everything
that even the best men can do. It is their aim to cheapen
and vilify, and, if possible, utterly damn them with their
foul calumny. Like cattle they go bellowing their idiocy
about as if it were really a high distinction; then sounding
the depths of their baseness, they set greatest store by
elaborate suppers, carnality, and utter idleness; in taverns
and brothels, alternately pledging themselves in foaming
beakers and vomiting their liquor, they try to spoil the
lucubrations, thoughts, and studies, the unassuming and
honest labors of learned men by obscene raillery. Thus at
first sight of my work they jeer: "What a dull person!
How much fair leisure and good time he has lost, how
much silly pains he has spent, how many parchments
wasted, and how many doggerel verses burned, and all to
no purpose! Were it not better to love, drink, sleep, and
devote all this time to pleasure rather than turn out such
stuff as this? Certainly they who pursue a reputation for

wisdom are the biggest fools! For with all their time spent
in study and disapproval of what is profitable, ere they
know a single happy day of their lives, they meet death
who spares none."

A wise verdict indeed, and a reverend, proceeding as it
does from panders' revels, from a senate of Gnathos,[3]
from dives of gluttons, and wine-bibbers, and from the
dens of whoremongers. In brief the reproaches of such as
these are to me like the glorious praise of great men, when
I consider that only a rascal can win a rascal's praise. Let
such men go, therefore, and gabble their applause to inn-
keepers, trainers, fishmongers, and queans; and sodden
with wine and sleep, bestow their praises upon such as
these, but leave the wise to labor in their own light. For
there is nought so ugly as an ignoramus; none so unreason-
able as a fool. Such are they who, long ere the miserable
hour of their death, have made the body the grave of an
unhappy soul.[4] Why, these men so reek with their foul infamy that the judicious, who can endure the bray of an
ass, the grunt of hogs, the bellowing of cattle, cannot listen
to them. Again I say, let them go their ways, serve their
bellies, and blush, not merely to revile others, but even to
appear, if ever they are sober, in the presence of men.

III. AGAINST THOSE WHO, WITHOUT LEARNING OR TASTE, PRETEND TO BOTH

THE second class[1] of men awaiting this book are perhaps
less open to criticism of moral character than the
first, but are surely not more intelligent. These are they
who, before ever darkening the door of a school, have
sometime or other overheard the names of certain philosophers, and thus consider themselves philosophers; or,
at least they desire to be thought so of others. They then
affect a certain weighty style and ponderous bearing, glance
over a few popular books[2] only in as far as they touch upon
more important points; then, to get their reputation, they

forgather with really erudite men, start question after question about the highest truths: for example, whether one Deity can consist of three persons; whether God can create anything in His own image; why He did not create the world a million years sooner; and the like. When they hear the answers of the wise, they offer a few silly considerations in reply. Then, after the teachers have rejoined and concluded the matter, not to seem too easily satisfied, they give a doubtful little shake of the head, smile knowingly, then stand about, glance at the bystanders, as if to say that they deferred merely to the reverence of their interlocutor. At length, whatever their slack and puny minds have caught from the lips of righteous men, and retained, they carry away to spout to a lot of websters, or at best, to an ignorant mob gaping at the corner.[3] There they fetch a deep sigh, then blab away about having consulted God himself, to give an impression that only by the greatest effort of speculative genius were their words torn from the very penetralia of the divine mind. Then, as a final proof to the unskilful of their absolute wisdom, they expand their discourse in anything but a consistent order, jumping[4] hither and yon through all sorts of subjects, never reaching a conclusion, but ever more and more hopelessly entangling both themselves and their hearers; as if they were filled to surfeit with liberal arts, many of whose names in point of fact they do not even know. They refer also with peevish sneer to Priscian,[5] Aristotle, Cicero, Aristarchus, Euclid, Ptolemy, and such, to show that they have neglected them for the sweet attraction of Theology to higher things. In like manner they treat moral character, the deeds of heroes, sacred laws and institutes, and all legislators.[6] But if ever the talk falls upon poetry and poets, then as if they enjoyed supreme knowledge and discrimination, they condemn, revile, and vilify both poets and poetry with such scorn, and make such a display of spurning them, that even the unsophisticated can hardly stand their outburst. They call the Muses fools and babblers, while Helicon, the Castalian spring, the grove of Phoebus and the like are the raving of lunatics, or mere elementary exercises in grammar.

From such fatuity I can easily infer what, at first sight of the monster, they will say of me, my work, and poets in general. But one should rather bear with their folly, I think, than urge reasons against it; for since they do not understand themselves, far less are they likely to understand others. Besides they are ignorant, and wanting as they do the light of truth, they let themselves be carried away by sensuality. And I would tell them for charity's sake—not that they deserve it—to mind their own business and let others alone. If they really are impelled by this desire for glory, and seek a reputation for wisdom, let them go to school, listen to teachers, pore over their books, study late, learn something, frequent the halls of brilliant debaters; and lest they rush into teaching with undue haste, let them remember the Pythagorean caveat, that no one who came to his school to speak on philosophical subjects should open his mouth till he had listened five years.[7] When they shall win praise in this respect, and earn genuine title, then, if they wish to come forward, let them lecture, or dispute, or refute, or inveigh, and vigorously press their opponents. But any other course is proof rather of madness than wisdom.

IV. TO THE JURISTS, WITH A BRIEF DIGRESSION IN PRAISE OF POVERTY[1]

THERE is further a class of men, recognizable by the golden buckles of their togas and almost regal decorations, and yet not less remarkable for their impressive gait and bearing and their fluency of speech. Clients swarm at their heels, and they are conspicuous and influential men. In reality they are eminent teachers of the law, and judges,

and, in their proper administration of the law, hold a
tight rein on the evil forces that pervert society. Thus by
their help innocence is exalted, each man gets just rights,
and the State is not only maintained in its natural strength,
but, through an increasing tradition of justice, grows
stronger and better. These men[2] therefore deserve special
reverence and honor.

But wisely as they purge the stains of others, yet are
they themselves marked, almost to a man, with one taint—
the love of money;[3] they think nothing and nobody deserves approval that is not aglitter with gold. These, I
expect, will come along with the rest, to see whether there
is not some offence in my work against which they may
take the law; and I know perfectly, if they stick to their
precedent, what objection they will make. It is their practice, especially during a lull in their duties, to leave bench
and court, and join an informal gathering of friends; if,
in the course of the conversation, anyone happens to mention poets, they always praise them highly of course, as
men of great learning and eloquence. But at length with
the honey they mingle poison—not deadly, to be sure. They
say poets can hardly be called wise to have spent their
whole time following a profession that, after years of
labor, yields never a cent. This explains, they add, why
poets are always stark poor; they never make brilliant
showing with dress, money, nor servants; from this they
argue that, because poets are not rich, their profession is
good for nothing. Such reasoning along with its unex-
pressed conclusion, finds easy access to the ears and minds
of others, since we are all somewhat given to love of
money, and foolishly take wealth to be the greatest thing
in the world. If they come to examine my work, I daresay
they will be enough smitten of this disease to say: "Oh yes,
a very pretty work, but of no use whatever!" And they will
dub my endeavors futile because they tend in a direction

exactly opposite to that of the efforts of others. Thus they
will not only seem to pass sentence on me, but, by implication, to condemn poets themselves, together with their
works and their poverty, as a supreme and detestable evil.
Well, this objection seems at once God-fearing and humane
and popular, and would, indeed, deserve a vote of thanks if
it really flowed from a charitable source. But arising, as in
point of fact it does, from the obfuscated judgment of men
without taste, it should be laughed to scorn; while we only
pity this itch for money. Yet some deference to high position of such men is fitting; and, that they may not feel
they have been snubbed, I think their objection should be
traced to its origins somewhat more at length.

I readily grant[4] therefore their contention, that poetry
does not make money, and poets have always been poor—
if they can be called poor who of their own accord have
scorned wealth. But I do not concede that they were fools
to follow the study of poetry, since I regard them as the
wisest of men,[5] provided they have, like good Catholics,
recognized the true God. And now to resume—that I may
not by so free a confession appear to have abandoned the
field of conflict altogether to my opponents and yielded
them the victory—let me bring forward their first objection.

These gorgeous interpreters of the law say, then, that
poetry does not get wealth, thus hoping, as one may easily
see, to separate it from all things worthy of imitation as a
subject of no moment among the various branches of
knowledge. I repeat, poetry certainly never does make one
rich, yet I do not admit their claim that it thereby makes
for meanness. For money-getting is *not* the function and
end of the speculative sciences, but of the applied sciences
and finance. Indeed these last aim at nothing else, and, to
achieve it quickly, they never render any service absolutely
gratis. Likewise the court lawyers, out of their acquain-

tance with the law and out of the failings of their fellow men, rear offices wherein they fairly coin money with the stamp of a venal tongue, and make gold out of the tears of the wretched by the transmuting power of their own verbosity. But poetry, mindful of its high origin, utterly abhors and rejects such a practice, and if it is to be condemned and despised for this, then Philosophy, mistress of things,[6] who teaches us the causes of all that exists, must sink into low price, or to none at all. The same is true of Theology, by which we attain to a true knowledge of God. I never have heard that *these* sciences implied zeal for the acquisition of wealth. But, though my opponents may not be aware of it, Poetry devotes herself to something greater; for while she dwells in heaven, and mingles with the divine counsels, she moves the minds of a few men from on high to a yearning for the eternal, lifting them by her loveliness to high revery, drawing them away into the discovery of strange wonders, and pouring forth most exquisite discourse from her exalted mind. And if at any time in answer to gentle prayers, she leave her lofty throne, and descend to earth with her meinie of sacred Muses, she never seeks a habitation in the towering palaces of kings or the easy abodes of the luxurious; rather she visits caves on the steep mountainside, or shady groves, or argent springs, where are the retreats of the studious, often plain enough and ill lighted with the light that fails; and there she dwells.[7] All of which I shall treat more fully elsewhere[8] in its proper place. Thus, ethereal and eternal as she is, she has no dealings with things that perish, but holds of little worth all splendors made with hands as things useless and empty, for she is content with her proper benefits, and cares not to heap up wealth.

But further my opponents, proceeding from their first charge, subjoin that poets have not been very wise to hold a creed whose followers never get rich. To answer this

objection properly, I think we very much need the help
of one who can make a wise choice, and I hope my
opponents will agree with me as to whether jurist or poet
deserves a reputation of wiser discernment. Without
question it is wiser, in my opinion, to select that mind
which transports us on high, instead of that which bears
us down to earth; a mind firmly established instead of
one tottering on the verge of a fall; a mind which offers
lifelong benefit rather than briefest felicity. At any rate
the poets have chosen a science[9] or pursuit of knowledge
which by constant meditation draws them away into
the region of stars, among the divinely adorned dwellings
of the gods and their heavenly splendors. Whether this be
true testimony let the poems of the prophets bear witness
in their own words, written down as they are in excellent
style[10] by the pen of poets under direct impulse of this
divine knowledge. Lawyers, in their practice of law, are
skilled in mere memory of what is written, and dispense
the decisions and rulings of legislators literally, but without intelligence. Obviously it is not their business to consider high or remote matters—whether, for example, the
sun moves from India to Spain in a right or an oblique line
—but rather whether John Doe or Richard Roe holds a
trifle of land by right hereditary, or in tenure of emphy-
teusis or precary, or whether a certain sum is to be de-
clared just or extortionate, or whether a high-spirited
woman should have a divorce on grounds of incompati-
bility. Great and noble matters these—exalted far above
the lap of nature!

Furthermore poetry, such as the poor poets have chosen
to cultivate, constitutes a stable and fixed science founded
upon things eternal, and confirmed by original principles;
in all times and places this knowledge is the same, un-
shaken by any possible change. Not so with the law; the
Slav, for example, knows not the same civil laws as the

African. In the toil of war men feel less the authority of the law than in the happy tranquillity of peace. Then too city ordinances and statutes of the realm may greatly increase or diminish the power of a law; and the proclaimed adjournment[11] of court may silence them. Laws even become antiquated and sometimes actually dead; for some were long ago held in very high regard which in our times are either neglected or wholly obsolete; and consequently not invariable like poetry. In a word, then, it is clear enough from what has been said that we should speak of the practice of law, not of the science of law; and how much a science transcends mere practice[12] the wise of all times know—both ancient and modern.

Furthermore, if the privilege of long life is not granted a man in any other way, poetry, at any rate, through fame vouchsafes to her followers the lasting benefit of survival —rightly enough called a benefit, since we all long for it. It is perfectly clear that the songs of poets, like the name of the composer, are almost immortal.[13] As for jurists, they may shine for a little while in their gorgeous apparel, but their names in most cases perish with the body. Short is a lifetime, if you count up the lifetimes that Homer has lived. And now to come to the point I had in mind: no educated man will doubt that the poets have chosen wisely, while the jurists have shown less sense in their choice, since they have actually made fools of themselves in trying to impute to those who do not deserve it the fault which really is their own.

They say again that poets have always been very poor, pouring out the charge, as it were, from excess of drinking at the source already mentioned, and that too, as if their great wealth as lawyers made poverty infamous and detestable. It is obvious enough, as I said, that lawyers have raked together a heap of gold from the tears, troubles, dangers, nay often the actual suffering of others.[14] This is

the way they go about becloaked and befringed, loaded
with all kinds of fur, aglitter with large gold pins, a string
of clients trailing at their heels, since this sort of display
is what humanity is mad about. Likewise it is not idleness
but innocence and deliberate choice[15] that have made the
poets poor, as no one will deny. Yet contrary to their desire, they have been marked by a certain eminent and enduring lustre of renown; and I can easily cite examples to
prove it. Thus we are assured that Homer[16] was so poor
that, when he lost his eyesight, he had not enough to pay a
boy to lead him. Wait but a little and you shall see whether
adornment is not in store for this poverty. When Darius,
the rich and powerful king of the Persians, had been con-
quered by Alexander of Macedon, some jewels fell into
Alexander's possession, among which was found a rare
gold casket, most exquisitely wrought and adorned; this
casket, by unanimous consent both of Alexander and his
generals, was set apart not for his jewels, but for his volumes of Homer. What honor as splendid as this was ever
bestowed upon bedizened jurists? Nobody ever saw less of
the good things of this world than Plautus of Sarsina.[17]
He, to feed himself honestly in his destitution, used all day
to wear himself out working at the hand-mills for a pit-
tance, then sit up all night writing his comedies; yet their
number and workmanship is such that the laurel of victory,
the special decoration of triumphant emperors, was not
too proud a distinction to encircle his brow. To the glory
of his name it remains green and fragrant even unto
this day, while the birettas of jurists, for all their wealth,
have become food for mice and worms. Again, Ennius of
Brundisium,[18] a highly illustrious man, and seer as well,
had means so slender that he dwelt on the Aventine, content with the service of one little maid. His want of servants has found full recompense in the wealth of his
honors. Of these, since, on his own merits, his fame is very

great, I need mention but one. When the day of life was over, his friends, the Scipios, had him buried in their tomb, showing that they did not scorn to have a Brundisian's ashes mingled with those of the Cornelii. Again, everybody has heard that Vergil[19] was the poor son of a potter; he was worth only the little paternal plot in the village of Andes, the modern Pietola, near Mantua, nor did he hold that free of litigation. But so deserving were his attainments that he enjoyed the friendship of Octavius Augustus, master of all the world. When, on his deathbed, the poet ordered in his will that the *Aeneid* be burned, the Emperor trampled all the authority of the laws under foot to save this great poem, and in an exquisite lyric published his order that it be preserved and studied. What lawyer, I should like to know, however gorgeous in gems and gold, ever received so splendid an honor at the hands of so glorious a prince? And many another distinguished example follows of poets happy in their modest means, while marked with like honors. But time fails for fuller illustration.

These and earlier proofs are enough to show that poets, though poor, have been wise, and even illustrious, and that they live with the eternity of their fame, while the wealth and names of jurists vanish like smoke into thin air. By the same course of reasoning I have shown also that this work of mine, if poetry is worth anything, is least of all superfluous, nor were my labors in compiling it vain.

At this point let me turn a little aside in hope of curbing the violence of those who inveigh against poverty. This poverty, then, which most people flee as an intolerable ill, is really a mere paucity of perishable goods. Yet I should call poverty also a mental disease that often afflicts even the rich. The first kind—mere paucity of perishable goods —where one cares naught for increase, is highly desirable as a bringer of tranquillity and infinite comforts. The second—a mental disease—is the enemy of peace and quiet, and cruelly tortures the mind it possesses.[20] The first has been the lot of the poets whom my opponents call poor, but who were satisfied with enough to live on. For, with such poverty as our leader, we by choice attain to liberty and peace of mind, and thereby to honorable ease; whereby, while we dwell in the midst of earth, we taste the delights of heaven. Such poverty is founded upon a rock, fearing neither threat nor thrust of Fortune, who confounds this world. Let thunders fall and mad winds smite the earth; incessant rain submerge the fields, rivers wash them away; let trumpets sound to battle and tumultuous wars arise, and plunder rage on every hand. Amid all, Poverty smiles at fire and ruin, and rejoices in sweet security. Nay it was Poverty that the Delphic oracle, in person of Aglaus of Psophis,[21] who owned a handful of land, set above the wealth of King Gyges. Poverty hath lured poets to adorn their souls with virtues, to spend time in meditation on things divine, to weave poetic fabrics in high-sounding verse, and to seek for themselves an enduring name. She lured Diogenes,[22] most illustrious and richest of the Cynics in his time, to spend his huge substance upon those who needed it, and he actually spent it all. Then by choice he dwelt in a tub—a sort of movable house— instead of a palace, and fared on wild lettuce prepared by his own hands, rather than pay court to Dionysius for the sake of enjoying the dainties of kings. Such deliberate rejection of wealth, together with his fame for learning, were enough to draw a certain proud young man to an interview with him—no less than Alexander of Macedon, who was already meditating the rule of the world. He sought the philosopher's friendship, and offered him great gifts, but in vain. Poverty lured Xenocrates,[23] who was content with a small garden, to prompt a desire in this same young man's mind for his good will. To win it he

sent a splendid embassy laden with royal gifts. She lured
Democritus[24] of his own accord to give his paternal lands
and untold wealth to the republic of Athens, since he would
rather enjoy the liberty to study in poverty, than be harassed
with the slavish care for money. She lured Anaxagoras to
renounce great rewards for the sake of sweet philosophy,
alleging as he did so, that, if he had preferred to cultivate
them, he would have lost himself. She enabled Amyclas,[25] a
poor sailor, alone on the shore by night, to hear unperturbed
the voice of Caesar, of which the proud kings stood in fear,
as the great man called and knocked at the door of his
hut. In like manner Aruns,[26] a poor seer, when all Italy
was ablaze with civil war, stood without a tremor among
the marble mountains of Luna, and studied the motions of
heavens, sun, and moon. Now all these facts they fail to
consider who first violently attack Poverty, then run away.
Pray, let them say whether it was incumbent upon Homer
to go to law with his overseer about the management of his
farm, or exact an account of household affairs from his
housekeeper, as long as he could produce the *Iliad,* and
hand down his name bright in starry splendor even unto
this day. I might ask the same regarding Vergil or the
others who have cultivated the art of poetry in poverty.
They, then, who are clothed in purple need not despise her
for going forth clad in a thin mantle; for this is the first
glory of them who endeavor aright. Nor would they say
that she walks alone, nor call her low and filthy. I know
not—or rather I do know—how much good it does to dress
the body in cloth of gold, while the mind[27] grows foul with
vice. This kind of poverty, though you heed it not, is
adorned with heavenly charms invisible to eyes that are
darkened with the clouds of avarice. Nor does Poverty go
forth alone, though it may seem so to them who are followed by an anxious crowd of clients. Ever in her train are
seers crowned with laurel, emperors wearing tunics em-

broidered with palms. She goes adorned with divine song
by Homer,[28] whose name is in many a mouth, by Hesiod,
Euripides, Ennius, Terence, Vergil, Flaccus, and many
another. Her the Camilli,[29] the Quintii, the Curtii, the
Fabricii, the Scipios and Catos have adorned with marvellous triumphs, richer in emulation and the glory of their
deeds than in gold. Her they have set above exalted kings,
and thus made her empress of the world. With all this
state and following will the lawyers then say that she walks
poor and alone?

Much besides might I utter in praise of such poverty,
but for my desire to touch upon the sort of poverty that
afflicts those who in so large a number imagine themselves
rich. For the second kind of poverty—that of the imagination—is theirs who try to flee it as they would the enemy;
little they realize that the harder they follow riches, the
more they are throwing themselves into poverty's very
arms. What else is such poverty, I wonder, than persecu-
tion in the midst of vast wealth by a desire to get more?
Can I call Tantalus[30] rich, who, though surrounded with
food and drink, dies of hunger and thirst? Nay he is surely
the poorest of all.

Yet suppose our jurists as rich as Darius, would they get
any enjoyment from their wealth? If we may trust experience, so-called rich men suffer from a constant fever of
anxiety. Let a tiny cloud appear, and the rich man immediately dreads rain, and fears that his crops will be
ruined. If a breeze springs up, he is all of a tremble lest
his fruit-trees be uprooted or his buildings blown down.
If fire breaks out in his neighborhood, he is ready to drop
with fright lest it reach his house. If war, then he miserably forecasts the plundering of flocks and herds—poor
wretch! If a lawsuit is settled, he sets up a groan over it
as his misfortune. The envy of friends, the stealth or

[31]

violence of thieves, the intriguing of relatives, civil dis-
orders—one or more of these keeps him in constant and
foolish terror. I could mention many another care—all of
which make these rich people not only poor, but actually
destitute. The gifts of fortune stand on slippery ground
without support. Therefore let these wretches no longer
insult deserving men, and remember that men who are
really rich and wise do not produce mere burdens for the
shoulders, but treasure to be kept in a pure heart. Let them
consider how foolish it would be to suppose, even if wealth
were desirable, that Nature would be so harsh, or God so
cruel, as to plunge us naked into this transient life. Men
are naturally content with little, and enough is granted us
without our effort, so that even if we would, we cannot
be destitute. Besides, virtue, not robes, is man's natural
ornament. I therefore beseech these egregious tamers of
human nature, to leave poets in peace. For properly and
essentially they have no business with poets—nor poets
with them. Poets sing their songs in retirement; lawyers
wrangle noisily in the courts amid the crowd and bustle of
the market. Poets long for glory and high fame; lawyers
for gold. Poets delight in the stillness and solitude of the
country; lawyers in office buildings, courts, and the clamor
of litigants. Poets are friends of peace; lawyers of cases
and trials. But if they will not listen to my plea, let them
at any rate give ear to the authority of Solon,[31] himself a
most learned lawyer, who, when he had finished his tables,
forsook the law for poetry, and who would have proved
another Homer, if he had lived.

V. OTHER CAVILLERS AT THE POETS AND THEIR
IMPUTATIONS

THERE is also, O most serene of rulers, as you know far
better than I, a kind of house established in this world by
God's gift, in the image of a celestial council, and devoted

only to sacred studies. Within, on a lofty throne, sits
Philosophy,[1] messenger from the very bosom of God,
mistress of all knowledge. Noble is her mien and radiant
with godlike splendor. There she sits arrayed in royal robes
and adorned with a golden crown, like the Empress of all
the World. In her left hand she holds several books, with
her right hand she wields a royal sceptre, and in clear and
fluent discourse she shows forth to such as will listen the
truly praiseworthy ideals of human character, the forces of
our Mother Nature, the true good, and the secrets[2] of
heaven. If you enter you do not doubt that it is a sanctuary
full worthy of all reverence; and if you look about, you
will clearly see there every opportunity for the higher
pursuits of the human mind, both speculation and knowledge, and will gaze with wonder till you regard it not
merely as one all-inclusive household, but almost the very
image of the divine mind. Among other objects of great
veneration there, behind the mistress of the household, are
certain men seated in high places, few in number, of gentle
aspect and utterance, who are so distinguished by their
seriousness, honesty, and true humility, that you take them
for gods not mortals. These men abound in the faith and
doctrine of their mistress, and give freely to others of the
fullness of their knowledge.

But there is also another group[3]—a noisy crowd—of all
sorts and conditions. Some of these have resigned all pride,
and live in watchful obedience to the injunctions of their
superiors, in hopes that their obsequious zeal may gain
them promotion. But others there are who grow so elated
with what is virtually elementary knowledge, that they fall
upon their great mistress' robes as it were with their
talons, and in violent haste tear away a few shreds as
samples; then don various titles which they often pick up
for a price; and, as puffed up as if they knew the whole
subject of divinity, they rush forth from the sacred house,

setting such mischief afoot among ignorant people as only
the wise can calculate. Yet these rascals are sworn conspirators against all high arts. First they try to counterfeit a good man; they exchange their natural expression
for an anxious, careful one. They go about with downcast
eye to appear inseparable from their thoughts. Their pace
is slow to make the uneducated think that they stagger
under an excessive weight of high speculation. They dress
unpretentiously, not because they are really modest, but
only to mask themselves with sanctity. Their talk is little
and serious. If you ask them a question they heave a sigh,
pause a moment, raise their eyes to heaven, and at length
deign to answer. They hope the bystanders will infer from
this that their words rise slowly to their lips, not from
any lack of eloquence, but because they are fetched from
the remote sanctuary of heavenly secrets. They profess
piety, sanctity, and justice, and often, forsooth, utter
the words of the prophet,[4] "The zeal of God's house hath
eaten me up."

Then they proceed to display their wonderful knowledge, and whatever they don't know they damn—to good
effect too. This they do to avoid inquiry about subjects
of which they are ignorant, or else to affect scorn and indifference in such matters as cheap, trivial, and obvious,
while they have devoted themselves to things of greater
importance. When they have caught inexperienced minds
in traps of this sort, they proceed boldly to range about
town, dabble in business, give advice, arrange marriages,
appear at big dinners, dictate wills, act as executors of
estates, and otherwise display arrogance unbecoming to a
philosopher. Thus they blow up a huge cloud of popular
reputation, and thereby so strut with vanity that, when they
walk abroad, they want to have everybody's finger pointing them out, to overhear people saying that they are
great masters of their subjects, and see how the grand

folk rise to meet them in the squares of the city and call them "Rabbi," speak to them, invite them, give place and defer to them. Straightway they throw off all restraint and become bold enough for anything; they are not afraid to lay their own sickles to the harvest of another; and haply, while they are basely defiling other people's business, the talk may fall upon poetry and poets. At the sound of the word they blaze up in such a sudden fury that you would say their eyes were afire. They cannot stop; they go raging on by the very momentum of their wrath. Finally, like conspirators against a deadly enemy, in the schools, in public squares, in pulpits, with a lazy crowd, as a rule, for an audience, they break out into such mad denunciation of poets that the bystanders are afraid of the speakers themselves, let alone the harmless objects of attack.[5]

They say[6] poetry is absolutely of no account, and the making of poetry a useless and absurd craft; that poets are tale-mongers,[7] or, in lower terms, liars; that they live in the country among the woods and mountains because they lack manners and polish. They say, besides, that their poems are false, obscure, lewd, and replete with absurd and silly tales of pagan gods, and that they make Jove,[8] who was, in point of fact, an obscene and adulterous man, now the father of gods, now king of heaven, now fire, or air, or man, or bull, or eagle, or similar irrelevant things; in like manner poets exalt to fame Juno and infinite others under various names. Again and again they cry out that poets are seducers of the mind, prompters of crime, and, to make their foul charge, fouler, if possible, they say they are philosophers' apes, that it is a heinous crime to read or possess the books of poets; and then, without making any distinction, they prop themselves up, as they say, with Plato's authority to the effect that poets ought to be turned out-of-doors—nay, out of town, and that the Muses, their mumming mistresses, as Boethius says, being sweet with deadly sweetness, are detestable, and should be driven out with them and utterly rejected. But it would take too long to cite everything that their irritable spite and deadly hatred prompt these madmen to say. It is also before judges like these—so eminent, forsooth, so fair, so merciful, so well-inclined— that my work will appear, O glorious Prince; and I know full well they will gather about it like famished lions,[9] to seek what they may devour. Since my book has entirely to do with poetic material, I cannot look for a milder sentence from them than in their rage they thunder down upon poets. I am well aware that I offer my breast to the same missiles that their hatred has already employed; but I shall endeavor to ward them off.

O merciful God, meet now this foolish and ill-considered clamor of mad men, and oppose their rage. And thou, O best of kings, as I advance upon their line, support me with the strength of thy noble soul, and help me in my fight for thee; for courage and a stout heart must now be mine. Sharp and poisonous are their weapons, but weak withal. Foolish judges though they be, they are strong in other ways, and I tremble with fear before them, unless God, who deserteth not them that trust in Him, and thou, also, favor me. Slender is my strength and my mind weak, but great is my expectation of help; borne up by such hope, I shall rush upon them with justice at my right hand.

VI. POETRY IS A USEFUL ART

I AM about to enter the arena, a manikin against these giant hulks—who have armed themselves with authority to say that poetry is either no art at all or a useless one. In the circumstances, for me first to discuss the definition and function of poetry would be hunting a mare's nest.[1] But since the fight must be fought I wish these past masters of all the arts would declare upon what particular point they desire the contest to bear. Yet I know full well that with a sneer and a brazen front they will unblushingly utter the same ineptitudes as before. Come, O merciful God, give ear to their foolish objections and guide their steps into a better way.

They say, then, in condemnation of poetry, that it is naught.[2] If such is the case, I should like to know why, through generation after generation, so many great men have sought the name of poet. Whence come so many volumes of poems? If poetry is naught, whence came this word poetry? Whatever answer they make, they are going out of their way, I think, since they can give no rational answer that is not directly against their present vain contention. It is absolutely certain, as I shall show later,[3] that poetry, like other studies, is derived from God, Author of all wisdom; like the rest it got its name from its effect. From this name "poetry" at length comes the glorious name of "poet"; and from "poet," "poem." In that case poetry apparently is not wholly naught, as they said.

If then it prove a science, what more will those noisy sophists have to say? They will either retract a little, or rather, I think, flit lightly over the gap thus opening in their argument to the second point of their objection, and say that if poetry *is* a mere art,[4] it is a useless one. How rank! How silly! Better to have kept quiet than hurl themselves with their frivolous words into deeper error. Why, do not the fools see that the very meaning of this word "art" or "faculty" always implies a certain plenitude? But of this elsewhere.[5] Just now I wish that these accomplished gentlemen would show how poetry can reasonably be called futile when it has, by God's grace, given birth to so many famous books, so many memorable poems, clearly conceived, and dealing with strange marvels. They will keep quiet at this, I think, if their vain itch for display will let them.

Keep quiet, did I say? Why they would rather die than confess the truth in silence, not to say with the tip of their tongues. They will dart off on another tack, and by their own arbitrary interpretation, will say, with slight addition, that poetry must be regarded a futile and empty thing, nay, damnable, detestable, because the poems which come of it sing the adulteries of the gods they celebrate, and beguile the reader[6] into unspeakable practices. Though this interpretation is easy to refute—since nothing can be empty that is filled with adulteries[7]—in any case it may be borne with a calm mind; nay their contention based upon it may be granted in all reason, since I readily acknowledge that there are poems of the kind they describe, and if the bad kind were to corrupt the good, then the victory would be theirs. But, I protest; if Praxiteles or Phidias, both experts in their art, should choose for a statue the immodest subject of Priapus on his way to Iole[8] by night, instead of Diana glorified in her chastity; or if Apelles,[9] or our own Giotto[10]—whom Apelles in his time did not excel—should represent Venus in the embrace of Mars[11] instead of the enthroned Jove dispensing laws unto the gods, shall we therefore condemn these arts? Downright stupidity, I should call it!

The fault for such corruption lies in the licentious mind of the artist. Thus for a long time there have been "poets," if such deserve the name, who, either to get money or popularity,[12] study contemporary fashions, pander to a licentious taste, and at the cost of all self-respect, the loss of all honor, abandon themselves to these literary fooleries. Their works certainly should be condemned, hated, and spurned, as I shall show later.[13] Yet if a few writers of fiction erred thus, poetry does not therefore deserve universal condemnation, since it offers us so many inducements to virtue, in the monitions and teaching of poets whose care it has been to set forth with lofty intelligence, and utmost candor, in exquisite style and diction, men's thoughts on things of heaven.[14]

But enough! Not only is poetry more than naught, but it is a science worthy of veneration; and, as often appears in the foregoing as well as in succeeding pages, it is an art[15] or skill, not empty, but full of the sap of natural vigor for those who would through fiction subdue the senses with the mind. So, not to be tedious, it would seem that at the first onset of this conflict these leaders have turned tail, and, with slight effort on my part, have abandoned the arena. But it is my present duty to define Poetry, that they may see for themselves how stupid they are in their opinion that poetry is an empty art.

VII. THE DEFINITION OF POETRY, ITS ORIGIN, AND FUNCTION[1]

THIS poetry, which ignorant triflers cast aside, is a sort of fervid and exquisite invention, with fervid expression, in speech or writing, of that which the mind has invented.[2] It proceeds from the bosom of God,[3] and few, I find, are the souls in whom this gift is born; indeed so wonderful a gift it is that true poets have always been the rarest of men.[4] This fervor of poesy is sublime in its effects: it impels the soul to a longing for utterance; it brings forth strange and unheard-of creations[5] of the mind; it arranges these meditations in a fixed order,[6] adorns the whole[7] composition with unusual interweaving of words and thoughts; and thus it veils truth in a fair and fitting garment of fiction.[8] Further, if in any case the invention so requires, it can arm kings, marshal them for war, launch whole fleets from their docks, nay, counterfeit sky, land, sea, adorn young maidens with flowery garlands, portray human character in its various phases, awake the idle, stimulate the dull, restrain the rash, subdue the criminal, and distinguish excellent men with their proper meed of praise: these, and many other such, are the effects of poetry. Yet if any man who has received the gift of poetic fervor shall imperfectly fulfil its function here described, he is not, in my opinion, a laudable poet. For, however deeply the poetic impulse stirs the mind to which it is granted, it very rarely accomplishes anything commendable if the instruments[9] by which its concepts are to be wrought out are wanting—I mean, for example, the precepts of grammar and rhetoric, an abundant knowledge of which is opportune. I grant that many a man already writes his mother tongue[10] admirably, and indeed has performed each of the various duties of poetry as such; yet over and above this, it is necessary to know at least the principles of the other Liberal Arts,[11] both moral and natural,[12] to possess a strong and abundant vocabulary, to behold the monuments and relics[13] of the Ancients, to have in one's memory the histories of the nations, and to be familiar with the geography of various lands, of seas, rivers and mountains.

Furthermore, places of retirement, the lovely handiwork of Nature herself, are favorable to poetry, as well as peace of mind and desire for worldly glory;[14] the ardent period of life[15] also has very often been of great advantage. If these conditions fail, the power of creative genius frequently grows dull and sluggish.

Now since nothing proceeds from this poetic fervor, which sharpens and illumines the powers of the mind, except what is wrought out by art,[16] poetry is generally called an art. Indeed the word poetry has not the origin that many carelessly suppose, namely *poio, pois,* which is but Latin *fingo, fingis;* rather it is derived from a very ancient Greek word *poetes,*[17] which means in Latin exquisite discourse (*exquisita locutio*). For the first men who, thus inspired, began to employ an exquisite style of speech, such, for example, as song[18] in an age hitherto unpolished, to render this unheard-of discourse sonorous to their hearers, let it fall in measured periods; and lest by its brevity it fail to please, or, on the other hand, become prolix and tedious, they applied to it the standard of fixed rules, and restrained it within a definite number of feet and syllables. Now the product of this studied method of speech they no longer called by the more general term poesy, but poem.[19] Thus as I said above, the name of the art, as well as its artificial product, is derived from its effect.

Now though I allege that this science of poetry has ever streamed forth from the bosom of God[20] upon souls while even yet in their tenderest years, these enlightened cavillers will perhaps say that they cannot trust my words. To any fair-minded man the fact is valid enough from its constant recurrence. But for these dullards I must cite witnesses to it. If, then, they will read what Cicero, a philosopher rather than a poet, says in his oration delivered before the senate in behalf of Aulus Licinius Archias,[21] perhaps they will come more easily to believe me. He says: "And yet we have it on the highest and most learned authority, that while other arts are matters of science and formula and technique, poetry depends solely upon an inborn faculty, is evoked by a purely mental activity, and is infused with a strange supernal inspiration."

But not to protract this argument, it is now sufficiently clear to reverent men, that poetry is a practical art,[22] springing from God's bosom and deriving its name from its effect, and that it has to do with many high and noble matters that constantly occupy even those who deny its existence. If my opponents ask when and in what circumstances, the answer is plain: the poets would declare with their own lips under whose help and guidance they compose their inventions when, for example, they raise flights[23] of symbolic steps to heaven, or make thick-branching trees[24] spring aloft to the very stars, or go winding about mountains to their summits. Haply, to disparage this art of poetry now unrecognized by them, these men will say that it is rhetoric which the poets employ. Indeed, I will not deny it in part, for rhetoric has also its own inventions. Yet, in truth, among the disguises of fiction rhetoric has no part, for whatever is composed as under a veil, and thus exquisitely wrought, is poetry and poetry alone.[25]

VIII. WHERE POETRY FIRST DAWNED UPON THE WORLD

IF YOU inquire, O King, under what sky, in what period, and by whose agency Poetry first came to light,[1] I hardly trust my ability to answer. One group of writers thinks it arose with the holy rites of the Ancients, that is, among the Hebrews,[2] since Holy Writ records that they were the first to offer[3] sacrifice to God; for we read that the brothers, Cain and Abel, the first men born on earth, sacrificed to God; so also did Noah when the flood subsided and he went forth from the ark; and so Abraham for victory over his foes, when he offered Melchisedek the priest wine and bread. But since these accounts do not yield altogether the desired answer, writers of this opinion—rather by divination than proof, it must be said—insist that these rites were accomplished with some sort of formal discourse. They add that Moses, when, with the people of Israel, he had passed the Red Sea dry-shod, performed a complete sacrifice, since we read that he established rites, priests, and a tabernacle[4] like the temple that was to be, and appointed prayers to placate the Divine Will. So it seems that poetry had its origin among the Hebrews not earlier than Moses, leader of the Israelites; and he led the people forth and performed his rites about the time that King Marathius[5] of the Sicyoni died, which was the three thousand, six hundred and eightieth year of the world.

A second group would give the Babylonians the glory of inventing poetry. Among these the Venetian,[6] bishop of Pozzuolo, a tremendous investigator, was wont to argue at length in bantering fashion, that poetry was far older than Moses, having had its origin about the time of Nembroth. Nimrod, he said, was the founder of idolatry, for when he saw that fire was useful to men, and that he could, to some extent, foretell the future from its various motions and sounds, he averred that it was a god; wherefore he not only worshipped it instead of God, and persuaded the Chaldeans to do likewise, but built temples to it, ordained priests, and even composed prayers. Now, according to the Venetian these prayers showed that he employed formal, polished discourse. Possibly; but the Venetian never clearly showed his authority[7] for his statement. Yet I have read often enough[8] that religious worship, the study of philosophy, and the glory of arms all had their origin among the Assyrians. But I cannot easily believe, without more trustworthy evidence, that an art so sublime as that of poetry arose first among peoples so barbarous and wild.

The Greeks also[9] maintain that poetry originated with them, and Leontius[10] supports this view with all his might. I am a little inclined his way, as I recollect hearing my famous teacher once say that among the primitive Greeks, poetry had some such origin as this: While they were still rude, some of them, above the rest in intellectual power, began to wonder at the works of their Mother Nature; and as they meditated they came gradually to believe in some one Being,[11] by whose operation and command all visible things are governed and ordered. Him they named God. Then, thinking that He sometimes visited earth, and considering Him holy, they raised buildings for Him at enormous expense, that He might on His visits find abiding places consecrated to His name. These we now call temples. Then, to propitiate Him, they devised peculiar honors to be rendered Him at appointed seasons, and called them rites. Finally, in their belief that, as He excelled all others in divinity, so ought He in honor also, they had silver tables made for His rites, and fashioned of gold the drinking-cups, candelabra, and whatever other vessels they used; they also selected men from among the wisest and gentlest of the people, whom they afterwards called priests, and these they would have appear in no common garb at the celebration of rites, but made them resplendent in costly robes with tiaras and crosiers. Then, since it seemed absurd for the priests to perform rites to the Deity in utter silence, they had certain discourses composed to show forth the praise, and great works of the Deity himself, to express the petitions of the people, and offer him the prayers of men in their various needs. And since it would appear inappropriate to address the Deity as you would a farmhand, an underling, or a familiar friend, the wiser among them wanted a polished and artistic manner of speech devised, and they committed this task to the priests. Some of these, though few—and among them, it is thought, were Musaeus, Linus, and Orpheus[12]—under the prompting stimulus of the Divine Mind, invented strange songs in regular time and measure, designed for the praise of God. To strengthen the authority of these songs, they enclosed the high mysteries of things divine in a covering of words, with the intention that the adorable majesty of such things should not become an object of too common knowledge, and thus fall into contempt. Now since the art thus discovered seemed wonderful and wholly new, they named it, as I have said, from its *effect,* and called it poetry or *poetes,* that is, in Latin *exquisita locutio;* and they who had composed the songs were named poets. And, as the name favors the effect, the belief is that both the musical accompaniment of poetry and all its other accoutrements arose among the Greeks.

But the date of its origin is very doubtful. Leontius, for one, used to say that he had heard his teacher, Barlaam[13] of Calabria, and other learned authorities on the subject, more than once assign the date to the time of Phoroneus,[14] King of Argos, who came to the throne in the three thousand, three hundred and eighty-fifth year of the world. They also said that Musaeus, whom I mentioned above as one of the inventors of poetry, was eminent among the Greeks, and that Linus flourished about the same time; their fame, which is still great, bears witness even in our day that they presided over the rites of the Ancients. To these is added Orpheus of Thrace; they are therefore considered the earliest theologians.[15]

But Paul of Perugia[16] used to infer from the same ancient authorities, that poetry was much younger, and alleged that Orpheus, who is recorded as one of the earliest poets, flourished in the reign of Laomedon, King of Troy, when Eurystheus ruled Mycenae, about the three thousand, nine hundred and tenth year of the world, that he was the Orpheus[17] of the Argonauts, and not only a successor of Musaeus, but the teacher of the same Musaeus, son of Eumolpus. Such, at least, is the testimony of Eusebius in his *Liber Temporum*. Whence Paul's statement, cited above, that poetry was more recent among the Greeks than his opponents held. Leontius, however, in reply maintained that learned Greeks thought there were several by the name of Orpheus and Musaeus, but that the ancient Orpheus was a Greek contemporary with the ancient Musaeus and Linus, whereas it is a younger one who is called the Thracian. Indeed, since this younger Orpheus invented the rites of Bacchus, and the nocturnal gatherings of the Maenads, and made many innovations in the liturgy of the Ancients, and especially had great powers of eloquence —all of which won him high esteem in his generation—he was therefore regarded as the great Orpheus by posterity.

Perhaps this is the right view especially since some of the
Ancients bear witness that there were poets before the birth
of the Cretan Jove, and it is known from Eusebius that
Orpheus the Thracian flourished after Jove's rape of
Europa.[18]

But with scholars thus at variance, and me unable to
find reliable evidence in ancient authors to support their
theories, I cannot tell which to follow. It is at least evident
from all accounts that, if one is to follow Leontius, poetry
originated with the Greeks before it did with the Hebrews;
if the Venetian, then with the Chaldeans before it did
among the Greeks; but if we prefer to believe Paul, it follows that Moses was a master of poetry before either Babylonians or Greeks. Aristotle,[19] to be sure, perhaps for
reasons just urged, asserts that the first poets were theologians, by that meaning Greeks; and herein he favors
somewhat the opinion of Leontius. Nevertheless I cannot
believe that the sublime effects of this great art were first
bestowed upon Musaeus, or Linus, or Orpheus, however
ancient, unless, as some say, Moses and Musaeus[20] were
one and the same. Of the beast Nimrod[21] I take no
account. Rather was it instilled into most sacred prophets,
dedicated to God. For we read that Moses,[22] impelled by
what I take to be this poetic longing, at dictation of the
Holy Ghost, wrote the largest part of the Pentateuch not in
prose but in heroic verse. In like manner others have set
forth the great works of God in the metrical garment of
letters, which we call poetic. And I think the poets of the
Gentiles in their poetry—not perhaps without understanding—followed in the steps of these prophets; but whereas
the holy men were filled with the Holy Ghost, and wrote
under His impulse, the others prompted by mere
energy of mind,[23] whence such a one is called "seer." Under
fervor of this impulse they composed their poems. But
since I have nothing further to say on the origin of poetry,

do thou, O glorious King, choose whichever opinion accords with thy serene judgment.

IX. IT IS RATHER USEFUL THAN DAMNABLE TO COMPOSE STORIES

THESE fine cattle bellow still further to the effect that poets are tale-mongers, or, to use the lower and more hateful term which they sometimes employ in their resentment —liars.[1] No doubt the ignorant will regard such an imputation as particularly objectionable. But I scorn it. The foul language of some men cannot infect the glorious name of the illustrious. Yet I grieve to see these revilers in a purple rage let themselves loose upon the innocent. If I conceded that poets deal in stories, in that they are composers of fiction, I think I hereby incur no further disgrace than a philosopher would in drawing up a syllogism. For if I show the nature of a fable or story, its various kinds, and which kinds these "liars" employ, I do not think the composers of fiction will appear guilty of so monstrous a crime as these gentlemen maintain. First of all, the word "fable"[2] (*fabula*) has an honorable origin in the verb *for, faris,* hence "conversation" (*confabulatio*), which means only "talking together" (*collocutio*). This is clearly shown by Luke[3] in his Gospel, where he is speaking of the two disciples who went to the village of Emmaus after the Passion. He says:

"And they talked together of all these things which had happened.

"And it came to pass, that, while they communed together, and reasoned, Jesus himself drew near, and went with them."

Hence, if it is a sin[4] to compose stories, it is a sin to converse,[5] which only the veriest fool would admit. For nature has not granted us the power of speech unless for purposes of conversation, and the exchange of ideas.

But, they may object, nature meant this gift for a useful purpose, not for idle nonsense; and fiction is just that—idle nonsense. True enough, if the poet had intended to compose a mere tale. But I have time and time again proved that the meaning of fiction is far from superficial.[6] Wherefore, some writers have framed this definition of fiction[7] (*fabula*): Fiction is a form of discourse, which, under guise of invention, illustrates or proves an idea; and, as its superficial aspect is removed, the meaning of the author is clear. If, then, sense is revealed from under the veil of fiction, the composition of fiction is not idle nonsense. Of fiction I distinguish four kinds:[8] The first superficially lacks all appearance of truth; for example, when brutes or inanimate things converse. Aesop, an ancient Greek, grave and venerable, was past master in this form; and though it is a common and popular form both in city and country, yet Aristotle,[9] chief of the Peripatetics, and a man of divine intellect, did not scorn to use it in his books. The second kind at times superficially mingles fiction with truth, as when we tell of the daughters of Minyas at their spinning, who, when they spurned the orgies of Bacchus, were turned to bats; or the mates of the sailor Acestes,[10] who for contriving the rape of the boy Bacchus, were turned to fish. This form has been employed from the beginning by the most ancient poets, whose object it has been to clothe in fiction divine and human matters alike; they who have followed the sublimer inventions of the poets have improved upon them; while some of the comic writers[11] have perverted them, caring more for the approval of a licentious public than for honesty. The third kind is more like history than fiction, and famous poets have employed it in a variety of ways. For however much the heroic poets seem to be writing history—as Vergil in his description of Aeneas tossed by the storm, or Homer[12] in his account of Ulysses bound to the mast to escape the lure of the Sirens' song—yet their hidden meaning is far other than appears on the surface. The better of the comic poets, Terence and Plautus,[13] for example, have also employed this form, but they intend naught other than the literal meaning of their lines. Yet by their art they portray varieties of human nature and conversation, incidentally teaching the reader and putting him on his guard. If the events they describe have not actually taken place, yet since they are common, they could have occurred, or might[14] at some time. My opponents need not be so squeamish—Christ, who is God, used this sort of fiction again and again in his parables!

The fourth kind contains no truth at all, either superficial or hidden, since it consists only of old wives' tales.[15]

Now, if my eminent opponents condemn the first kind of fiction, then they must include the account in Holy Writ describing the conference of the trees[16] of the forest on choosing a king. If the second, then nearly the whole sacred body of the Old Testament will be rejected. God forbid, since the writings of the Old Testament and the writings of the poets seem as it were to keep step[17] with each other, and that too in respect to the method of their composition. For where history is lacking, neither one concerns itself with the superficial possibility, but what the poet calls fable or fiction our theologians[18] have named figure. The truth of this may be seen by fairer judges than my opponents, if they will but weigh in a true scale the outward literary semblance of the visions of Isaiah, Ezekiel, Daniel, and other sacred writers on the one hand, with the outward literary semblance[19] of the fiction of poets on the other. If they find any real discrepancy in their methods, either of implication or exposition, I will accept their condemnation. If they condemn the third form of fiction, it is the same as condemning the form which our Savior Jesus Christ, the Son of God, often used when He was in the flesh, though

Holy Writ does not call it "poetry," but "parable";[20] some call it "exemplum," because it is used as such.

I count as naught their condemnation of the fourth form of fiction, since it proceeds from no consistent principle, nor is fortified by the reinforcement of any of the arts, nor carried logically to a conclusion. Fiction of this kind has nothing in common with the works of the poets, though I imagine these objectors think poetry differs from it in no respect.

I now ask whether they are going to call the Holy Spirit, or Christ, the very God, liars, who both in the same Godhead have uttered fictions. I hardly think so, if they are wise. I might show them, your Majesty, if there were time, that difference of names constitutes no objection where methods agree. But they may see for themselves. Fiction, which they scorn because of its mere name, has been the means, as we often read, of quelling minds[21] aroused to a mad rage, and subduing them to their pristine gentleness. Thus, when the Roman plebs seceded from the senate, they were called back from the sacred mount to the city by Menenius Agrippa,[22] a man of great influence, all by means of a story. By fiction, too, the strength and spirits of great men worn out in the strain of serious crises, have been restored. This appears, not by ancient instance alone, but constantly. One knows of princes who have been deeply engaged in important matters, but after the noble and happy disposal of their affairs of state, obey, as it were, the warning of nature, and revive their spent forces by calling about them such men as will renew their weary minds with diverting stories and conversation. Fiction has, in some cases, sufficed to lift the oppressive weight of adversity and furnish consolation, as appears in Lucius Apuleius;[23] he tells how the highborn maiden Charis, while bewailing her unhappy condition as captive among thieves, was in some degree restored through hearing from an old woman the charming story of Psyche. Through fiction, it is well known, the mind that is slipping into inactivity is recalled to a state of better and more vigorous fruition. Not to mention minor instances, such as my own,[24] I once heard Giacopo San-severino,[25] Count of Tricarico and Chiarmonti, say that he had heard his father tell of Robert,[26] son of King Charles, —himself in after time the famous King of Jerusalem and Sicily—how as a boy he was so dull that it took the utmost skill and patience of his master to teach him the mere elements of letters. When all his friends were nearly in despair of his doing anything, his master, by the most subtle skill, as were, lured his mind with the fables of Aesop into so grand a passion for study and knowledge, that in a brief time he not only learned the Liberal Arts familiar to Italy, but entered with wonderful keenness of mind into the very inner mysteries of sacred philosophy. In short, he made of himself a king whose superior in learning men have not seen since Solomon.

Such then is the power of fiction that it pleases the un-learned by its external appearance, and exercises the minds of the learned with its hidden truth; and thus both are edified and delighted[27] with one and the same perusal. Then let not these disparagers raise their heads to vent their spleen in scornful words, and spew their ignorance upon poets! If they have any sense at all, let them look to their own speciousness before they try to dim the splendor of others with the cloud of their maledictions. Let them see, I pray, how pernicious are their jeers, fit to rouse the laughter only of girls. When they have made themselves clean, let them purify the tales of others, mindful of Christ's commandment[28] to the accusers of the woman taken in adultery, that he who was without sin should cast the first stone.

X. IT IS A FOOL'S NOTION THAT POETS CONVEY NO MEANING BENEATH THE SURFACE OF THEIR FICTIONS

SOME of the railers are bold enough to say, on their own authority, that only an utter fool would imagine the best poets to have hidden any meaning in their stories; rather, they have invented them just to display the great power of their eloquence, and show how easily such tales may bring the injudicious mind to take fiction for truth. O the injustice of men! O what absurd dunces! What clumsiness! While they are trying to put down others, they imagine in their ignorance that they are exalting themselves. Who but an ignoramus would dare to say that poets purposely make their inventions void and empty, trusting in the superficial appearance of their tales to show their eloquence? As who should say that truth and eloquence cannot go together. Surely they have missed Quintilian's saying;[1] it was this great orator's opinion that real power of eloquence is inconsistent with falsehood. But this matter I will postpone that I may come to the immediate subject of this chapter. Let any man, then, read the line in Vergil's *Bucolics*:[2]

> He sung the secret seeds of Nature's frame,

and what follows on the same matter: or in the *Georgics*:[3]

> That bees have portions of ethereal thought
> Endued with particles of heavenly fires.

with the relevant lines; or in the *Aeneid*:

> Know first that heaven and earth's compacted frame,
> And flowing waters, and the starry frame, etc.

This is poetry from which the sap of philosophy runs pure. Then is any reader so muddled as not to see clearly that Vergil was a philosopher; or mad enough to think that he, with all his deep learning, would, merely for the sake of displaying his eloquence—in which his powers were indeed extraordinary—have led the shepherd Aris-

teus[4] into his mother Climene's presence in the depths of
the earth, or brought Aeneas to see his father in Hades?
Or can anyone believe he wrote such lines without some
meaning or intention hidden beneath the superficial veil
of myth? Again, let any man consider our own poet Dante
as he often unties with amazingly skilful demonstration
the hard knots of holy theology; will such a one be so in-
sensible as not to perceive that Dante was a great theologian[5] as well as philosopher? And, if this is clear, what
intention does he seem to have had in presenting the picture of the griffon[6] with wings and legs, drawing the
chariot on top of the austere mountain, together with the
seven candlesticks, and the seven nymphs, and the rest of
the triumphal procession? Was it merely to show his dex-
terity in composing metrical narrative? To mention another instance: that most distinguished Christian gentle-
man, Francis Petrarch, whose life and character we have,
with our own eyes, beheld so laudable in all sanctity—and
by God's grace shall continue to behold for a long time; no
one has saved and employed to better advantage—I will
not say, his time, but every crumb[7] of it, than he. Is there
anyone sane enough to suppose that he devoted all those
watches of the night, all those holy seasons of meditation,
all those hours and days and years—which we have a right
to assume that he did, considering the force and dignity of
his bucolic verse, the exquisite beauty of his style and diction—I say, would he have taken such pains merely to
represent Gallus begging Tyrrhenus[8] for his reeds, or
Pamphilus and Mitio[9] in a squabble, or other like pastoral
nonsense? No man in his right mind will agree that these
were his final object; much less, if he considers his prose
treatise on the solitary life, or the one which he calls *On
the Remedies for all Fortunes,* not to mention many others.
Herein all that is clear and holy in the bosom of moral
philosophy is presented in so majestic a style, that nothing

could be uttered for the instruction of mankind more replete, more beautified, more mature, nay, more holy. I
would cite also my own eclogues,[10] of whose meaning I
am, of course, fully aware; but I have decided not to,
partly because I am not great enough to be associated with
the most distinguished men, and partly because the discussion of one's attainments had better be left to others.

Then let the babblers stop their nonsense, and silence
their pride if they can; for one can never escape the conviction that great men, nursed with the milk of the Muses,
brought up in the very home of philosophy, and disciplined
in sacred studies, have laid away the very deepest meaning in their poems; and not only this, but there was never
a maundering old woman,[11] sitting with others late of a
winter's night at the home fireside, making up tales of Hell,
the fates, ghosts, and the like—much of it pure invention
—that she did not feel beneath the surface of her tale, as
far as her limited mind allowed, at least some meaning—
sometimes ridiculous no doubt—with which she tries to
scare the little ones, or divert the young ladies, or amuse
the old, or at least show the power of fortune.

XI. POETS PREFER LONELY HAUNTS AS FAVORABLE TO CONTEMPLATION[1]

I HAVE remarked above[2] the objection of my clamorous
opponents that poets, for lack of urbanity and manners,
prefer the open country, the mountains and woods, as a
habitation. Boors! Why they are too mad and blind to see
that, in trying to prove truth by a false opinion, they
have actually turned liars. I admit that poets seek the
country, mountains and woods, and if my opponents hadn't
spoken of it, I was resolved to myself, and may have done
so already.[3] The reason, however, is not, as these windbags
allege, a lack of sophistication; indeed the poets' own
works witness enough to the contrary. But, if these cav-

illers scorn to trust such evidence, let them turn the pages
of the Ancients, the annals of philosophers; there they are
sure to find many instances of poets who enjoyed at their
pleasure the friendship and domestic intercourse of kings
and nobles, such as never fall to the lot of crude and oafish
men. In proof whereof not a few examples occur to me
off hand. I could if I wished show that the poet Euripides[4]
was a tent-comrade of Archelaus, King of Macedon, Ennius[5] of Brundisium lived with the Scipios, and Vergil
was a very intimate friend of Octavius. And, if ancient
instances do not appeal to them, there are enough modern
ones. Our Dante[6] was a friend to Frederick of Arragon,
King of Sicily, and to Can Grande della Scala, the illustrious duke of Verona. I know, and in fact so does everybody, that Francis Petrarch[7] has been on terms of great
intimacy and affection with the Emperor Charles, with
John, King of France, with Robert,[8] King of Jerusalem
and Sicily, and with many an exalted prelate besides, and
will continue to be, as long as he pleases, and they are
alive.

But these mutterers probably are not aware that poets
have sought and still seek their habitation in solitudes because contemplation of things divine is utterly impossible
in places like the greedy and mercenary market, in courts,
theatres, offices, or public squares, amid crowds of jostling
citizens and women of the town. Yet unless such contemplation is practically uninterrupted, the poet can neither
conceive his works, nor complete them.

But all this aside, I should hardly expect their charges,
had they ever in a moment of sanity read Horace's words[9]
to Florus. After he has reviewed in his own elegant manner certain disadvantages of life in the city, he asks,

> At Rome, amidst its toils and cares,
> Think you that I can write harmonious airs?

meaning thereby that it cannot be done. Not content with

this, he adds other of the inconveniences that for ever disturb the lives of city people, and then says with some irony,

> Go then, and bustle through the noisy throng,
> Invoke the Muse, and meditate the song,

as much as to say—if you can!

Then come the quizzical lines:

> How then in noise unceasing tune the lay,
> Or tread, where others hardly find their way?

Then, with some indignation,

> What then—at Rome? in this tumultuous town,
> Toss'd by the noisy tempest up and down,
> Can I, though even the willing Muse inspire,
> Adapt the numbers to the sounding lyre?

So, without going further, the reason why poets seek to dwell in sylvan spots is clear. We read also that Paul the Hermit did thus, and Antonius, Macharius, Arsenius,[10] and many other reverend and holy men, not from want of sophistication, but to serve God with a freer mind. It seems then that it is no such abomination as these critics appear to think, to dwell in the woods where there is nothing artificial nor counterfeit, nor noxious to the mind, for all nature's works are simple.

There the beeches stretch themselves, with other trees, toward heaven; there they spread a thick shade with their fresh green foliage; there the earth is covered with grass and dotted with flowers of a thousand colors; there, too, are clear fountains and argent brooks that fall with a gentle murmur from the mountain's breast. There are gay song-birds, and the boughs stirred to a soft sound by the wind, and playful little animals; and there the flocks and herds, the shepherd's cottage or the little hut untroubled with domestic cares; and all is filled with peace and quiet. Then, as these pleasures possess both eye and ear, they soothe the soul; then they collect the scattered energies of the mind, and renew the power of the poet's genius, if it be weary, prompting it, as it were, to long for contemplation of high themes, and yearn for expression[11]—impulses wonderfully reinforced by the gentle society of books, and the melodious bands of the Muses moving in stately dance. In the light of all this what studious man would not prefer remote places to the city?

But it is not the reproach of poets in preferring lonely spots—if reproach is the right word—that moves these insolent men to recrimination; it is rather a reprehensible ambitious infection of their own minds; and because poets differ from them in this respect they call them abominable. It is a trait of abandoned characters to wish above all that others should be like them, either in self-defense, or to enjoy the privilege of being shocked at another's crime. Let them blush then and be still, if the poet's ways are not theirs. Decent men detest and abhor their trick of disfiguring their faces with artificial pallor. They detest and abhor this constant strolling about the cities. They detest and abhor this purchase of cheap popularity among idlers, of notoriety among the ignorant, by foul and hideous hypocrisy. They abhor not merely to ask, but even to desire the badges of office, or to haunt the halls of kings, to flatter any man with a head higher than the rest, to be on the track of pontifical robes, for pure idleness and their bellies' sake to flatter poor women into a deposit of money from which they graft, and get by foul means what they could never get on their merits. They detest and abhor with all their hearts this practice of sending souls of usurers to heaven for a price, and assigning them seats in glory according to their contributions.[12]

But the poets whom these fellows blaspheme are content with plain living and little sleep, with constant speculation and the laudable exercise of composition; thus they aspire to a glorious fame that shall endure to the end of time. O strange sort of men, so easily defiled with the hubbub of towns; O hateful solitude!

Enough! I could say more, were not the shining purity, the eminent virtue, the commendable lives of the great poets a stronger defence against such enemies than I can urge.

XII. THE OBSCURITY OF POETRY IS NOT JUST CAUSE FOR CONDEMNING IT

THESE cavillers further object that poetry is often obscure, and that poets are to blame for it, since their end is to make an incomprehensible statement appear to be wrought with exquisite artistry; regardless of the old rule of the orators, that a speech must be simple and clear.[2] Perverse notion! Who but a deceiver himself would have sunk low enough not merely to hate what he could not understand, but incriminate it, if he could? I admit that poets are at times obscure. At the same time will these accusers please answer me? Take those philosophers among whom they shamelessly intrude;[3] do they always find their close reasoning as simple and clear as they say an oration should be? If they say yes, they lie; for the works of Plato and Aristotle, to go no further, abound in difficulties so tangled and involved that from their day to the present, though searched and pondered by many a man of keen insight, they have yielded no clear nor consistent meaning. But why do I talk of philosophers? There is the utterance of Holy Writ, of which they especially like to be thought expounders;[4] though proceeding from the Holy Ghost, is it not full to overflowing with obscurities and ambiguities? It is indeed, and for all their denial, the truth will openly assert itself. Many are the witnesses, of whom let them be pleased to consult Augustine,[5] a man of great sanctity and learning, and of such intellectual power that, without a teacher, as he says himself, he learned many arts, besides all

that the philosophers teach of the ten categories. Yet he did
not blush to admit that he could not understand the beginning of Isaiah.[6] It seems that obscurities are not confined
to poetry. Why then do they not criticise philosophers as
well as poets? Why do they not say that the Holy Spirit
wove obscure sayings into his works, just to give them an
appearance of clever artistry? As if He were not the
sublime Artificer of the Universe![7] I have no doubt they
are bold enough to say such things, if they were not aware
that philosophers already had their defenders, and did not
remember the punishment[8] prepared for them that blaspheme against the Holy Ghost. So they pounce upon the
poets because they seem defenseless, with the added reason
that, where no punishment is imminent, no guilt is involved. They should have realized that when things perfectly clear seem obscure, it is the beholder's fault. To a
half-blind man, even when the sun is shining its brightest,
the sky looks cloudy. Some things are naturally so profound that not without difficulty can the most exceptional
keenness in intellect sound their depths; like the sun's
globe, by which, before they can clearly discern it, strong
eyes are sometimes repelled.[9] On the other hand, some
things, though naturally clear perhaps, are so veiled by
the artist's skill that scarcely anyone could by mental effort
derive sense from them; as the immense body of the sun
when hidden in clouds cannot be exactly located by the eye
of the most learned astronomer. That some of the prophetic poems are in this class, I do not deny.

Yet not by this token is it fair to condemn them; for
surely it is not one of the poet's various functions to rip
up and lay bare the meaning which lies hidden in his inventions. Rather where matters truly solemn and memorable are too much exposed, it is his office by every
effort to protect as well as he can and remove them from
the gaze of the irreverent, that they cheapen not by too

common familiarity. So when he discharges this duty and does it ingeniously, the poet earns commendation, not anathema.

Wherefore I again grant that poets are at times obscure, but invariably explicable if approached by a sane mind; for these cavillers view them with owl eyes, not human. Surely no one can believe that poets invidiously veil the truth with fiction, either to deprive the reader of the hidden sense, or to appear the more clever; but rather to make truths which would otherwise cheapen by exposure the object of strong intellectual effort and various interpretation, that in ultimate discovery they shall be more precious.[10] In a far higher degree is this the method of the Holy Spirit; nay, every right-minded man should be assured of it beyond any doubt. Besides it is established by Augustine in the *City of God,* Book Eleven,[11] when he says:

"The obscurity of the divine word has certainly this advantage, that it causes many opinions about the truth to be started and discussed, each reader seeing some fresh meaning in it."

Elsewhere he says of Psalm 126:[12]

"For perhaps the words are rather obscurely expressed for this reason, that they may call forth many understandings, and that men may go away the richer, because they have found that closed which might be opened in many ways, than if they could open and discover it by one interpretation."

To make further use of Augustine's testimony (which so far is adverse to these recalcitrants), to show them how I apply to the obscurities of poetry his advice on the right attitude toward the obscurities of Holy Writ, I will quote his comment on Psalm 146:[13]

"There is nothing in it contradictory: somewhat there is which is obscure, not in order that it may be denied thee, but that it may exercise him that shall afterward receive it," etc.

But enough of the testimony of holy men on this point, I will not bore my opponents by again urging them to regard the obscurities of poetry as Augustine regards the obscurities of Holy Writ. Rather I wish that they would wrinkle their brows a bit, and consider fairly and squarely, how, if this is true of sacred literature addressed to all nations, in far greater measure is it true of poetry, which is addressed to the few.

If by chance in condemning the difficulty of the text, they really mean its figures of diction and oratorical colors and the beauty which they fail to recognize in alien words, if on this account they pronounce poetry obscure—my only advice is for them to go back to the grammar schools,[14] bow to the ferule, study, and learn what license ancient authority granted the poets in such matters, and give particular attention to such alien terms as are permissible beyond common and homely use. But why dwell so long upon the subject? I could have urged them in a sentence to put off the old mind,[15] and put on the new and noble; then will that which now seems to them obscure look familiar and open. Let them not trust to concealing their gross confusion of mind in the precepts of the old orators; for I am sure the poets were ever mindful of such. But let them observe that oratory is quite different, in arrangement of words, from fiction, and that fiction has been consigned to the discretion of the inventor as being the legitimate work of another art than oratory. "In poetic narrative above all, the poets maintain majesty of style and corresponding dignity." As saith Francis Petrarch in the Third Book of his *Invectives,* contrary to my opponents' supposition, "Such majesty and dignity are not intended to hinder those who wish to understand, but rather propose a delightful task, and are designed to enhance the reader's pleasure and support his memory. What we acquire with difficulty and keep with care is always the dearer to us;" so continues Petrarch.[16] In fine, if their minds are dull, let them not blame the poets but their own sloth. Let them not keep up a silly howl against those whose lives and actions contrast most favorably with their own. Nay, at the very outset they have taken fright at mere appearances, and bid fair to spend themselves for nothing. Then let them retire in good time, sooner than exhaust their torpid minds with the onset and suffer a violent repulse.

But I repeat my advice to those who would appreciate poetry, and unwind its difficult involutions. You must read, you must persevere, you must sit up nights, you must inquire, and exert the utmost power of your mind. If one way does not lead to the desired meaning, take another; if obstacles arise, then still another; until, if your strength holds out, you will find that clear which at first looked dark. For we are forbidden by divine command[17] to give that which is holy to dogs, or to cast pearls before swine.

XIII. POETS ARE NOT LIARS[1]

THESE enemies of poetry further utter the taunt that poets are liars. This position[2] they try to maintain by the hackneyed objection that poets write lies in their narratives, to wit, that a human being was turned into a stone[3] —a statement in every aspect contrary to the truth. They urge besides that poets lie in asserting that there are many gods,[4] though it is established in all certainty that there is but One—the True and Omnipotent. They add that the greatest Latin poet, Vergil, told the more or less untrue story of Dido,[5] and allege other like instances. I fancy they think their point is already won, and so indeed it would be, were there no one to repel their boorish vociferations with the truth. Yet further discussion seems hardly necessary for I supposed that I had already answered this objection above,[6] where at sufficient length I defined a story, its kinds, what sorts the poets employ, and wherefore.

But if the matter is to be resumed, I insist that, whatever those fellows think, poets are not liars. I had supposed that a lie was a certain very close counterfeit of the truth which served to destroy the true and substitute the false. Augustine[7] mentions eight kinds of lies, of which some are, to be sure, graver than others, yet none, if we employ them consciously, free from sin and the mark of infamy that denotes a liar. If the enemies of poetry will consider fairly the meaning of this definition, they will become aware that their charge of falsehood is without force, since poetic fiction has nothing in common with any variety of falsehood, for it is not a poet's purpose to deceive anybody with his inventions; furthermore poetic fiction differs from a lie in that in most instances it bears not only no close resemblance to the literal truth, but no resemblance at all; on the contrary, it is quite out of harmony and agreement with the literal truth.

Yet there is one kind of fiction very like the truth, which as I said,[8] is more like history than fiction, and which by most ancient agreement of all peoples has been free from taint of falsehood. This is so in virtue of their consent from of old that anyone who could might use it as an illustration in which the literal truth is not required, nor its opposite forbidden. And if one considers the function of the poet already described, clearly poets are not constrained by this bond to employ literal truth on the surface of their inventions; besides, if the privilege of ranging through every sort of fiction be denied them, their office[9] will altogether resolve itself into naught.

Again: if all my preceding argument should deserve reprobation—and I hardly think it possible—yet this fact remains irrefutable, that no one can in the proper discharge of his duty[10] incur by that act the taint of infamy. If the judge, for example, lawfully visits capital punishment upon malefactors, it is not called homicide. Neither is a soldier who wastes the enemy's fields called a robber. Though a lawyer[11] gives his client advice not wholly just, yet if he breaks not the bounds of the law he does not deserve to be called a falsifier. So also a poet, however he may sacrifice the literal truth in invention, does not incur the ignominy of a liar, since he discharges his very proper function not to deceive, but only by way of invention.

Yet if they will insist that whatever is not literally true is, however uttered, a lie, I accept it for purposes of argument; if not, I will spend no more energy in demolishing this objection of theirs. Rather I will ask them to tell me what name should be applied to those parts of the Revelation of John the Evangelist—expressed with amazing majesty of inner sense, though often at first glance quite contrary to the truth—in which he has veiled the great mysteries of God.[12] And what will they call John himself? What too will they call the other writers[13] who have employed the same style to the same end? I certainly should not dare answer for them "lies" and "liars," even if I might. Yet I know well they will say what I myself in part am about to say—should anyone ask me—that John and the other prophets[14] were men of absolute truthfulness, a point already conceded. My opponents will add that their writings are not fiction but rather figures, to use the correct term, and their authors are figurative writers. O silly subterfuge! As if I were likely to believe that two things to all appearances exactly alike should gain the power of different effects by mere change or difference of name.

But not to dispute the point, I grant they are figures.[15] Then, let me ask, does the truth which they express lie on their surface? If they wish me to think it does, what else is it but a lie thus to veil the eyes of my understanding, as they also veil the truth beneath? Well then, if these sacred writers must be called liars, though not held such, since indeed they are none, no more are poets[16] to be considered liars who lean with their whole weight upon mere invention.

Yet without question poets do say in their works that there are many gods, when there is but One. But they should not therefore be charged with falsehood, since they neither believe nor assert it as a fact, but only as a myth or fiction, according to their wont. Who is witless enough to suppose that a man deeply versed in philosophy hasn't any more sense than to accept polytheism? As sensible men we must easily admit that the learned have been most devoted investigators of the truth, and have gone as far as the human mind can explore; thus they know beyond any shadow of doubt that there is but one God.[17] As for poets, their own works clearly show that they have attained to such knowledge. Read Vergil[18] and you will find the prayer:

If any vows, Almighty Jove, can bend Thy will—

an epithet which you will never see applied to another god. The multitude of other gods they looked upon not as gods, but as members or functions of the Divinity; such was Plato's opinion,[19] and we call him a theologian. But to these functions they gave a name in conformity with Deity because of their veneration for the particular function in each instance.

But I do not expect these disturbers to hold their peace here. They will cry out the louder that poets have written many lies about this one true God—whom, as I have just said, they recognize—and on that count deserve to be called liars. Of course I do not doubt that pagan poets had an imperfect sense of the true God, and so sometimes wrote of him what was not altogether true—a lie, as their accusers call it. But for all that I think they should hardly be called liars. There are two kinds of liars: first, those who knowingly and wilfully lie, whether to injure another person or not, or even to help him. These should not be called merely liars, but, more appropriately, "wilful deceivers."[20] The second class are those who have told a falsehood without knowing it. Among these last a further distinction[21] is in order. For in some cases ignorance is neither to be excused nor endured. For example, the law forbids any man privately to hold a citizen prisoner. John Doe has detained Richard Roe, his debtor, and pleads exemption from fine through ignorance of the law; but since such ignorance of the law seems stupid and negligent, it can constitute no defense. Likewise a Christian who is of age should find no protection in ignorance of the articles of faith. On the other hand there are those whose ignorance is excusable, such as boys ignorant of philosophy or a mountaineer ignorant of navigation, or a man congenitally blind who does not know his letters. Such are the pagan poets who, with all their knowledge of the Liberal Arts,[22] poetry, and philosophy, could not know the truth of Christianity; for that light of the eternal truth which lighteth every man that cometh into the world[23] had not yet shone forth upon the nations. Not yet had these servants gone throughout all the earth bidding every man to the supper of the Lamb. To the Israelites alone had this gift been granted of knowing the true God aright, and truly worshipping Him. But they never invited anyone to share the great feast with them, nor admitted any of the Gentiles at their doors. And if pagan poets wrote not the whole truth concerning the true God, though they thought they did, such ignorance is an acceptable excuse and they ought not to be called liars.

But my opponents will say, that whatever ignorance occasioned the lie, he who told it, is none the less a liar. True; but I repeat, they who sinned in pardonable ignorance are not to be damned[24] by the same token as the offenders whose ignorance was crass and negligent; for the law, both in its equity and its austerity, holds them excused, wherefore, they incur not the brand of a lie.

If these disparagers still insist in spite of everything that poets are liars, I accuse the philosophers, Aristotle, Plato, and Socrates of sharing their guilt. Now, I expect, these expert critics will again lift their voices to heaven and cry to the sound of harp and cithera that this objection of theirs has suffered no harm. Fools! Though one small shield be shattered, the whole front does not waver. Let them not exult, but remember how often they have now been belabored and beaten back.

Their objection to Vergil—that no wise man would ever consent to tell the story of Dido[25]—is utterly false. With his profound knowledge of such lore, he was well aware that Dido had really been a woman of exceptionally high character, who would rather die[26] by her own hand than subdue the vow of chastity fixed deep in her heart to a second marriage. But that he might attain the proper effect of his work under the artifice of a poetic disguise, he composed a story in many respects like that of this historic Dido,[27] according to the privilege of poets established by ancient custom. Possibly someone more worthy of a reply than my opponents—perhaps even thou, O Prince—may ask to what purpose this was necessary for Vergil. By way of fitting answer let me then say that his motive was fourfold.[28]

First, that in the same style which he had adopted for the *Aeneid* he might follow the practice of earlier poets, particularly Homer, whom he imitated in this work. For poets are not like historians, who begin their account at some convenient beginning and describe events in the unbroken order of their occurrence to the end. Such, we observe, was Lucan's method, wherefore many think of him rather as a metrical historian than a poet.[29] But poets, by a far nobler device, begin their proposed narrative in the midst of the events,[30] or sometimes even near the end; and thus they find excuse for telling preceding events which seem to have been omitted. Thus Homer, in the *Odyssey*, begins, as it were, near the end of Ulysses's wanderings and shows him wrecked upon the Phaeacian shore, then has him tell King Alcinous everything that had happened to him hitherto since he left Troy. Vergil chose the same method in describing Aeneas as a fugitive from the shore of Troy after the city was razed. He found no place so appropriate on which to land him before he reached Italy as the coast of Africa; for at any nearer point he had been sailing continuously among his enemies the Greeks. But since the shore of Africa was at that time still the home of rude and barbarous rustics, he desired to bring his hero to somebody worthy of regard who might receive him and urge him to tell of his own fate and that of the Trojans. Such a one above all he found in Dido, who, to be sure, is supposed to have dwelt there not then, but many generations later;[31] yet Dido he presents as already living, and makes her the hostess of Aeneas; and we read how at her command he told the story of his own troubles and those of his friends.

Vergil's second purpose,[32] concealed within the poetic veil, was to show with what passions human frailty is infested, and the strength with which a steady man subdues them. Having illustrated some of these, he wished particularly to demonstrate the reasons why we are carried away into wanton behavior by the passion of concupiscence; so he introduces Dido, a woman of distinguished family, young, fair, rich, exemplary, famous for her purity, ruler of her city and people, of conspicuous wisdom and eloquence, and, lastly, a widow, and thus from former experience in love, the more easily disposed to that passion. Now all these qualifications are likely to excite the mind of a high-born man, particularly an exile and castaway thrown destitute upon an unknown shore. So he represents in Dido the attracting power of the passion of love, prepared for every opportunity, and in Aeneas one who is readily disposed in that way and at length overcome. But after showing the enticements of lust, he points the way of return to virtue by bringing in Mercury, messenger of the gods, to rebuke Aeneas, and call him back from such indulgence to deeds of glory. By Mercury, Vergil means either remorse, or the reproof of some outspoken friend, either of which rouses us from slumber in the mire of turpitude, and calls us back into the fair and even path to glory. Then we burst the bonds of unholy delight, and, armed with new fortitude, we unfalteringly spurn all seductive flattery, and tears, prayers, and such, and abandon them as naught.

Vergil's third purpose, is to extol, through his praise of Aeneas, the *gens Julia* in honor of Octavius; this he does by showing him resolutely and scornfully setting his heel upon the wanton and impure promptings of the flesh and the delights of women.

It is Vergil's fourth purpose[33] to exalt the glory of the name of Rome. This he accomplishes through Dido's execrations at her death; for they imply the wars between Carthage and Rome, and prefigure the triumphs which the Romans gained thereby—a sufficient glorification of the city's name.

Thus it appears that Vergil is not a liar, whatever the unthinking suppose; nor are the others liars who compose in the same manner.

XIV. THE FOOLISHNESS OF CONDEMNING WHAT ONE DOES NOT READILY UNDERSTAND

FURTHERMORE my opponents curse the poet and clamor for the extinction of poetry as replete with pranks and adulteries of pagan gods. Besides they can in no way bear the practice of the poets who assign many forms and names to one and the same god, such as Jove and the like. My adversaries come on like a foolish soldier, who is so fierce and eager to hunt the enemy that he does not look out for himself; with the usual result that he bares himself to the blows he intended for another. I supposed that these objections taken in the lump had already found their answer above[1] where I remember saying time and again that in various licentious or grotesque incidents and names are implied many wise and pure thoughts; and these I am aware of having revealed[2] to the best of my ability by removing the outer mythological covering.

But those seductive performances of the gods presented chiefly by comic poets,[3] in whatever way, I neither praise nor commend, but detest, and I hold such writers to be as execrable as the scenes themselves. Wide indeed is the field of fiction, and Poetry's horn as she advances overflows with her many inventions; wherefore fair and decent disguises have never been lacking for any possible thought which an author may wish to express.

Indeed this complaint has now long since been laid to rest and removed. At one time outrageous songs were sung on the stage of the theatre by mimes and actors and spongers and the like; but, according to Cicero,[4] the ancient Romans abolished and repudiated them, condemned both the stage and its debased art, punished those who practised it with the censor's brand, and erased them from the roll of their tribes. Furthermore warning was published by Pretorian edict that whoever went upon the stage for the purpose of acting in such plays should in so doing lose his good name. Then after the time of the Emperor Constantine and Pope Sylvester,[5] as the Catholic faith sprang up everywhere and waxed daily, the songs of such comic purveyors to the stage disappeared from the world, and

left the writings of noble and worthy poets; wherein they
exhibited the works of both men and nature in a nobler
style, in artistic form, in more eloquent diction, under an
appropriate guise of myth and image. But those whom
the godly Plato[6] would have expelled from the city, and
whom my present adversaries in their ignorance really revile, are now cast out and abolished.

In reply to the second clause of my adversaries' objection, I may say that, if they had exercised some prudence
in the onset, and been more alert to discover where they
were exposed to attack, they would have been sure to see
that the weapon they cast at the Gentile poet rebounds upon
themselves. They would cease to wonder that the poets
call Jove, now god of heaven, now lightning, now an eagle,
or a man, or whatever,[7] if they had only reminded themselves that Holy Writ itself from time to time represents
the one true God as sun, fire, lion, serpent, lamb, worm,
or even a stone. Likewise our most venerable mother the
Church is prefigured in the sacred books, sometimes as a
woman clothed with the sun, or arrayed in varied garb,
sometimes as a chariot, or a ship, or an ark, a house, a
temple, and the like. No less is this true of the Virgin
Mother, or of the Great Enemy of mankind, as I remember to have read, time and again.[8] I can say the same also
of the multiplicity of sacred epithets; those applied to God
alone are indeed innumerable at present, as are those of the
Virgin Mary and the Church. Such forms and epithets
are not devoid of mystic meaning; no more are those employed by poets.

Why then keep up this bray? They suffer from a mor-
bid envy that will not endure what it cannot explain.

XV. DETESTABLE JUDGMENT OF THE INCOMPETENT

YET another charge is urged by these zealots—that poets
seduce their readers into criminal practices. If they urged

this charge with some distinction, I might concede it in part. It is, of course, a well-known fact that long ago there were comic poets[1] of doubtful honor who were such either at the prompting of their own unrighteous minds, or at the demand of an age as yet corrupt. For example, Ovid, the Pelignian, a poet of great eminence but licentious imagination, wrote a book on the Art of Love[2] in which, to be sure, he suggested many a wrong practice; yet it was in no respect really dangerous, since no youth is so mad with passion, and no young woman so simple, that under the impulse of carnal appetite they are not much keener in inventing expedients to achieve their desires than he who thought to make himself an eminent advisor in such matters. If, then, poets like these, who, I admit, should in some cases be rejected, have not kept fair the fame of the art of poetry, why, pray, should others of resplendent fame incur the same taint, and share the blame of the guilty? Why, it is not to be endured!

Yet to show why these objectors attack the really great poets, I beg them to tell whether they have ever read a book of Homer, or Hesiod,[3] or Vergil, or a poem of say Horace or Juvenal? If they say yes, will they then tell what prompting to criminal practices they find therein; thus we who are blind may profit by their insight, and likewise condemn the blameworthy.

But such questions are vain. Who can hear their charge without seeing that they never have read these poets? We may rest assured that, if they had, they would never have arrived at their absurd conclusion. I am afraid, however, that such interrogation as this may only move them to add one sin to another; for they cannot keep still, so great is their fear that silence will impair their reputation for omniscience. They will talk away with bold effrontery, puffed cheeks, and unblushing brow, as if they were travelling the straight road to the summit of praise.

But why listen to such nonsense? Foh! I neither do, nor wish to—something better claims my interest. Great God, now mayest Thou rest from Thine eternal labor. If Thine eyes, O God, long for slumber, Thou mightest now be satisfied. For these creatures assume Thine office; nightly they watch in Thy place, and sweat in Thy stead. Among their greater duties, they very likely will drive the Primum Mobile. Tremendous undertaking! And they are equal to it, if Thou, O Lord, wilt suffer it.

Base perverted souls, that in petty disparagement of others miserably lay bare their own ignorance! We can, if we are not the greater fools, easily see how just, holy and acceptable is this charge of theirs. And that no one may think the answer I am about to make proceeds from mere idle speculation, let me say that it derives from most accurate deduction. Some time ago I heard several men engaged in making perhaps too scrupulous a reply to cross-questioning of this very sort; and—what was of especial interest to me—a certain venerable man,[4] in other respects of eminent sanctity and learning, did not stop at a mere answer, but launched into a gratuitous diatribe in the worst of bad taste. God knows, I speak the truth. O King! This man, as it seemed, was so fierce an enemy of the poet's name that he apparently could not endure the word without retching. He once exhibited this prejudice on an occasion not altogether to his credit. For it happened one morning in our University[5] that he was reading from the desk the Gospel according to St. John[6] to a large audience when suddenly he came upon the name of poet. Forthwith he became flushed, his eyes took fire, and raising his voice, he broke into a perfect frenzy and poured out one false charge after another against poets. And finally, to show the justice of his case, he averred—nay, almost swore: "I never have seen, nor do I wish to see, a volume of poetry!" Good God! What may we expect from the ignorant, if an aged and revered man, and, in other respects, learned, spake thus? Could a madman speak worse nonsense? I should like to know of these censors extraordinary, if they can spare a moment from their greater concerns, how, if they haven't seen, much less become acquainted with the poets, they make out that poets are corruptors of morals. Why then, do they keep up this ignorant yelping? Why do such incompetents usurp the bench to judge that of which they know nothing? Why thunder out their verdict where one side of the case has never been examined, let alone heard? Perhaps they will say the Holy Spirit inspires them to this harsh judgment against poets. So I might suppose, if I thought the Holy Spirit ever enters, not to say dwells, in souls so foul. O base impiety, vile offence, hateful presumption—that a child born blind should openly attempt to distinguish colors. The practice[7] of these venerable judges, forsooth, is that reported of Phoroneus among the Argives, Lycurgus among the Lacedaemonians, Minos among the Cretans, and Aeacus among the Myrmidons.

But to come now to my main point. The prattle of these reverend judges notwithstanding, poets are not corruptors of morals. Rather, if the reader is prompted by a healthy mind, not a diseased one, they will prove actual stimulators to virtue, either subtle or poignant, as occasion requires. Not to appear content with insufficient proof, I should like to call the attention of these noisy objectors to a few examples which may enable them, if they will, to acknowledge this fact. I will not pause with Homer, who, being a Greek writer, is less familiar to the Latins. But let them, if they will, read, yes, and re-read those lines in the *Aeneid*[8] where Aeneas exhorts his friends to endure patiently their labors to the last. How fine was the ardor of his wish to die a fair death from his wounds, to save his country! How noble his devotion to his father when he bore him to safety on his shoulders through the midst of the enemy and a shower of flying weapons, while buildings were ablaze and temples crashing down at every turn! What gentleness he showed to his enemy Achaemenides! What strength of character in spurning and breaking the chains of an obstreperous passion! What justice and generosity, too, in distributing well-earned rewards among friends and aliens alike, at the conclusion of the anniversary games to Anchises at the court of Acestes! What circumspect wisdom he showed in his descent into Hades! What noble exhortations to glorious attainment were those of his father! There too was his tact in cultivating friendly relations, and his high and loyal courtesy in keeping them afterwards; and there were his devoted tears for the death of his friend Pallas, and his frequent admonitions to his friend's son. But enough! I crave their attention—these who bray at the name of poetry: let them weigh carefully both the words and thought of this poet, and, if they are intelligent enough, derive from them all possible fruition. Please God, they will then see whether the poet allures the reader to eat the fruit of sin. Surely if Vergil[9] could have known and worshipped God in due form, nothing but that which is holy could be found in his works. But if my opponents object that legally nothing is proved by one witness, they may add Horace of Venusia, Persius of Volterra, and Juvenal[10] of Aquinum. For the satires of these poets inveigh against vice and the vicious with such righteous energy that they seem likely to do away with them. If then, these several examples suffice, let them who accuse poets of corrupting their readers be silent, subdue their rage with gentleness, nor scorn to learn, before they pass absurd judgment upon the labors of others; lest in hurling the darts of their dull injustice at others, they call down the thunderbolts of divine vengeance upon themselves.

XVI. THE READING OF POETS CONDUCES TO RIGHTEOUSNESS

IN THE next place, they who so spitefully lie in wait for the poet, say that he is an allurer of the mind, since the charming music of his verse, his polished language, his ornate discourse, inspire folly in his readers, or what is worse, seduce the unsophisticated. Now any ignoramus as unfamiliar with the poets, particularly the great poets, as these know-nothings, or one who has glanced at them, but was too feeble of mind to appreciate them, will readily believe that these men are most righteous, just, and holy in their attack upon poetry. May God, and they to whom he has granted the light of intelligence, behold this! Thou, heavenly harper, thou, O David, who art wont to quiet Saul's rage with thy sweet song, if ever thou didst utter a soft, melodious note, silence now thy song. And thou, O Job,[1] who hast recorded thy labors and longsuffering in heroic verse, if it should prove agreeable or fair, do thou likewise. And ye too, all holy men besides who have sung the divine mysteries in exalted notes, do ye accordingly. In like manner would I call upon Orpheus, Homer, Vergil, Horace, and the rest—when we reach the point where men are heard to say with impunity that the practice of framing metrical discourse sweetly, agreeably, and with care, is one and the same with perverting the minds of men. Ah, Bavius and Maevius,[2] rejoice when these great names are fallen; for ample time and room have been conceded to you when least I expected it.

My antagonists will now say, I know, that it was the practice of writing and reading nonsense in sonorous verse that they called pernicious. I grant this qualification is of no small moment, unless I have already shown too often the nature of the absurdities in great poets which they now attack. Yet, for the sake of giving a direct answer to the charge that poets seduce the mind, I should first like to know—since there are many poets—which of them my opponents accuse. Of course they can mention only those they study themselves. But their own accusation[3] shows which these are. Why, bless me, these zealots[4] love, and are loved, make eyes at laughing girls, dictate love-notes, write verses, dash off ditties, which they charge with their thrills and sighs, and when their own ingenuity fails, resort for timely aid to professors in the art of love. Wherefore they search the pages of Catullus, Propertius, and Ovid,[5] and from the foolish suasion of such, expressed in sweet-sounding verses, and in easy but ornate style, with whole-hearted inclination they surrender to its influence, are deluded, seduced, and enthralled. Thus it is they have discovered the allurements of the poets, thus they ungratefully turn and accuse their teachers, and thus they call them seducers of the mind, whom they have followed uninvited and of their own free will. Great, thrice great, employment for our opponents. And worthy indeed is their homage to Love, whose power overcame first Phoebus, then Hercules—each victorious over monsters. Ah, how much better it would have been for these ignorant men to hold their peace, rather than speak to their own undoing. With a little thought, they may see that in the act of accusing the poets they have only proved themselves to blame. Whence we readily infer the true worth of their studies, their desires, their so-called justice. What might one expect of them in case a girl by licentious glance and gesture, and soft utterance, held out an unholy promise to them, if they are allured by unuttered verses perused in silence? Well may the wretches blush and revise their mad counsel, considering how Ulysses, noble soul, spurned the sound, not of songs read in the closet, but the dulcet music of the Sirens, whom he passed by for fear of harm at their hands.

As for the force of this epithet "allurer"[6] which these men hurl at the poets in hope of disparagement, they might have seen that, though Jews hurled it at Christ our Savior when they called him "allurer," yet not for ever was it destined to vilify Him. For these rascal perverters could not rob the word of its pristine force. It may, at times, have a good connotation. Skilful herdsmen may, for example, lure from an infected herd the cattle as yet untainted; much more do cultivated men by their instruction lure away nobler souls from those foundering under moral disease. Thus, I think, do the great poets most frequently lure the credulous to their improvement, while these unjust judges are lured and deluded into an evil course more by their own wickedness than by that of even the less honorable poets, and they try their utmost to show it. O blessed Jesus, turn aside this plague from the ignorant and credulous! Take these babblers and so instruct them that by Thy example they may be willing first to do, and then to teach!

XVII. THAT POETS ARE MERELY APES OF THE PHILOSOPHERS

A FEW of the enemies of poetry who would outdo the rest in their attack say that poets are but apes of the philosophers.[1] I cannot make sure whether such eructation comes from a wish to raise a general laugh, like their cheap jokes among silly girls, or whether it rises from real conviction, or from a mere low and idle desire to ridicule. If the first, then the wise should suffer it to pass, though with some feeling of indignation. For they often see eminent men bantered by the ignorant, who at many a street corner appear disguised as filleted asses, or hogs in their trappings, or in fringed and variegated skins of different beasts; and thus disguised freely utter, with less impropriety, any ribald lampoons they can make up. But if this charge against poets comes from conviction or from desire to ridicule, it is, in either case, both stupid and

vicious. The apes' natural and invariable habit (as I remember saying elsewhere[2]) is to imitate as far as they can
everything they see, even to the actions of men. Whence
these men speciously infer that poets, being imitators, are
therefore apes of the philosophers: now this is not so
absurd, even if it were true; for philosophers have been
for the most part honorable men, and inventors of noble
arts.[3] But the ignorant deceive themselves. If they but
understood the works of the poets, they would see that,
far from being apes, they should be reckoned of the very
number[4] of the philosophers, since they never veil with
their inventions anything which is not wholly consonant
with philosophy as judged by the opinions of the Ancients.
And then, too, the pure imitator never sets foot outside
his model's track—a fact not observed in poets. For
though their destination is the same as that of the philosophers, they do not arrive by the same road. The philosopher, everyone knows, by a process of syllogizing,
disproves what he considers false, and in like manner
proves his theory, and does all this as obviously as he can.
The poet conceives[5] his thought by contemplation,[6] and,
wholly without the help of syllogism, veils it as subtly
and skilfully as he can under the outward semblance of
his invention. The philosopher as a rule employs an un
adorned prose style, with something of scorn for literary
embellishment. The poet writes in metre, with an artist's
most scrupulous care, and in a style distinguished by exquisite charm. It is, furthermore, a philosopher's business
to dispute in the lecture-room, but a poet's to sing in
solitude. With such discrepancy between them, the poet
cannot prove to be "the ape of the philosopher." If they
called them apes of nature, the epithet might be less
irritating, since the poet tries with all his powers to set
forth in noble verse the effects, either of Nature herself,
or of her eternal and unalterable operation. If my op-

ponents care to consider it, they will perceive the forms, habits, discourse, and actions of all animate things, the courses of heaven and the stars, the shattering force of the winds, the roar and crackling of flames, the thunder of the waves, high mountains and shady groves, and rivers[7] in their courses—all these will they find so vividly set forth[8] that the very objects will seem actually present in the tiny letters of the written poem. In this sense, I admit, the poets are apes, and I hold it a task full of honor to attempt with art what nature performs in the fullness of her power. So much upon this point. It would be better for such critics if they would use their best efforts to make us all become apes of Christ, rather than jeer at the labors of poets, which they do not understand. Sometimes people who try to scratch another's itching back feel someone's bloody nails in their own skin—and not so pleasantly either!

XVIII. IT IS NOT A DEADLY SIN TO READ THE POETS[1]

THESE judges of equity—or rather of iniquity—in the heat of their mad desire to destroy the name of poet, as if they had not already said enough, keep shrieking and bellowing to this effect: "O ye distinguished men, ye redeemed of the blood of the Lord, ye chosen people of God, if in your hearts is piety, devotion, love of Christianity, fear of God, cast from you these unhallowed books of the poets; burn them with fire; scatter their ashes to the winds! For to have them at home, to read them, or even incline to read them is a mortal sin! They infect the soul with deadly poison, they drag you down into hell, and hurl you into endless exile from the heavenly kingdom!" Then with a louder voice they call Jerome to witness, and allege his words in the *Epistle to Damasus*[2] on the Prodigal Son: "The songs of poets are the food of devils." This and much else of the same sort they yell at the top of their voices at their poor ignorant hearers. O piety! O pristine faith! O great and patient God! How longsuffering art Thou! Thou Founder of all things, why dost Thou aim Thy thunderbolts at high towers and lofty mountain-tops? These, most Holy Father, these are Thy proper mark who with a treacherous tongue and false pursue empty celebrity through the destruction of others who are innocent. Doctors[3] bury their mistakes in the ground. These charlatans try to hide their ignorance in prohibitions and flames. What ingenuous man could listen to these impostors without thinking that poets are most pernicious, nay, enemies of the name of God, familiars of demons, cruel, evil-doers, always ready for crime, heedless of every good, utterly devoid of piety, faith, or holiness? By such ignorant and unfair procedure, men of real distinction are brought to ignominy which they least deserve. I hope God will some day find them out.

Let us now consider, as we can, the real nature of this inexpiable sin which, they keep roaring, consists in possessing, looking at, or reading the songs of poets. I have already explained clearly enough what their books contain—the tendency of their influence, and what they teach and what they condemn. But, all that aside, I grant for the moment what is in reality untrue, that poets describe all manner of crimes, and make them attractive to their readers. What of it? They were Gentiles,[4] who knew not Christ, and who upheld their own religion, because they regarded it as holy, and in publishing their works, they often held out to others the fruit that was most pleasing and acceptable to their own palates. And if further excuse were required, I wish these most exquisite babblers would tell me whether any teaching, ancient or modern, has forbidden their describing the wickedness of their gods in any style they choose. Surely not, if the Christian has not been forbidden to write such poetry as yields nothing, under intelligent scrutiny, contrary to Catholic Truth. If not, and if neither the Law, nor the Prophets, nor the holy rulings of the pontiffs, forbid the perusal of poetry, what harm is there in possessing and reading them? My opponents will say again that they seduce the mind with their sweetness. But this objection I have answered just above.[5] And if these imbeciles are in any wise tractable, let them recall the saw about stones and glass houses[6] and take care.

Yet I grant freely that it would be far better to study the sacred books than even the best of these works, and I suppose they who do so are more acceptable to God, to the high Pontiff, and to the Church. But we are not all at all times subject to one inclination, and occasionally some men incline to poetical writers. And if we so incline,[7] or turn to them of our own accord, what sin or harm is there in that? We can in all innocence hear of the customs of barbarians, or, if we please, actually receive them among us, treat them hospitably, give them the benefit of our justice, if they ask it, and make of them friends and feast-mates. And yet—God's will! These learned men forbid us to read the poets! Why, there are Manichaeus, Arius, Pelagius, and such heresiarchs. No one forbids our knowing their vile errors, so that we may recognize them.[8] Yet it is a frightful thing to read poetry, they keep clamoring, "nay, a deadly sin." We may watch wandering clowns doing their low tricks at the corner; or hear entertainers sing their dirty songs at banquets, or buffoons at restaurants, or panderers in the brothels—yes, even let them blaspheme—and still escape hell. But poetry! Alas, it drives us forth into exile from the Kingdom of Heaven! It is thought proper for the painter to paint, within the holy precincts of the church itself, pictures[9] of the triple dog Cerberus guarding the gate of Pluto, or sailor Charon plying the waters of Acheron, or the Furies with snaky fillets and flaming brands, or even Pluto himself, prince of the unhappy realm, in the act of visiting punishment upon the damned. Then is it wrong for poets to describe them in resounding verse, and is the reader guilty of unpardonable sin? The painter has even been permitted to decorate the palaces of princes and nobles with subjects chosen from the amours of ancient myth, the crimes of gods and men, and all sorts of fabrications, without an interfering word from the Fathers; and anyone who will may look at these pictures all he pleases. But a poet's creations, blazoned in ornate letters, they find more vicious to the wise than are pictures to the ignorant.

Well, I confess I could not, in spite of me, tell how violent and stubborn are the consuming spleen and ignorance which have driven these cattle so mad. Certainly they should know the testimony of the Vessel of Election,[10] that sin consists not in the knowledge of evil, but in the act.

But not thus content, these raw and upstart pedagogues make bold to say—perhaps to gain more reputation for wisdom among their female admirers,[11] and so get the fatter leavings—they make bold to say, that it is most pernicious even to read the poets, much more to know them. What bores! If poets are altogether to be scorned, then it will be wrong to pick up a pearl from the mud, since the dirt, though it may be wiped off, will make it less precious. Nor do these expounders blush, though their arrogant and sweeping prohibition would turn the truth to a lie, provided it comes from the mouth of a poet; they will deny at the top of their voices that poets ever speak the truth. It is absurd to say that the devil, the enemy of man, can utter a good word, but that the poets can never do so. For though I granted a moment ago, only for argument's sake, that they *are* evil, yet many of them can not justly be accused of any dishonor but that of being

Gentiles. Yet the devil's testimony is frequently cited by holy men, while to cite the poets is, on the authority of these accusers, an unpardonable sin.

At this point I beseech these prohibitors and proscribers of poets to tell in what way Poetry has sinned worse than Philosophy. For while Philosophy is without question the keenest investigator of truth, Poetry[12] is, obviously, its most faithful guardian, protecting it as she does beneath the veil[13] of her art. If Philosophy errs, Poetry cannot keep in the right path. She is Philosophy's maidservant, and must follow in the steps of her mistress; so that necessarily the error of the one makes the other deviate. What right, then, have we, if we constantly cite the pagan philosophers, and cherish their thoughts, and consider nothing really well founded unless it rests upon their authority— what right have we fearfully to shun the poets and their words and condemn them in scorn? Socrates is lauded, Plato honored, Aristotle studied, not to mention the rest; and yet they were pagans, and often capable of erroneous and condemned opinion. But Homer is driven off with reproaches, Hesiod condemned, Vergil and Horace[14] despised, though their creations carry no other meaning than do the dissertations of the philosophers. But since these cavillers have studied the philosophic writings a little, and, by dint of slight but painful effort, have caught certain very elementary fragments[15] from them, they commend them as if they fully understood them. Yet the poets, whose works they neglect, and therefore do not appreciate, they despise and condemn. In spite of all this howling and barking, exhorting and pleading, if philosophical writings, and the life and customs of barbarians, and the perverted teaching of heretics, are allowable, certainly the works of the poets may be read, kept, and listened to with impunity, yet with a pure and steadfast mind, lest the poets, being, as it were, aliens from the orthodox faith, should now and then say something contrary to it, and the reader should slip unawares.

Finally, the last point of these noisy upstarts calls for really sharp and extended reproof; for they think that they have established their whole contention thus far by the authority of one devout and famous man. They keep shouting the dictum of Jerome to Pope Damasus,[16] that the songs of poets are the food of devils. But a moment's consideration of my previous words would have shown them that I myself confirmed this point, particularly in condemning and repudiating more than once the obscenity of the comic poets.[17] But since they are too obfuscated with envy to make any distinction between poets, and only rush hither and yon in their blindness; their cheap prejudice ought to be repelled and silenced for ever. If they had read carefully the epistles and other works of Jerome,[18] or even this particular one they call to witness, they would find the real meaning of his dictum explained by Jerome himself, and their objection removed. I have in mind particularly the figure of the captive woman described as naked, shaven, and with closely pared nails; the Israelitish bride with hair close-cropped. If they would not appear more fastidious in their piety than these holy doctors they will find that this "food of devils" is not only snatched from the fire into which they have ordered it to be cast, but kept with care, and dressed and tasted by no less a person than Fulgentius,[19] the Catholic doctor and pontiff; the fact is proved by his book which he himself has named the *Book of Myths*, and in which he recounts and explains the fables of the poets in highly finished style. In like manner they will discover that the great teacher Augustine[20] was not afraid of poetry and its creations, but indeed studied it with patience and sagacity, and understood it. Certainly they could not deny it, in spite of themselves, for the holy man often cites Vergil and other poets; in

fact he almost never mentions Vergil without a laudatory
epithet. To repeat, then; the great and most holy Jerome,
master of three languages, whom these men in their ignorance cite with so much ado, studied and remembered
the poets with such care, as they may see, that their contention gains practically nothing by citing. him. If they
are not convinced, let them note for example the preface[21]
of his *Hebraicae Quaestiones* on Genesis, and see whether
it is not throughout in the manner of Terence, and whether
he does not frequently cite Horace and Vergil as his advocates, so to speak, or even Persius and others. Let them
read beside Jerome's eloquent letter to Augustine,[22] and
see that the learned author there numbers among illustrious
men the very poets that these men try in every possible
way to overwhelm with their clamor. And if they are
still unconvinced, they may read through the Book of
Acts and see how studiously Paul, the Vessel of Election,[23]
sought acquaintance with the words of the poets. In his
attempt to persuade the obstinate Athenians, on the Areopagus, he did not disdain, they will find, to cite the testimony of poets; and in another place he quotes a verse of
Menander, the comic poet: "Evil communications corrupt
good manners." I think it is the poet Epimenides whose
line he cites elsewhere: "The Cretans are always liars, evil
beasts, slow bellies"—a good description, by the way, of
my opponents. Thus he who was caught up into the third
heaven,[24] unlike these more pious persons, thought it
neither a sin nor a shame to read and teach the works of
poets.[25] Again, let them examine the words of Dionysius[26]
the Areopagite, a disciple of Paul, and glorious martyr of
Christ, in his book on the *Celestial Hierarchy*. He takes
the matter up from the first premise, and gives complete
proof that divine theology employs, with its other instruments, poetic inventions. He says: "For in truth Theology
with much skill hath employed sacred poetic forms and

figures to convey non-figurative meaning, at the same time
opening our minds, as I have already said, providing them
with means of right conjectural interpretation, and presenting the Holy Scriptures to them in anagogical form";
and he continues with much more to the same effect. And
lastly, to omit the other instances that I could cite against
their bestial ravings, did not our Lord and Savior speak
often in parable[27] appropriate to the style of comic poet?
Did he not, with his own voice, employ a verse of Terence[28]
against the stricken Paul—"It is hard for thee to kick
against the pricks?" Far be it from me to suppose that
our Lord took these words from Terence, though Terence
lived long before they were uttered. It serves to prove my
point that our Savior ever willed that a word and thought
of His own should have been first uttered through the
mouth of Terence, showing that the songs of poets are not
wholly the food of devils.

What now have these cattle left to bellow about? Will
they keep on howling and hurling their insults at poetry,
though refuted by their own evidence, and vanquished by
the testimony of many saints? They will, I suppose, make
as much noise as ever, so incurable is their madness; but
the justice of their claim thou, O excellent King, and others,
may judge, who are friends of reason, and love not their
shameless obstinacy. But God is a just judge and will in
time visit proper punishment upon these envious and arbitrary destroyers; and the same measure[29] shall be measured
unto them that they mete unto others.

XIX. IT IS UNTRUE THAT PLATO WOULD ABOLISH
ALL POETS FROM HIS REPUBLIC[1]

A MERE trifle it seems to these barkers—the exposure of
their vain attempt to drive the poets out of the homes and
hands of men. For see! they rally and rush to the attack,
and flourishing like a weapon the authority of Plato they

belch out with hideous roar, that Plato ordered the poets banished from the cities. Then, as if Plato were weak and needed help, they add as their own reason, that poets may vitiate the commonwealth with their immorality. Though I have already[2] answered this objection at sufficient length, I shall not now shrink from a fuller reply. For I admit that the authority of this philosopher is of the highest order; and deserves all respect if rightly understood; but these men pervert or altogether misprise his meaning, as I shall prove.

I have said[3] that the poets prefer to dwell in solitude, wherefore their disparagers called them backwoodsmen and boors. But if poets chose the hurly-burly of towns, what would these backbiters say of them? They would call them tyrants! It seems that they have changed their minds, and now call the poets dwellers in cities; if so, they are wrong. It is an established fact that Homer,[4] after wandering the world over, settled at last in extreme poverty on the shore of Arcadia, amid crags and mountain-forests; and there, overtaken by blindness, but with "mind irradiate," conceived those great and marvellous works; works anointed not with the sweetness of Hybla, but of Castaly—the *Iliad* and the *Odyssey*. And Vergil,[5] who was no less a genius than Homer, forsook Rome, then mistress of the world, and deserted Octavius, ruler of all the earth, whose friendship was the poet's peculiar and happy privilege, all to seek out an abode not far from the famous principality of Naples in central Campania, a spot even in that day abounding in beauty and comfort; and there, according to the account of John Barillus,[6] a man of much intelligence, he chose a spot still and removed, near a lonely shore, between the cape of Posilipo and the old Greek colony Pozzuolo, whither none would come except to visit him. There he composed both his *Georgics* and the divine *Aeneid*. And when at Vergil's death, Octavius wished to commemorate his choice of this lonely spot, he caused his bones to be brought from Brundisium, and buried close by his favorite retreat near the road still called the Puteolan Way; thus his bones lie near the abode of his choice.

But I will not confine myself to ancient examples, for, however happy and authentic, my opponents will none of them. Francis Petrarch,[7] a man of heaven-sent genius, and the greatest poet of our time, scorned the western Babylon, and ignored the favor of the Pope, for which nearly every Christian longs and contends his utmost—not to say the favor of bonneted cardinals and other princes—and departed to a secluded valley, in an exceptionally lonely part of France, where the Sorga, the greatest of springs, takes its rise. There, in meditation and composition, he spent nearly the whole flower of his youth, content with one servant. The proofs of his deed still remain and will so remain for a long time—a little house and garden, and, as long as God pleases, a number of living witnesses. These examples suffice to show what a waste of effort it is to try to drive poets out of the city whence they have departed of their own choice.

I wish my opponents would say whether they think that Plato, in his *Republic,* passed the stricture they mention upon Homer, so that Homer would have been an exile from his ideal city. Whatever they say, I cannot think so, having read so much in praise of Homer.[8] The most sacred laws of the Caesars call him father of all virtues; and time and again their proposers, to win reverence for them, and support them with holy testimonial have mingled with them lines from Homer. Thus at the close of the proem of the Justinian Code occurs such a quotation, as likewise under the titles, On Justice and Law, On Contract of Sale, On Legacies and Trusts, and so forth: the curious may see it for themselves in the Pandects of Pisa.[9] It was Homer whom many of the leading cities of Greece would have dignified as their citizen, though he had died in poverty; nay, they contended with one another for this honor. This is clearly shown in Cicero's speech for Archias[10] where he says: "Homer is claimed as their fellow-citizen by the men of Colophon, while the Chians demand, and the Salaminians aspire to the same honor; Smyrna also insists that he is here, and has gone so far as to dedicate a shrine to him. Many others are there who likewise strive and contend for the same honor." Nor is Cicero the only witness; I remember reading it in an old Greek verse[11] familiar to the learned which says: "Seven cities dispute for the honor of Homer's birth—Samos, Smyrna, Chios, Colophon, Pylos, Argos and Athens." Nay Plato himself calls Homer to witness in the very book[12] of the *Republic* in which he condemns poets, and elsewhere. If then the laws call him the father of virtues, and glory of the law, and if he is claimed as citizen of so many states, and if Plato, our very monitor, cites him to prove a point, isn't it utter folly to think so wise a man as he would have ordered such a poet to be excluded from his commonwealth?

Are we to believe that by the same token Ennius[13] must be banished? He was a man who lived content in honest poverty, and yet was greatly endeared to the Scipios by his goodness; and they, besides their distinction of noble birth and exploits in war, were at home in philosophy, and singularly pure in character. They so loved the poet that at his death they desired that he be buried in the tomb of their family, and his ashes mingled with those of their fathers and their own. Then I for one will never agree with these idiots; nay, rather am I convinced that Plato would have wished his state brim-full of such as these. What of Solon,[14] who in his old age, after he had made the laws of Athens, devoted himself to poetry? Must he be also expelled who restored a broken and ruined city to civil and moral health? There again is Vergil,[15] who withal was so pure that he blushed in mind as well as in countenance when he overheard an indecent remark among his coevals or others, and thus won the nickname "Parthenias," that is, "virgin," or more correctly "virginity." It is often said that his works contain as many admonitions to virtue as they do words. To save his divine poem from being burned according to his own dying command, Octavius interrupted the cares of his vast empire to compose some prohibitory verses, which are still extant. The poet's name enjoys such honor at his native Mantua that when Augustus moved his ashes, and the Mantuans were not suffered to have the keeping of them as they wished, they began to honor the little farm where he had lived, and named it after him as if it had been alive; and the old men of the place still point it out to the younger generation as something sacred and venerable. They even take care to call strangers' attention to it, as if to augment their own glory. Such things do not happen unprecedented by conspicuous virtue. Shall we suppose then, that Plato would have men of such virtue expelled from the state? Blockheads! I could say as much of Horace, and Persius of Volterra, and Juvenal of Aquinum,[16] all to prove that it never entered Plato's mind to expel such men. But it is my purpose to cite contemporary instances, immediately visible, so that they can not repudiate them by any possible tergiversation. Can one imagine that Plato would have been mad enough to banish Francis Petrarch? From his youth Petrarch has lived celibate, and such has been his horror at impure and illicit love, that his friends know him for a perfect model[17] of saintly and honorable living. A lie is his mortal enemy, and he abhors all the vices. Truth finds in him her sanctuary, and virtue her adornment and delight. He is a pattern of Catholic piety—dutiful, gentle, devout, and so modest that he is called a second

Parthenias. He is, besides, the present glory of the art of
poetry, an eloquent and sweet-tongued speaker, a man to
whom the whole heart of Philosophy is open and familiar,
of penetration more than human, endowed with tenacious
memory, and enjoying knowledge commensurate with the
mind of man. His prose, and his more extensive works in
verse,[18] are so splendid, so redolent with sweetness, so
loaded down with the bright bloom of his eloquence, so
honey-sweet with rounded cadence, so pungent with the
sap of his wonderful wisdom, that they seem like the
creations of a divine not a human genius. What more
could one say? For surely he exceeds human limits and
far outstrips the powers of man. Such praise I utter not
of an ancient who died centuries ago, rather of one who,
please God, is alive and well; of one whom you, my snarl-
ing monsters, if you trust not my words, may see with
your own eyes, and seeing, believe. I have no fear that
he will share the common fate of great men, whose presence, as Claudian[19] says, impairs their fame. Nay, rather,
I insist that his actual presence far surpasses his reputation. So dignified is his bearing, so flowing and delightful
his discourse, so gentle his manners, so tranquil his old
age, that one may say of him what Seneca[20] writes of
Socrates, that his hearers were even more edified by his
character than by his words. I pause in my eulogy of this
great man to ask these objectors whether such are the
poets Plato would banish from his state. If men of this
kind are shut out, what sort would even Plato admit in
their stead? Will they be panderers, body-snatchers, para-
sites, roisterers, fishmongers, or jailbirds and the like?
Long life and happiness to Plato's state, if she rids herself of poets to receive such as the safeguards of life and
morals. But let us never suppose the learned man meant
what these "interpreters" say he did; for I can only believe
that great poets and their kind are to be rightly regarded

not as merely citizens of his state and all others, but as
the princes and rulers thereof.

But they will spleen and say: "If not these, then what
poets would Plato expel?" There is only one answer to
such nonsense. Find out for yourselves, you incompetents!
To be sure, allowance must be made for ignorance of all
sorts. Every art, like every liquor, hath its lees; the lees
may be but so much foul draff; yet an art, like a liquor,
without lees is cheapened. What, for example, is truer
than Philosophy, mistress[21] of all sciences and arts? Yet
she hath had as her dregs,[22] so to speak, the Cynics and
Epicureans—not to mention any more—who having got
themselves tangled up in unspeakable errors, proceeded in
various ways to defame her more like enemies than sup-
porters. But shall we say that for the sake of these we
must abandon also Socrates,[23] Xenocrates, Anaxagoras,
Panetius, and others adorned with the fair title of Philosopher? Such is the way of the knave and the fool!
What is holier than the Christian religion? Yet she hath
her Donatists, her Macedons, her Fotini,[24] and far worse
dregs of heresy than they; and we do not therefore regard
Basil, and St. John Chrysostom, and Ambrose, and Pope
Leo, and many another holy and reverend man as profane.
Thus also poetry, like the other arts, contains likewise its
dregs. There have been certain so-called comic poets,[25]
who, to be sure, included a few upright men such as
Terence and Plautus, but who for the most part defiled
the bright glory of poetry with their filthy creations. Even
Ovid at times makes one of these. Whether from innate
foulness of mind, or greed for money, or desire of popularity, they wrote dirty stories and presented them on
the stage, and thus prompted lascivious men to crime,
unsettled those who were established in virtue, and weak-
ened the moral order of the whole state. What was worst
of all, though the pagan religion was already in other

respects reprehensible, yet they seduced various peoples into the practice of such licentious rites that its own disciples had to blush for it. It is such poets, I repeat, that paganism no less than Christianity abhors, and such it is that Plato would banish. Indeed I think they ought to be not expelled, but exterminated. But for the sake of these, must Hesiod[26] also go, and Euripides, and Statius, and Claudian, and the like? I think not. I beseech these cavillers, then, to make a distinction, to avoid their hateful and unworthy prejudice, to single out for their attacks the really undeserving, and leave honorable men in peace.

XX. THE MUSES NOT INJURED BY THE DEFECT OF A SINGLE GENIUS[1]

LASTLY, O noble King, these blasphemers of poetry have dared with unspeakable effrontery to invade the very threshold of the Gorgonian cave,[2] so still, remote, and holy, and thrust themselves into the fair sanctuary of the adorable art, where maidens dance together and raise the divine song. Amid clamor and discord they flourish the words of the most holy and learned Boethius, particularly those found near the beginning[3] of his book on *Consolation*. It is the point where Philosophy speaks saying: "Who hath let these drabs of the stage approach unto this sick man; for they apply no manner of remedy to his sufferings, but only nurse them with sweet poisons," etc. Thus they shriek in triumph, and fill the place with hubbub, and try with cowardly insult to frighten them who take innocent sport therein. Little do they understand Boethius' words: they consider them only superficially; wherefore they bawl at the gentle and modest Muses, as if they were women i the flesh, simply because their names are feminine. They call them disreputable, obscene, witches, harlots, and, forcing the meaning of Boethius' diminutive,[4] they would push them to the bottom of society, nay in the

lowest brothel make them supine to the pleasure of the
very dregs of the crowd. From this slander they deduce
their contention that poets are dishonorable; for if, according to Boethius, the Muses are lewd, and disreputable,
so also must be their familiars, the poets; since friendship and familiarity rest only upon affinity of character,
and hence the Muses obviously are close familiars of
the poets, as their songs aver, and therefore share their
shame. Here mayest thou see, O sapient King, to what
end the cleverness of these busy-bodies allures them. But
whatever that end may be, it spells confusion in the face
of pure truth. The number, quality, and names of the
Muses, and their significance as perceived by great men,
I have shown, if I remember rightly, in the Eleventh
Book[5] of this work; but the impiety of my opponents is
still alive and calls for further effort on my part. I think
it safe to infer from previous demonstration that there
are two kinds of poets—one worthy of praise and
reverence, always acceptable to good men, the other obscene and detestable, who, I said,[6] should be both expelled
and exterminated. Now the same distinction holds of the
Muses, of which there is one genus but two species. For
though they all enjoy the same power, and are governed
by the same laws, yet the fruits of their labors are unlike, since one beareth sweet, the other bitter. Accordingly
one may be held in honor, the other in dishonor. The one
deserves every title and epithet of praise; she dwells in
laurel groves, near the Castalian spring, or in whatsoever
places we hold sacred; she is the companion of Phoebus;
she goeth forth adorned with garlands of flowers, and
graced with the sweet sound of voices in song. The other
is she who is seduced by disreputable comic poets[7] to
mount the stage, preempt theatres and street-corners: and
there for a fee she calmly exhibits herself to loungers in
low compositions, destitute of a single commendable

grace. It is not hers to relieve or heal the sufferings of those who languish, with the consolations of goodness, and with holy remedies of salvation; she only enhances their suffering even unto death amid groans and complaints, and strangles them in the toils of sensual delight. Hence these poet-haters may learn what they were too stupid to see, that when Boethius called the Muses drabs of the stage, he spoke only of theatrical Muses. This the cavillers might have seen clearly enough, if they had understood what Philosophy says a little later.[8] Her words are: "But leave him to the ministering and healing care of *my* Muses." And, by way of clearer proof that he was talking of the second sort of Muses, Philosophy later cites[9] many a fragment of verse and poetic fable to soothe and console Boethius. So if these good Muses have a share in the healing art of Philosophy, they must be reputable perforce. And if reputable, so are their familiars, it would seem by my opponents' arguments. Thus both poets and Muses are honorable, in spite of this attempt to befoul and disgrace them.

XXI. TO THE KING

WITH such reasons as I could command, O most beneficent King, have I now repulsed the obloquy of these skulking enemies. Had I less self-respect, I should have sharpened and barbed my shafts with far more deadly effect against their character and manner of life, as well as their bold presumption. But I suppose this would only have led to more of their talk, and the desire to answer it would protract my discourse beyond reason. Prolixity is usually distasteful to a mind taken up with great affairs, like a king's, and may offend even those that are free and at leisure. So I would not tire your Highness, nor seem bent on the utter extermination of my opponents; compassion for their ignorance is better even than their destruction, however deserved. I will therefore pause at this point, and in conclusion do for them, with your indulgence, what of their own accord they would not do: setting aside all the resentment they have earned, and overlooking their weaknesses, I will address to them a friendly word, if by chance I may convert them to a better course.

XXII. THE AUTHOR ADDRESSES THE ENEMIES OF POETRY IN HOPE OF THEIR REFORM

AND now, O men of sense, ye will do wisely to calm your indignation and quiet your swollen hearts. Our contest has grown perhaps too bitter. You began by taking up the cudgel against an innocent class of men, with the intention of exterminating them. I came to their defence, and, with God's help and the merits of the case, did what I could to save deserving men from their deadly enemies. Yet, if the poets in person had fairly taken the field against you, you would see how far their powers surpass both yours and mine, and repent at the eleventh hour. But the fight is over; with some glory of war, and a good deal more sweat, we have reached the point where the lust for victory may be a bit qualified, and we may part company with a fair settlement. Come then, let us freely unite to rest from our labors, for the prizes of the contest have been awarded. You forfeit to me your theory, and I to you a bit of consolation; this leaves ample room for peace. I have no doubt you are willing, since you are sorry to have begun the contest, and by this arrangement we shall both enjoy its benefits. To prove my sincerity, I, who am the first to tire of it, will be the first to resume friendly relations; that you may do likewise, I beg of you to consider with fair and unruffled mind the few words which I, in all charity and friendship, am about to say to you.

You recall, gentlemen, that, as well as I could, I have shown you the nature of poetry, which you had counted as

naught, who the poets are, their function, and their manner
of life, whom you cried out upon as depraved liars, moral
perverters, corrupt with a thousand evils. I have shown
also the nature of the Muses, whom you had called drabs
and consigned to the stews. Yet being actually so worthy
of regard as I have shown, you should not only cease to
condemn them, but should cherish, magnify, love them,
and search their books to your improvement. And that
old age may not prevent you, or the popularity of other
arts, try your best to do what an aged prince was not
ashamed to attempt; I refer to that shining example of
all virtues, famous King Robert[1] of Sicily and Jerusalem,
who besides being king, was a distinguished philosopher,
an eminent teacher of medicine, and an exceptional theologian in his day. Yet in his sixty-sixth[2] year he retained
a contempt for Vergil, and, like you, called him and
the rest mere story-tellers, and of no value at all apart from
the ornament of his verse. But as soon as he heard Petrarch
unfold the hidden meaning of his poetry, he was struck
with amazement, and saw and rejected his own error;
and I actually heard him[3] say that he never had supposed
such great and lofty meaning could lie hidden under so
flimsy a cover of poetic fiction as he now saw revealed
through the demonstration of this expert critic. With
wonderfully keen regret he began upbraiding his own
judgment and his misfortune in recognizing so late the
true art of poetry. Neither fear of criticism, nor age, nor
the sense of his fast expiring lease of life were enough
to prevent him from abandoning his studies in the other
great sciences and arts, and devoting himself to the
mastery of Vergil's meaning. As it happened, an early
end broke off his new pursuit, but if he might have
continued in it, without doubt he would have won much
glory for the poets, and no little advantage for the Italians engaged in such studies. Will you, then, hold that

gift not worth the taking which was holy in the sight of
this wise king? Impossible! You are not mere tigers or
huge beasts, whose minds, like their ferocity, cannot be
turned to better account.

But if my pious expectation is doomed to disappointment, and the heat of your hatred still burns against them
who deserve it not, then whenever your tongues itch to
be at it again, I beseech you, for the sake of your own
decency, mind my words. I adjure you, by the sacred breast
of Philosophy,[4] which haply in other days has nourished
you, not to rush in headlong fury upon the whole company
of poets. Rather, if you have sense enough, you must observe right and timely distinction among them—such distinction as only can bring harmony out of discord, dispel
the clouds of ignorance, clear the understanding, and set the
mind in the right way. This you must do if you would
not confuse the poets we revere—many of them pagans,
as I have shown—with the disreputable sort. Let the lewd
comic writers[5] feel the stream of your wrath, the fiery
blast of your eloquence; but be content to leave the rest in
peace. Spare also the Hebrew authors. Them you cannot
rend without insulting God's majesty itself. I have already
cited Jerome's statement[6] that some of them uttered their
prophetic song in poetic style as dictated by the Holy
Ghost. By the same token must Christian writers[7] escape
injury; for many even of our own tongue have been
poets—nay, still survive—who, under cover of their compositions, have expressed the deep and holy meaning of
Christianity. One of many instances is our Dante.[8] True, he
wrote in his mother tongue,[9] which he adapted to his artistic
purpose; yet in the book which he called the *Commedia* he
nobly described the threefold condition of departed souls
consistently with the sacred teaching of theology.[10] The
famous modern poet Petrarch has, in his *Bucolics*,[11] employed the pastoral guise to show forth with marvellous

effect both the praise and the blame visited by the true
God and the glorious Trinity upon the idle ship of Peter.
Many such volumes are there which yield their meaning
to any zealous inquirer. Such are the poems of Prudentius,[12] and Sedulius,[13] which express sacred truth in disguise. Arator,[14] who was not merely a Christian, but a
priest and cardinal in the church of Rome, gave poetic
form to the Acts of the Apostles by recounting them in
heroics. Juvencus,[15] the Spaniard, also a Christian, employed the symbolic device of the man, the ox, the lion,
and the eagle, to describe all the acts of Christ our Redeemer, Son of the Living God. Without citing further
examples, let me say that, if no consideration of gentleness can induce you to spare poets of our own nation, yet
be not more severe than our mother the Church; for
she, with laudable regard, does not scorn to favor many
a writer; but especially hath she honored Origen.[16] So
great was his power in composition that his mind seemed
inexhaustible and his hand tireless; so much so that the
number of his treatises on various subjects is thought to
have reached a thousand. But the Church is like the wise
maiden who gathered flowers among thorns without tear-
ing her fingers, simply by leaving the thorns untouched;
so she has rejected the less trustworthy part of Origen,
and retained the deserving part to be laid up among her
treasures. Therefore distinguish with care, weigh the
words of the poets in a true balance, and put away the
unholy part. Neither condemn what is excellent, as if, by
raising a sudden hue and cry against poets, you hoped to
seem Augustines or Jeromes[17] to an ignorant public.
They were men whose wisdom equalled their righteousness; they directed their attack not against poetry, or the
art of poetry, but against the pagan errors contained in
the poet's works. At these they hurled fearless and outspoken condemnation because it was a time when Catholic

truth was surrounded and beset with harassing enemies. At the same time they cherished them and ever recognized in these works so much art, and polish, such seasoning of wisdom and skilful application of ornament, that whoever would acquire any grace of Latin style apparently must derive it from them.

Finally in the words of Cicero pleading for Archias:[18] "These studies may engage the strength of our manhood and divert us in old age; they are the adornment of prosperity, the refuge and solace of adversity; delightful at home, convenient in all places; they are ever with us through the night season; in our travels; in our rural retreats. And if we may not pursue them ourselves nor enjoy them in person, yet should we admire them as seen in others," etc. Poetry, then, and poets too, should be cultivated, not spurned and rejected; and if you are wise enough to realize this there is nothing more to say. On the other hand, if you persevere in your obstinate madness, though I feel sorry for you, contemptible as you are, yet no writing in the world could help you.

Thus ends the Fourteenth Book of the
Genealogy of the Gentile Gods.
Here happily begins the
Fifteenth and Last Book,
wherein the Author
clears himself
of Various
Charges.

BOOK XV

I HAVE now steadied and trimmed my little craft,[1] O most clement King, by such means as I could, for fear she be driven ashore by the wash of a stormy sea or the counter-force of the wind, with joints sprung and timbers crushed. And I have spread above her such protection as seemed opportune against lowering clouds that dissolve in rain or deadly flashes of lightning, lest she be either swamped or burned. Finally I have made her fast to the rocks, with stays and hawsers, that the ebb tide might not drag her into the depths. But mortal precaution avails naught against the wrath of God; and I have therefore resolved that the fate of my venture must be left in His hands without Whose favor naught shall endure. May He in His mercy keep her!

It now remains to offer some protection to the exhausted sailor from the weapons of his enemies, and in some way save him, if I can. No doubt he is pursued of many. But though aforetime I may have seemed impatient of the false charges against poetry and poets, yet shall I endure with the utmost patience the attacks upon the sailor, how-ever violent. Such a course is perfectly reasonable; for in my opinion, the vituperative attack upon fair poetry and the skilful practicers of that art was unworthy, pro-ceeding as it did from either pride or ignorance, I am not sure which. Not so with the sailor. For if he have put forth his utmost strength and nautical skill to bring his craft past roaring whirlpools and rocky shoals to safety, one can find no just fault with him. But I am fully aware of his great ignorance, and haply he deserves reproof for many an error of inadvertence. I will do my best, then, with God's help, to make his endeavor look less arrogant. And may He who snatched the young Israelites[2] unscathed from the fiery furnace, save me from the jaws of my maligners, and bring me to the end of this my last work to the glory and honor of His holy name.

I. THAT WHICH AT FIRST HAS LITTLE USE MAY SOME DAY BE OF GREAT PRICE

I AM well aware that the aforementioned cavillers, or others of the sort, will glance sharply about this scene of our contest, and will then say—perhaps with pious intention, for mind-reading is difficult enough—"Such an immense work, of no utter use[1] either now or in time to come!" Thus briefly they in effect demolish the whole book, especially as their objection seems colored by, or rather founded upon, a half-expressed fact. Of course anyone would at first glance say that the tales of the poets that make up this whole work are useless and even superfluous. But this, I think, is a mistake.[2] I admit the work consists altogether of fables; and if I grant that such material is of little present use, yet will I show that many things of little present use, and among them this work, will eventually be of great worth. Then will I prove that, affording as it does, public and private benefits, it must be reckoned among useful things. Much then that we possess is of the very highest value, though not useful in the ordinary sense; and this applies as well to nature's products as to the inventions of man. When we wish to build a house[3] we engage stone-workers, and masons, and carvers, and distinguished architects; yet for all practical purposes a common overseer could make as good a house out of mud and wattles. We build temples, and capitols, and royal palaces at tremendous cost both to people and prince, and adorn them with unnecessary painting. We use vases of gold and relief work, when cheap Samian[4] ware would serve all needs. So with crowns and gay clothes, and gold armlets; we enjoy wearing them, when a plain woollen cloak is enough for any man. Thus artistic embellishment acquires value though it is of no practical use whatever. But since it derives this value from human ambition and pretence, let us see whether Nature, who is in every thing most prudent and discerning, has not also her desire for superfluous decoration. For example, of what use is the hair on the head? None, as all agree. Yet many claim such value for it that, if Venus were without it, she could not please Mars, for all her attendant graces. Caesar,[5] as dictator, set such value upon hair, that he asked the senate for the perpetual privilege of wearing the laurel to cover his baldness. What use has a man for a beard?[6] Yet if he come of age without one, he blushes for it before his fellows. Why does a stag have horns, or birds gay plumage? For embellishment[7] and nothing else. This is enough to show that a thing precious for no other reason, may become so for ornament's sake. And if this is true of other things it certainly will be so of this book of mine. What is fairer in the oral intercourse of men than an occasional story[8] mingled with the substance? What is more fitting than to unite with such discourse the pregnant meaning of a myth? Both of which—myth and meaning—this book offers in abundance. Great beauty accrues to weighty and elaborate speeches, as one may see who reads the works of Cicero or Jerome[9] and other wise men, wherein myth and fable are mingled throughout. And this is enough to prove my work a valuable one merely on the score of ornament.

But there remains its usefulness, public and private, in which its greater value resides. Some men[10] have thought that the learned poet merely invents shallow tales, and is therefore not only useless, but a positive harm. This is because they read discursively and, of course, derive no profit from the story. Now this work of mine removes the veil from these inventions, shows that poets were really men of wisdom, and renders their compositions full of profit and pleasure to the reader. And thus if poets who seemed to have perished through want of appreciation are now brought back to life,[11] as it were, and to a high place in the state, while their usefulness to the individual, which was ignored because it was unrecognized, is now revealed by this work of mine, thus they rouse the reader's mind to higher feelings. Furthermore, I hope[12] that, God willing, men will rise up as they have done in the past who will devote themselves to the study of poetry. As they peruse the memorials and remains of the Ancients they cannot fail to derive much help from this work of mine, which will prove valuable to them, if not to others. But enough. For, though these words of mine fail with every-one else, yet if your desire, O excellent Prince, by whose order I began the work, is satisfied, that in itself I hold a measure of high value, however praiseworthy success at large may be. Yet if my book shall have failed to please your Highness, though it be favorably received by others, it will be worth little to me. It lies with you, then, to give the book its value, or, if it be your pleasure, to reject it.

II. THINGS WHICH SEEM PERISHABLE OFTEN ENDURE LONGEST

WITH the same pious intention, some will say, as soon as they see how loose and inarticulate my work is, that a thing so full of holes and rifts is doomed not to last. My hearty thanks to these prognosticators; for they wake me up, and make me alert to the immediate necessity of pre-caution. If you remember, O renowned King, I antici-pated[1] this possibility even before I began my work, and

at the outset showed as well as I could my reasons for
thinking that the book must needs be fragmentary and
mutilated. It appears from their comment, and in other
ways, that I was not mistaken. Therefore I claim a just
excuse for this defect. I have reinforced the work with
such support as I could command, and, once fortified in
this manner, it has developed no new or unexpected seams;
as for the old and expected ones, I do not look for the
sudden collapse that my critics forecast. If we may sur-
mise the future in the usual way, this work will last a
long time. One has often seen a fortress[2] founded upon
a rock fall to ruin sooner than a fisherman's hut on the
marshes. But a man who knows his house is not very
strong keeps constant watch, and as necessity demands,
renews his foundation, stops the cracks in his walls, props
his roof with timbers, and reinforces his galleries; so that
the building that seemed on the point of collapse often
lasts for ages. Who otherwise can be sure of his strength?
For, while he rests secure, lo, one huge stone, loosened
by its weight, slips, comes crashing down, and drags the
whole house into a heap of ruins.

Decay is not the only fate of a great building: envy
skulks in palaces, and hatred contrives their destruction;
but a small house, with few inmates, familiar to its owner
and his few friends, may last as long as God wills. Who
could have thought that Ilium, the new-built city of Priam,
fortified as it was, rich, gorgeous, the glory of all Asia's
realm, the menace of all Greece, would fall before the hut
of Aglaus[3] of Psophis? In like manner we have seen a
strong young man, full of life and health and beauty, by
a slight fever or other accident, plunge to sudden death,
while many an infirm old man drags out his life far beyond his wish.

But there is little need of discussion; human life teems
with illustrations. Say what they please, I cling to my

preference. Of one thing, at least, I am sure—"except the
Lord keep the city, the watchman waketh but in vain."[4]
His is the power to save or destroy: His, and His alone
is the knowledge of the term of all things mundane,
whether long or short. The hope of the wise is in Him
alone; the eye of the Lord be upon me! Knowing as I do
the defects of my work, and that He "giveth grace to the
humble," I have prayed Him to bestow all humility upon it.

But I have said enough. For defective, fragmentary,
and full of gaps as my composition may be, the best is
that it can at least reach your hands, my King, and prove
to you my obedience, if not my scrupulous care. Such brief
fame will be enough; but if my book survives, then shall
I have God's goodness, and the King's favoring fortune
to thank for it.

III. THE VARIOUS PARTS OF THE BOOK COULD NOT BE ARRANGED IN BETTER ORDER[1]

THERE will be other critics, I suspect, who, after examin-
ing what the rest have examined, will say that a sensible
man would rather have the whole compilation perish than
live on and on, since destruction will undo its defects, but
survival only exhibit them. They will, above all point to
a defect of construction—a broad chest protruding from
the pate,[2] legs from the chest, and feet from where the
head ought to be. Think of Socrates'[3] saying—"O happy
physicians, whose blunders are hidden underground!" But
with authors how different! For their choice utterances
are exposed to the fangs of hounds, or at least harassed
by their yelps. So this work of mine, wrought with the
utmost pains of selection and composition, backed as far
as possible by illustrious authority, is struck down by the
words of passers-by. Yet patience is needful, if insolence
is to be overcome of humility. I have no answer to such
talk except that I was aware from the beginning of this

Genealogy that many men would have many opinions, and that at the opening of the First Book I had not neglected to show that I chose the most ancient of the gods,[4] which would lead naturally to some mention of the others. To this most ancient head, as my researches enabled me, I have joined in order the chest and other members. If other genealogies are truer or better arranged—and I admit that it is quite possible—I confess I have not seen them, though I have taken great care and gone through many volumes. And I know not in what order and relation the members of so vast a body could be combined. Let my critics also bring forth their knowledge, and, if in view of that my treatise deserves to be condemned, then the reader may give them his whole confidence. But if they merely assert without proof that I have joined the breast to the pate, it amounts only to unjust detraction, not fair rejoinder nor useful emendation.

IV. WHAT IS OMITTED IS IRRELEVANT

BESIDES thus urging the book's crudity, a charge already rebutted, these critics—or others—will say that I have left out much that ought to be included. I cannot deny this, even if I would, especially when I recall that, in dealing with the external matter of the myths, I said near the beginning[1] of this work that for lack of proper books I should omit many human descendants of the gods. And though such books should prove to exist, who in the world will ever be hardy enough to come out and say that he has seen and read them all? Since I have not seen some which others have, I am not ashamed to admit that many authorities will be missed, perhaps in some cases even from lapse of memory.[2] I cannot remember everything I have seen. Wherefore I beg that with this in mind they will temper their judgment, and not set down to deliberate error what really comes of ignorance or forgetfulness.

There is another consideration upon which perhaps men of higher attainments will be ready to criticize. I refer to the interpretations of the myths. Far be it from me to withstand their strictures. Indeed I think the criticism very likely is just, since I would never have dared on my own initiative to undertake such a task, aware as I was of my unfitness. But who will expect a perfect performance from imperfect man? God only[3] can create the perfect thing, since He alone is perfect. If I have ventured too boldly, it has been at your command, O excellent King. And if in this respect my work is inferior, let the blame rest with your Highness. But I implore these more learned critics in the holy and venerable name of Philosophy,[4] for which, I think they have regard, that, as they are impelled by some authority of the wise to make a savage attack upon an imperfect piece of work, so likewise they temper their wrath with humane considerations. Though the learned more often perceive that which escapes the unlearned, yet it sometimes happens that an unlearned man may see what the learned have overlooked. I am human, and it is no new and strange thing for a human being to err. As Horace says:[5]

> Now and then
> Short fits of slumber creep on Homer's pen.

Argus[6] had a hundred eyes, waking and sleeping fifty at a time, turn and turn about; and yet on one occasion he could not help going to sleep in all of them. What wonder then, if I with only two am sometimes overcome? Let them, I pray, interpret such myths as I could not, altering any inadequate explanation, and correcting such as have been based upon erroneous opinion. If I have not written fully, I have tried at least to write piously. If I have failed in this, I am not too perverse humbly to confess my error and be grateful for correction. For I am one who, though I hasten with all speed towards old age,[7] am not afraid to learn—nay, I rather desire and long so to do. If, then, these critics do as I beg of them, my work will be improved and I shall gain by their generosity, both in learning and in praise.

V. THE BOOK CONTAINS ONLY SUCH MYTHS AND STORIES AS HAVE BEEN DERIVED FROM COMMENTARIES OF THE ANCIENTS

OTHERS will rise up and complain aloud that I have herein included myths and stories never heard of before, simply to make my work more impressive and elaborate. I deny having mingled any new myths or stories with the old, but I do admit having derived some from numerous Latin sources—stories unknown in this day and generation. None of these, however, is derived from any source other than the commentaries[1] of the Ancients; nor were they cited to make the book more impressive and elaborate, but under necessity. Yet such is the querulous plaint of these jaundiced critics, all at odds with themselves! You cannot satisfy them. If you write in a style that is easy to read,[2] loose, and obvious, they call it pedestrian, say it smells of the schoolroom, and throw it down in disgust. If you employ a somewhat harder style, they tire at the first step because the meaning does not strike the mind out of hand; then they find fault with the author for being harsh, and, however perfect his art, they reject him in scorn. But I do not think my style is involved or ambiguous; nor do I see that any difficulty or obscurity necessarily accrues to my work from inserted myths however unfamiliar to them—no, not even if I had made them up myself.

But I suspect my critics mean quietly and adroitly to condemn as false the myths and stories with which they are unfamiliar under the pretext that they are mere padding. I have already said that they are drawn from ancient commentaries, as I have shown by citing in each instance the names of the respective authors; if they have never seen them before, they should not therefore condemn them, as if nothing were true but what they had read. I am very sure they have read much that is unknown to me, just as I too may have read what has never come to their notice. No one but God has ever been able to enjoy omniscience. Then let them read my discoveries with the same mind in which they would have others read theirs. If perchance the text ever seems hard, let them exert their wits, and they will find that what they thought obscure is perfectly clear.[3]

VI. THE MODERN AUTHORS HEREIN CITED ARE EMINENT

I SUPPOSE they will also complain that I have cited as my authorities both such Ancients as are obscure or unheard of, and such moderns as have no reputation—in neither case such as they are ready to trust. Indeed this criticism carries some weight. However recent they once may have been who are now the Ancients, yet that which has been preserved through many ages has been approved by great lapse of time,[1] and thence gains its authority. But as to all moderns, the right verdict concerning them, whatever their merit, seems to many to be still in suspense. I am of opinion that no writer will last long whose very novelty is not approved, since their very novelty is the necessary source of approval. Thus I have dared cite as my authorities moderns whom I have known or know personally, or whom by their merits I recognize as exceptional and reliable men. I know by every sign that they have spent nearly their whole lives in sacred studies, that they have ever mingled with men eminent for their attainments both of learning and character, they have lived laudable lives, are without stain or taint of any kind, and that both their writings and conversation are approved by the wisest. On such terms, I think, their modernity should offset the age of others. But for fear anyone may think my cited authorities are without sufficient weight, or that I am trying to approve them by my own testimony, may I say something of each of the most modern of them, that, if I should speak with effect, others may also be judges of their excellence?

I have frequently cited that noble and venerable old man, Andalò[2] di Negro of Genoa, who was once my teacher of astronomy. Thou knowest well, O excellent King, how great his prudence, how serious his manner of life, and how deep is his knowledge of his subject. He was, as he used to say, very intimately associated with you, through similarity of studies which you pursued when a young man. You could see for yourself that he not only knew the motions of stars according to the laws discovered by the Ancients—which is our way of learning them—but he had travelled nearly all over the world, visiting every clime and horizon, and had used his experience and observation to inform himself at first hand of what we learn by mere hearsay. I am therefore disposed to trust him on all matters, but particularly on everything pertaining to astronomy, just as I should trust Cicero[3] on oratory or Vergil on poetry. Many of his studies explaining the motions of the stars and heavens are extant to show how eminent he was in that subject.

In like manner I have also occasionally cited Dante[4] Alighieri, the great Florentine poet and citizen, and have done it in all justice. He was a man of noblest birth and position among his compatriots, and however slender his means, or however great his suffering from cares at home, and at last from his long exile, yet he always found time to pursue his studies in at least physics and theology; witness the city of Paris, where he often entered the hall to dispute upon any subject of the curriculum with anyone who wished to submit theses or objections. He was moreover a poet of great learning and achievements, and nothing but his exile kept him from receiving the laurel crown. He had resolved that he would never accept it anywhere but in his native city, and that he was not allowed to do. But praise is superfluous. His greatness is proved by his famous work in rime, which he wrote in the Florentine dialect with amazing skill, and called the *Commedia*. In that he stands forth rather as a Catholic and sacred theologian than a mere mythographer, and since he is known nearly the whole world over, perhaps his reputation will have reached the ears of your Highness.

I have also cited, though rarely, Francis of Barberino,[5] a man of truly honorable character and illustrious life. Though more proficient in knowledge of sacred canons than in the art of poetry, he was the author of several essays in brilliant vernacular verse, which bear witness to the high order of his genius, and are much prized by the Italians. He was a man of purest faith, deserving all reverence, whom Florence did not scorn to include among her honored citizens. I have ever considered him an excellent and trustworthy authority on all points and worthy of being ranked with any men of distinction.

Not infrequently I quote Barlaam,[6] the monk of Basil Caesariensis, a Calabrian. Though his body was slight, he overtopped others in learning. Indeed he was so good a Hellenist that he enjoyed privileges at the hands of emperors and Greek princes and scholars, which show that neither in our time, nor for many a century, have the Greeks produced a man endowed with such vast and peculiar erudition. Shall I not do well to trust him, particularly in all that pertains to Greek? I have never seen any formal work from his hand, though I have heard that he has written several. I possess, however, some material derived from him, and, though it was never reduced to the form of a book with a title, and shows certain of Barlaam's deficiencies in Latin, yet it proves both his wide reading and observation, and his power in interpretative criticism.

Paul of Perugia,[7] a man of highest authority, is another of those to whom I refer. Advanced in years, of great and varied learning, he was long the librarian of the famous King Robert of Sicily and Jerusalem. If there was ever a man possessed of the curiosity of research he was the one. A word from his prince was sufficient to send him hunting through a dozen books of history, fable, or poetry. He thus enjoyed peculiar friendship with Barlaam, and though it could not be based upon common interests in Latin culture, it was a means by which Paul drank deeply of Greek lore. He wrote a huge book which he called *The Collections;* it included much matter on various subjects, but particularly his ingatherings of pagan mythology from Latin authors, together with whatever he could collect on the same subject from the Greeks, probably with Barlaam's help. I shall never hesitate to acknowledge that when still a youngster,[8] long before you drew my mind to this undertaking, I drank deep of that work, with more appetite than discretion. Especially did I prefer all that part set down under the name of Theodontius.[9] But to the very serious inconvenience of this book of mine, I found that his saucy wife Biella, after his death, wilfully destroyed this and many other books of Paul's. In short I am convinced that at the time when I knew him no one was his equal in studies of this sort.

Leontius Pilatus,[10] of Thessalonica, is another whom I often mention. By his own statement he was a pupil of the aforesaid Barlaam. He is a man of uncouth appearance, ugly features, long beard, and black hair, for ever lost in thought, rough in manners and behavior. For all that he is a most learned Hellenist, as any inquirer discovers, and a fairly inexhaustible mine of Greek history and myth. In

Latin he is not as yet so well versed. I have never seen any
work from his hand; and all my quotations from him I
have made at his oral dictation. For nearly three years I
heard him read Homer, and conversed with him on terms
of singular friendship; but so immense was the measure
of all he had to tell that my memory, quickened though it
was by pressure of other care, would not have been good
enough to retain it, had I not set it down in a notebook.

Then there is also Paul the geometrician,[11] my fellow-
townsman. I am sure, O illustrious King, that you know
him well by reputation; for I am convinced that to him
more than to any other man in this part of the world the
sciences of arithmetic, geometry, and astrology have
opened and revealed their very depths; indeed, it seems
as if no detail of them had escaped him. Wonderful as it
sounds, more wonderful yet is it to see him give immediate
ocular proof to anyone who asks, of every word he utters
about the stars or heavens. This he does by means of instruments that he has made for the purpose with his own
hands. His reputation is not confined to his native city, nor
even to Italy; his scholarship is more celebrated at Paris
than at home, as it is also in England, Spain, and particularly in Africa, where this subject enjoys special importance. Happy, indeed, the man whose zeal was more
intense, or who lived in a more liberal age than Paul.

Last and greatest of my authorities is Francis Petrarch,[12]
of Florence, my revered teacher, father, and master. Not
many years[13] ago at Rome, by vote of the senate and approval of the famous King Robert[14] of Sicily and Jerusalem, he received the decoration of the laurel crown from
the very hands of the senators. He really deserves to be
counted not among the moderns, but among the illustrious
ancients. His great eminence as a poet has been recognized
by—I will not say merely all Italians, for their glory is
singular and perennial—but by all France, and Germany,

and even that most remote little corner of the world, England;[15] and, I must add, many of the Greeks. Surely his great fame has reached Cyprus, and hence the ears of your Highness. Many memorable works from his hand in prose and verse yield patent proof to all the world of his heaven-sent genius. First is his divine poem *Africa,* written in heroics to extol the deeds of the first Africanus. It still lies in his drawer awaiting publication. Second, is his *Bucolics,* famous the world over. Third, the book of metrical epistles to his friends. Fourth are two great volumes of letters in prose, so replete with thought and fact, so resplendent with artistic embellishment, that no fair-minded reader would judge them in any respect inferior to Cicero's. Fifth are his *Invectives against the Physician.* Sixth his book *On the Solitary Life.* Last is one which will see the light in a few days—his book *On the Remedies of Fortune.* Besides these there are still in the works several, which at their early completion we shall yet read in his lifetime. Who then will repudiate his testimony? Who will refuse to trust him? Oh, had I not a little above[16] written of him in my feeble way, how much and how high the praise I could add to win more abundant faith in his utterance! But let what I have said suffice.

So much, then, about the moderns. But something remains to be said of those Ancients who are unfamiliar to my critics, lest I appear guilty of serious omission. They charge me with citing authors they never heard of, as if none were trustworthy whose names *they* have never heard. It is a common trait of the uneducated man to believe nothing that he does not see in a book, as though mere reading a fact made it credible. I confess I have cited myths and comment from many authors whose names are not generally current at present, because, as I said, their very antiquity accredited them. All these I have

either seen and read myself, or else found them quoted
by later writers. If these cavillers have not seen them
or even heard their names, it is not the authors' fault, but
that of their own idleness. They should blame themselves,
not find fault with me. The books cannot of their own
accord take wing from the libraries into the hands of
sluggards; and it is not the duty of those who are
familiar with them to act as proxies for those who are
not. Let them read and study for themselves. They will
discover much that is new to them, and be at home where
before they were strangers. They will find that these
unfamiliar authors carry as much weight as they assign
to those they have read before. So much, then, concerning both the modern and the ancient authors herein
adduced. If their merits did not justify my citations,
necessity would.

The great text of both civil and canon law has grown
in bulk throughout generations of human failing, by
editorial apparatus from many a doctor. The books of
the philosophers also carry with them their commentaries
compiled with great care and zeal. The books of medicine
are filled with marginal notes from countless pens that
resolve every doubt, and so with sacred writings, and
their numerous expositors; so also with the liberal and
the technical arts—each has its own commentary, from
which anyone may select on occasion according to his
preference. Poetry alone is without such honor. Few—
very few—are they with whom it has dwelt continuously.
Money-getters have found it unprofitable. It has therefore been neglected and scorned for many centuries, nay
even torn by many persecutions and stripped of the aids[17]
given to the other arts. Wherefore, wanting such range
of selection as they enjoy, one is forced to resort to this
and that authority and bring away such slight fragments
as one can. A discerning reader will readily see how

often this has happened, for I have not only appealed on occasion to modern authors, but have had recourse to anonymous notes.

Wherefore let these cavillers bow to expediency and accept the authority of both the unfamiliar Ancients and the moderns.

VII. GREEK POETRY[1] IS QUOTED IN THIS WORK NOT WITHOUT GOOD REASON

IT IS safe to say that these critics and others will charge me with purely gratuitous and ostentatious quoting from Greek poetry. I am well aware, of course, that the objection implies not a spark of charity, but proceeds from the malice of a blasted, withered, and impious heart. So be it; yet with God on my side, I shall not waver, but will, as usual, venture a humble response. Let me say then for the enlightenment of those unworthy slanderers, that it shows lack of judgment to derive from the stream what may be got at the fountainhead. I owned Homer's works,[2] and do yet, and drew from them much[3] that was of great use to my work. A great deal of this, as anyone may see, has been quoted by the Ancients, from whom of course I could have got it, as it were from the stream of tradition; in fact, I have frequently done so. But sometimes it has seemed better to draw from the source than from the stream, and more than once I have failed to find in the stream that which abounded in the fountain itself. Hence I have been guided sometimes by predilection, sometimes by necessity.

Authors occasionally delight to introduce digressive passages, which may indeed somewhat retard their readers, but contribute to their delectation and comfort, and keep them from leaving off their reading because they are tired with constant application or the monotony of the style. Such may be the effect of an occasional quotation of poetry. Furthermore my own bald statement of a fact thus gains corroboration from the witness of others in the face of any possible objector; if anyone distrusts the verse as quoted, he may consult the *Iliad* or the *Odyssey* to find out whether I quoted correctly; and if I was right, so much the greater certitude. Then, too, I am not the only one to quote Greek in a Latin discourse; the practice is old. Let them open the books of Cicero, or Macrobius, or Apuleius,[4] or, to go no further, the *Opuscula*[5] of Maximus Ausonius; these authors they will often find quoting Greek verses in their Latin writings, and their precedent I have followed.

But my objectors will now say that it may have been laudable in those days, but at present such pains are silly. Since nobody now knows Greek,[6] the old custom must perforce be obsolete. I am sorry, then, for Latin learning, if it has so completely rejected the study of Greek that we do not even recognize the characters. Though Latin literature be sufficient unto itself,[7] and enjoys the exclusive attention of the whole western world, yet without question it would gain much light through an alliance with Greek. Besides the ancient Latin writers have not by any means appropriated all that is Greek. Much yet remains unrevealed to us, and much by knowledge of which we might profit greatly. But I shall take up this matter again.[8]

My objectors do not consider to whom I dedicate my labor upon this book. If they did they would realize that he is a most erudite monarch,[9] said to be versed in Greek as well as Latin literature, who has learned Hellenists ever about him. *Such* will hardly agree with these dunces that Greek poetry is superfluous!

Well, enough! But I will now humor my accusers a bit. Suppose I *have* quoted Greek poetry for mere ostentation. What of it? Must they therefore set their teeth

in me? Whom do I hurt in the pure enjoyment of my
natural right? They may not know it, but it is my peculiar
boast and glory to cultivate Greek poetry among the
Tuscans. Was it not I who intercepted Leontius Pilatus[10]
on his way from Venice to the western Babylon, and with
my advice turned him aside from his long peregrination,
and kept him in our city? Did not I receive him into
my own house, entertain him for a long time, and make
the utmost effort personally that he should be appointed
professor in Florence, and his salary paid out of the
city's funds? Indeed I did; and I too was the first who, at
my own expense, called back to Tuscany the writings of
Homer and of other Greek authors, whence they had
departed many centuries before, never meanwhile to
return. And it was not to Tuscany only, but to my own
city that I brought them. I, too, was the first to hear
Leontius privately render the *Iliad* in Latin; and I it was
who tried to arrange public readings from Homer. And
though I did not understand Homer any too well, I got
such knowledge of him as I could; and if that wanderer
had dwelt longer among us, I should certainly have
learned much more. But little as I did gain of the vast
whole, some passages I came to understand very well by
frequent interpretation of my preceptor; these have I, on
occasion, embodied in this work. Now what possible harm
can come from this? Greek myths abound in this book,
yet no one accuses me of ostentation in recording them.
But let me insert a few verses in Greek letters, and down
they come upon me! Why, Marius of Arpinum, after his
several triumphs over the Africans, the Cimbri, and the
Teutons, made bold to do his drinking from the cantharus
like Father Bacchus himself. And so Caius Duellius,[11] the
first to beat the Carthaginians in a sea-fight, made it his
practice to go home from a public dinner by the light of a
wax torch. All this, however it exceeded the precedent of

the city of Rome, the Romans calmly accepted. Yet here
are swine who fly into a rage at me for mingling Greek
verses with Latin contrary to the modern custom, and
little glory do I get for my pains. I thought I was thus
adding a certain grace to my Latin, but lo, I have brought
down a storm of malice upon myself. I am sorry enough.
But it is no matter; from the judicious I do not look for
such objections, and as for the rest, if they claim my attention, patience will suffice to get along with them.
Finally, I beseech all my readers to endure such annoyance
unperturbed, mindful of Valerius' words[12] that there is no
life so lowly that the sweetness of glory does not appeal
to it.

VIII. THE PAGAN POETS OF MYTHOLOGY ARE THEOLOGIANS[1]

THERE are certain pietists who, in reading my words, will
be moved by holy zeal to charge me with injury to the
most sacrosanct Christian religion; for I allege that the
pagan poets are theologians—a distinction which Christians
grant only to those instructed in sacred literature. These
critics I hold in high respect; and I thank them in anticipation for such criticism, for I feel that it implies their
concern for my welfare. But the carelessness of their remarks shows clearly the narrow limitations of their reading. If they had read widely, they could not have
overlooked that very well-known work on the *City of
God*;[2] they might have seen how, in the Sixth Book,
Augustine cites the opinion of the learned Varro, who held
that theology is threefold in its divisions—mythical,
physical, and civil. It is called mythical, from the Greek
mythicon, a myth, and in this kind, as I have already[3] said,
is adapted to the use of the comic stage.[4] But this form of
literature is reprobate among better poets on account of its
obscenity. Physical theology is, as etymology shows, natural and moral, and being commonly thought a very useful

thing, it enjoys much esteem. Civil or political theology, sometimes called the theology of state worship, relates to the commonwealth, but through the foul abominations of its ancient ritual, it was repudiated by them of the true faith and the right worship of God. Now of these three, physical theology is found in the great poets since they clothe many a physical and moral truth in their inventions, including within their scope not only the deeds of great men, but matters relating to their gods. And particularly, as they first composed hymns of praise to the gods, and, as I have said, in a poetic guise, presented their great powers and acts, they won the name of theologians even among the primitive pagans. Indeed Aristotle[5] himself avers that they were the first to ponder theology; and though they got their name from no knowledge or lore of the true God, yet at the advent of true theologians they could not lose it, so great was the natural force of the word derived from the theory of any divinity whatsoever. Aware, I suppose, that the title "theologian" once fairly won, cannot be lost, the present-day theologians call themselves professors of sacred theology to distinguish themselves from theologians of mythological cast or any other. Such distinction admits no possible exception as implying an injury to the name of Christianity. Do we not speak of all mortals who have bodies and rational souls as men? Some may be Gentiles, some Israelites, some Agarenes, some Christians, and some so depraved as to deserve the name of gross beasts not men. Yet we do not wrong our Savior by calling them men, though with His Godhead He is known to have been literally human. No more is there any harm in speaking of the old poets as theologians. Of course, if any one were to call them sacred, the veriest fool would detect the falsehood.

On the other hand there are times, as in this book, when the theology of the Ancients will be seen to exhibit

what is right and honorable, though in most such cases
it should be considered rather physiology or ethology[6]
than theology, according as the myths embody the truth
concerning physical nature or human. But the old theology can sometimes be employed in the service of Catholic
truth, if the fashioner of the myths should choose. I have
observed this in the case of more than one orthodox poet
in whose investiture of fiction the sacred teachings were
clothed. Nor let my pious critics be offended to hear the
poets sometimes called even sacred theologians.[7] In like
manner sacred theologians turn physical when occasion
demands; if in no other way, at least they prove themselves physical theologians as well as sacred when they
express truth by the fable of the trees[8] choosing a king.

IX. IT IS NOT IMPROPER FOR CERTAIN CHRISTIANS
TO STUDY PAGAN ANTIQUITY[1]

OTHERS will say with equal emphasis that it is improper
for a Christian to investigate or publish wicked, super-
stitious beliefs and genealogies of the pagans, since they
tend to pervert the minds of readers to erroneous opinions
and involve them in imminent danger of false doctrine.
I grant it: the criticism proceeds from a most sacred
source.[2] A considerable number should, I doubt not, be
kept from studies of this sort. But just as safely others
can be admitted to them without the least danger of suspicion. If it had seemed necessary for every one to avoid
them, doubtless our holy Mother the Church would have
uttered a perpetual decree of prohibition against them.
Indeed, in the days when the Church was just taking root
among the pagans, the Christians found it expedient to
press hard against the pagan rites and observances, colored
as men's notions of religion were by the origin and by
the very perseverance of paganism. It was a precaution
lest readers of pagan literature be caught by the claw

of antiquity, and return as a dog[3] to their vomit. But today, by the grace of Christ, our strength is very great; the universally hateful doctrine of paganism has been cast into utter and perpetual darkness, and the Church in triumph holds the fortress of the enemy. Thus there is the very slightest danger[4] in the study and investigation of paganism. Of course it is better for a boy of tenacious memory but of mind as yet callow to avoid them, especially as he is not yet wholly familiar with the Christian religion. And a neophyte whose faith is not yet confirmed might, if the rein slackened, deviate into slippery places. Though there may be some men less sensitive who might let themselves slip into so dreadful a mistake, I cannot think it could happen to me even though I pursued nothing else. From my mother's womb I was brought to be washed at the fountain of our regeneration, and what my sponsors promised for me, a catechumen, I have kept from that hour to this as well as human frailty allowed. I have always held the Creed[5] as it is sung in the congregation of just men:

That there is one God in triple distinction of persons, true, eternal, Maker of all things, in perpetual reason their Governor, Preserver, and Ruler; containing all things within Himself, but contained of none. That, by a marvellous and unique creative act of this Divinity, through the adumbration of the Holy Ghost, His eternal Word was made to destroy the guilt of men incurred by the disobedience of our first parents. He was conceived of a pure Virgin, who was forewarned by the Heavenly Harbinger; He became incarnate, was born in due time of the Virgin, still a virgin, and was made mortal man. While yet an infant at His mother's breast He was adored by the Sabean Kings[6] with their offerings. As He grew, He went among doctors of the Law explaining to them its hard obscurities; yet they held Him not God, but

a boy of wonderful powers; for the unfading splendor of
truth had not as yet withdrawn the mist from their minds
that they might recognize here clothed in the flesh the God
that had been promised unto them. And I believe that He
who had thus left the heavenly mansions, and changed His
Godhead for a servant's guise, and grew a man among
men, in His thirtieth year was baptized in the River Jordan
by the prophet, unkempt and uncouth, one filled from his
birth with the Holy Ghost, and appointed to open the door
of eternal salvation; and the noise of thunder was heard,
and a clear sound from the overhanging cloud which was the
voice of God saying:[7] "This is my beloved Son in whom
I am well pleased; hear ye Him." And I believe, and hold
it proven, that first at Cana in Galilee He turned water
into wine to reveal the divinity within Him; then taking
the holy company of His apostles, He went throughout
Judea, and the cities of Phoenicia, and Samaria and Galilee, and in temple and synagogue taught the people the
heavenly truth, healed lepers, made the dumb speak, restored those who were blind by nature or accident, brought
back souls from death to their bodies, made fevers, winds,
and waves obey Him, and showed many other signs of
His divinity. At length when His hour was come through
the envy of the priests of the Jews, He washed His
friends' feet, and celebrated the great feast whereat was
wrought by His hands and words the ineffable sacrament
of our communion, in which He changed His body into
bread and His blood into wine, and revealed them so
changed unto those present and unto all generations to
come. Then was He sold by one of His disciples, and, as
He prayed in solitude, He was sought out by the rabble,
and taken with torches and staves, brought to the rulers,
basely accused, yet bearing with patient humility the false
witness of certain accusers; then He was mocked in the
judgment-hall, and cut with rods, crowned with a crown

of thorns, buffeted and spit upon, and at last condemned after the manner of thieves, hung high on the cross, and had vinegar and myrrh to drink. When His human strength was overcome by His punishment, His end came; or rather, I believe with Thomas Aquinas,[8] that He gathered up His strength, and of His own will gave up the ghost. And the whole earth shook, and the light of the midday sun turned to darkness for three hours, and the moon[9] opposite was darkened. I wonder that Dionysius the Areopagite, in writing to Polycarp explains it otherwise. Then with his spear a soldier, blind of heart, pierced the side of Jesus, and blood mingled with water gushed out, whence I believe proceeded all the sacraments[10] of our salvation. And I believe withal that when He had been taken from the cross and buried, He visited in spirit the abodes of hell, where He broke the iron bonds and shattered the walls of that ancient prison, then subdued Pluto, and brought forth to freedom all the ancient spoil of the place. Then by power of His deity, as sung by the prophets of old, the third day He rose from the bowels of the earth, like Jonah[11] from the whale's belly, and triumphed over death. Thereafter He appeared often among His own. At last, oppressed by no corporeal weight, in His true body that was sometime mortal, of His own strength He arose from before their eyes and ascended to Him who had sent Him forth. Hence He imparted to His brave champions the Heavenly Flame proceeding equally from Himself and His all-righteous Father, quickening all things and teaching all truth. In Its light they waged war upon the Prince of this world; and when they had sown the seed[12] of truth by their blood and wounds, and won the victory, they followed their Captain in triumph back into their own country. I believe also in the devout congregation of the just established by this only-begotten Son of God; in the holy baptism of regeneration, whereby the

sins of men are done away; and in the other rites and
sacraments of the Church by which we become sub-
missive to God, and rise again when, in our foolishness,
we have fallen, and by our own choice seek reconciliation
not accomplished by shedding human blood, as among
heathen savages, nor in the ancient manner, by sacrifice of
sheep and cattle. I have never ceased to believe, by testimony of the Fathers,[13] in the last great day when all
things perishable shall be done away, and by the might
of God we who were once mortal shall in our bodies
rise immortal, and enter into our appointed place. There
Christ Himself wearing all the marks of His passion,
shall sit enthroned as judge in His proper majesty, and
we shall hear Him speak final sentence upon our merits.
I believe also in the life to come, wherein I hope in the
body, through no merit of mine, but by divine compassion,
to behold God my Redeemer, and rejoice with the saints
in the land of the living.

This, then, briefly, is the sincere faith and eternal truth
which is so deeply implanted in my heart, that by no influence of pagan antiquity nor any other power can it
be torn out, or be cut off, or fall away. Sinner that I am,
I am not by grace of Christ like young Cherea, in Terence,[14] who by looking at a picture of Jove falling in a
shower of gold from the roof to the lap of Danae, was
inflamed to the desire of a similar misdeed. Any weak
susceptibility of that sort, if it ever existed—and I am
not at all sure that it did—left me with my youth. But
I knew well that our old adversary spreads snares and
nets[15] for us on every side, and, as a roaring lion, walketh
among the paths of men, seeking whom he may devour.
Like Mithridates,[16] the aged king of Pontus, who, with
great and bold spirit and a splendid outlay, waged fierce
and memorable war against Rome full forty years, and
ever from his youth up carried in his bosom an antidote

to deadly poison; so I have armed my breast[17] with the truth of the Gospel, the holy doctrine of Paul, and with the commands, advice, and admonitions of Augustine and many other very reverend Fathers. Wherefore little have I to fear from the weapons of paganism. If at thy bidding, O renowned King, I, a Christian, have handled the foolishness of the Gentiles, and so roused the disapproval of these credulous objectors, I have only done—to compare small things with great[18]—what many saintly men[19] have done with highest approval, such as Augustine, or Jerome, or among others the neophyte Lactantius. I have been fully aware from childhood, by the Psalmist's testimony,[20] that all pagan gods were devils, and have therefore disapproved of their absurd misdeeds; but I admit that, their manner of worship aside, the character and words of certain ancient poets have delighted me, and I have both praised them and defended[21] them as well as I could against their accusers; whereof this book is proof enough. This I have done to save from ignorant clutches men who, if they had known Christ, would have worshipped Him as reverently as the noblest of our faith. But, to go higher, some one will say: "You have done well; it is a commendable thing to forearm oneself. But remember, he that toucheth pitch shall be defiled.[22] Many a man at the very height of his trust in his strength has fallen at the hand of a weak enemy. Even if examples did not abound, Solomon is certainly a convincing proof of human weakness. He enjoyed at God's hand all wisdom, all wealth, great empire, held the Gentiles in just tribute, built a wonderful temple to God, wrought many good works; and yet in his old age forgot the Giver of so many honors, went up into the mountain of offence, and adored the Egyptian idol Moloch[23] on bended knee. And will you prove stronger or more circumspect than Solomon?" True, we deceive ourselves who trust too much in our own strength; the fact is true and undeniable. But my contention with paganism differs from that between Solomon and his Egyptian wife. Well aware in her woman's guile that she had ensnared the soul of an unhappy man with her beauty, and eager to glorify her own gods, she proceeded to ply him incessantly with amorous embraces, honeyed kisses, a woman's flattery, wantonness, prayers, and tears—a very ready means with her sex[24]—nay, with assumed indignation; and thus kept up the attack upon her lover day and night as well. Ah, how strong and irresistible are the love assaults of women, especially at night. For fear of losing her favor whom he loved above all the rest, Solomon turned and succumbed without defence to the armed force of a woman's wiles. But my strife with the absurdities of paganism is quite otherwise, for their power is disarmed by many a true reason familiar to me, and with their force thus spent and routed the fight is easy. I am fully aware that over-confidence is at all times a sin; but my trust is not in myself, but in the grace of Jesus Christ by whose precious blood I was redeemed. I am sure He will not suffer me, who have followed in His very steps so many years, even from my youth,[25] to go astray in my old age. And if I slip, He will stretch out the hand of His righteousness to me in my weakness, and lead my weary feet to quiet peace.

Finally, what I have said goes to show that while it is not desirable for everybody to study paganism, it is not equally improper for everybody.

X. WE CULTIVATE MOST THOSE STUDIES FOR WHICH WE HAVE THE STRONGEST NATURAL BENT

THERE are some who, though they admit the truth of all this, will not hesitate, I expect, to say that, instead of studying such a subject, it would have been far better to spend one's time on more sacred lore, which no one in his

right mind will deny. For example, there are the laws of
the Caesars, and canon law, and medicine[1]—subjects that
many consider most sacred, because they have so often
been the means of making greedy men rich. And there is
philosophy,[2] by whose excellent demonstration we learn
the causes of things, and the distinction between false and
true—surely a subject worthy of any great natural gifts.
There, too, are the sacred books,[3] that teach us to despise
perishable things, and declare the greatness of God and
His works, and point the way unto the Kingdom of
Heaven. This subject obviously takes precedence of all
others. A choice of any one of these subjects my objectors
would doubtless say was more righteous than the one I
made. Of course, if we were all doing what we ought,
judges and lawyers would go to court in vain. But it is
not so easy as some may think to desire all things that we
ought, and it is far harder to attain them, however much
we would. For example, the harp[4] has some strings
stretched more tightly than others, to make the difference
between high and low tones, and by this very difference,
when they are touched by the plectrum in a skilful hand,
they give forth sweetest harmony. So Mother Nature, of
her exhaustless strength and perfect skill, has produced
mortal aptitudes for various offices, by whose variety she
achieves the preservation of the human race, on which
she is particularly bent. For mere reproduction does not
imply preservation; and she sees that, if all men, not to
mention other beings, were made alike, nothing could, by
any device, be produced to last even a moment of time.
Hence by her wisdom this man is made a carpenter, that
a sailor, another a merchant, and some are fitted to be
priests, or kings, some lawyers, judges, poets, philosophers, or high theologians; and from their various pursuits results of necessity the preservation of this vast
number of men. If every one of us (since we are to

suppose it is every one's duty, if he can, to aspire to higher studies) should devote himself constantly to theology, we should then have no farmers; and without the farmer whence should we who pursue so noble a study have nourishment? Or without masons and carpenters where should we find protection from the rain and wind and cold and the sun's heat, and like inconveniences to which we are ever subject. Without the woolworker whence our clothes, or without the cobbler, our shoes? Why, for convenience of the human body Nature has given it a variety of members and functions, and so ordered their diversity that it is like a melody composed of a variety of tones; so for the preservation of the race we were of necessity born for different pursuits.[5] If we find Nature herself, who has disposed the heavens, and stars in their various orbits and courses, at God's will making us, as a matter of course, for different functions, then who will dare go over into another occupation than that to which he was born? Of course, I am fully aware of the power of free will, by which we may overcome Nature; we read of many such cases. But, after all, they must be counted rare, since the constraining force of natural bent is well-nigh invincible. Being, then, bred, born, and nourished for different pursuits, it is enough that we follow to the full our natural calling, and not stray into another, as some have done, who, at the end of a long and vain endeavor have finally lost their original gifts, and failed to attain what they were after. Whatever the vocation of others, mine, as experience from my mother's womb[6] has shown, is clearly the study of poetry. For this, I believe, I was born. I well remember how my father even in my boyhood directed all my endeavors towards business. As a mere child, he put me in charge of a great business man for instruction in arithmetic. For six years[7] I did nothing in his office but waste irrevocable time. Then, as there seemed to be some indication that I was more disposed to literary pursuits, this same father decided that I should study for holy orders, as a good way to get rich. My teacher[8] was famous, but I wasted under him almost as much time as before. In both cases I so tired of the work that neither my teacher's admonition, nor my father's authority, who kept torturing me with ever renewed orders, nor the pleas and importunities of my friends, could make me yield, so great was my one passion for poetry. It was not finally a sudden change of plan that sent me headlong into this pursuit, but rather a disposition of long standing. I remember perfectly that before I reached my seventh year, or had ever seen a story, or heard a teacher speak, or scarce knew my letters, a natural impulse to composition seized me. I produced some little inventions, slight as they may have been. Of course, at that tender age genius was as yet too weak for so great a function. But I had scarce reached my majority when my mind, by its own impulse, seized and assimilated the little I had already learned of poetry, and I pursued the art with the utmost zeal, and delighted myself above all things in reading, studying, and trying with all my might to understand poetry. This took place without a word of advice or instruction from anyone, while my father continually resisted and condemned such a pursuit. Strangely enough, before I knew the proper kinds and number of feet in a verse, my acquaintances, in spite of my most urgent protest, were all calling me a poet, a name I have never really deserved to this day. If my father had only been favorable to such a course at a time of life when I was more adaptable, I do not doubt that I should have taken my place among poets of fame. But while he tried to bend my mind first into business and next into a lucrative profession, it came to pass that I turned out neither a business man, nor a canon-lawyer,[9] and missed being a good poet besides. As to the other professions, though they interested me, their charm was not compelling, and I therefore followed them not. I have looked into the sacred writings, but was dissuaded from devoting myself to them by my increasing years and slender intellect; and besides I think it is highly disgusting to see what I may call an old man[10] take up elementary studies; in all respects it is most unbecoming to devote yourself to an undertaking which you are virtually certain you cannot carry through. Wherefore, since I believe that I am called to this profession by God's will, it is my purpose to stand fast in the same. These present studies show what I have done in it, and others may praise them as seems best. Then let those who allow the cobbler his awl and bristles, the wool-raiser his flock, the sculptor his statues, in all patience give me leave to cultivate the poets.[11]

XI. WE INTEREST OURSELVES IN PAGAN KINGS AND GODS TO OUR SERIOUS HARM

SOME of my readers will dart out of the beaten path and throw themselves in front of me shouting that I am a rash and presumptuous man to poke about as I do among the tombs of ancient kings,[1] and drag their ashes from their long sleep into public hatred again, or dim their ancient splendor with new clouds. They say I rouse the half-forgotten crimes of the very gods to the unhappy wakefulness of general notoriety, and under the honorable disguise of a genealogy of the gods, I recount merely their thieving and incest. This is a long and involved complaint of theirs, but it shows, I think, that they are aware of what I have written, particularly when they blame me for recounting the crimes of the pagan gods. Such blame smacks of a pagan mind. If their opinion really corresponds to their words, lo, that infamous error of paganism still flourishes in some minds! But I pray

God that He remove and dissolve it. As for the objections, they are answered easily enough. If I remember Aristotle's *Ethics*[2] aright, he only is bold and rash who goes to extremes of audacity. Now I think there is nothing extreme, and therefore nothing rash, in daring to perform what by every token has proved acceptable and necessary. I have never read of a prohibition against recounting the deeds of kings, be they good or bad. Of course it was better for kings to live in such a way that none but an honest report survive them. However, I have not written of them in any formal or appropriate style, but whatever account of them I have interpolated I have given simply and purely as the order of my task required. In so doing I have committed no new and unusual crime. There are the great and ancient volumes of famous historians,[3] wherein they recount the deeds of kings in splendid style and unbroken order. From these, I, a modern, have cited whatever was apposite to my work. If then, anyone is to be blamed, it is those rich and ancient historians whose works have long since spread their great fame throughout the whole wide world. If anyone is capable of resentment against the peaceful dead, he conceives it from these authors. But what sort of reverence is this? By what spark of charity was it kindled? What can possibly give rise to it? High-toned and noble souls of course! Anxious so to seem, at any rate, they display their concern for the honors of kings and make a show of being shocked at improper literature. How cheap the price they expect to pay for nobility—a distinction to be won only by an exalted manner of life, by justice, by sanctity, and by learning. If they were really noble, these simpletons would know that it is not merely a waste of time, but positively harmful to have sympathy with bad men of any sort, let alone pagans. If they have any sense, let them keep their reverence for a better object. The foul indecencies of the

pagan gods are not merely dormant or asleep; they have
been buried for ever, beyond any possibility of resurrection, by the holy teaching of Christ. They have been covered and pressed down by the enormous weight of
damnation, and I, as a Christian man, have tried to increase the weight of this mass, inadequately perhaps, but
as much as I could; and I looked for fitting praise of my
work, not for recriminations. But I take small account of
these mumblings and mouthings—the teeth of the curs are
not sharp enough to hurt. Then, if they really are Christian, let them stop talking and entertain a little regret
for their objection to the pagan gods; for this of all mis-
demeanors least becomes a Christian.

XII. WHETHER SCANT OR PROLIX, I DO NOT DESERVE THE RACK FOR IT[1]

PERCHANCE some will say that I am too concise, since
at times my recital and elucidation of myths and legends
is cursory; while others will, no doubt, find me for the
most part prolix.[2] I am forced to admit all this at once,
but there are many reasons for my misdemeanor. Several
articles I have been forced to treat very briefly; of course,
I might have spun out a myth or legend at length from
my own invention, but a man in his right mind would
shudder to do so. There were other legends which could
be fully told in a few words, and if a few words make
them clear, more would have been a mistake. There are,
besides, many that, without doubt, could not sustain more
words than I have spent upon them. But suppose I had
let myself say all that I could, or all that my matter
called for; suppose I had set down everything that came
to me as I was writing—every detail of the longest myths
or legends, every particular deed of gods or men, the
many varied meanings and versions of these myths, the
ancient authorities for the historical part, every opinion

or account of numerous writers on the subject—why, when do they think I could ever have got to the end of my work? A lifetime would hardly suffice for all that, and the result would have been so huge a tome[3] that it would have frightened off any reader at the first glance. Wherefore I have been content in what I have said merely to touch upon the most important points, for my audience is neither children nor the lazy rabble, but, as I say, a most learned King and such men of higher studies as this work may reach from the hands of your Serene Highness, O Prince. Besides, that the reader's mind may exert itself, one's book should not be too full; whatever is got at the cost of a little labor[4] is both more pleasing and more carefully observed than that which gets to the reader's mind of itself. Then, too, some chance to speak and write must be left to posterity for fear we may seem to begrudge future generations their talents, and arrogantly, as it were, usurp the glory to which they, like us, naturally aspire. My critics, therefore, should deal gently with me for all my condensing and omitting, since my reasons are altogether good.

As for those who may accuse me of prolixity, I will merely say that I have written more fully either when I judged it expedient to do so, or from pure delectation[5] of mind such as occasionally makes the pen of the better writers very generous. In short, as a condensed account exercises the educated mind, and a fuller appeals to the less educated,[6] I ask my more accomplished readers to remember that they were once untrained and so accept in patience a statement made somewhat fuller for the benefit of their juniors.

XIII. THE ROYAL COMMAND THAT CALLED FORTH THIS WORK IS GENUINE, NOT IMAGINARY

PERHAPS some will say, what has not infrequently been said of other eminent men, that purely for vainglory I

pretend to have compiled this book at thy command, O
famous King. How slow their trust! Or rather how
hopeless their minds! Conscious of their own failings,
they invidiously impute them to others. It is true, as Tully
says,[1] we are all actuated by a desire for praise,—and that
glory is a peculiar incentive to every excellent man. Now
since an obscure man finds a way to glory by paying court
to a great and excellent king, it may be readily believed
that some men, with the aim of exalting their humble
selves, have made pretensions of this sort; but that they
were authors who did so, I shall never believe. But of
this at another time. As for myself, I admit that I long
for fame,[2] but, desire it as I do, I am not so inflamed, so
unbridled in this desire, nor so averse to honor, that I
could have plunged into such duplicity without—I will
not say, a blush—but without loss of reason itself.
Herein, I confess, I am proud, if pride is the word. As
for the dedication of books, I should uninvited offer the
honor and title to nobody but God, nor accord it to every-
one that asked for it. You well know, O excellent King,
how much I protested and delayed, when your officer
Donino[3] urged and besought me to grant your request
and take up this labor. As the years went by, it happened
that your friend and my fellow-townsman, Bechino
Bellincioni,[4] on his way from Cyprus, met me at Ravenna.
After he expressed in agreeable manner your Highness'
kind consideration towards unworthy me, he began with
wonderfully urgent importunity to rouse my mind from
the drowsiness into which it had fallen over this work;
and this he said he did at your command. So also your
very dear friend, Paul, the geometrician,[5] has at times
shown me letters signed with your Majesty's seal,
enclosing your commands, and urged my attention to
them. God knows, and so does your Highness, that I
never have seen you nor you me; yet I took these orders

as genuine, and shouldered this enormous load. If this has been done without your knowledge, then I have been deceived by those I have just mentioned; and I admit that these persons who say that the book was not written at your command are telling the truth. But it is no fault of mine, unless it should be said that I was to blame for not replying that I would write the book only on condition of receiving letters to that effect directly from you. But it seemed presuming in me not to trust the distinguished officer Donino. He died, I have heard, in almost the very year that he met me, so that I cannot now appeal to him; but Bechino and Paul are alive,[6] and I have as my witnesses before the world both them and your royal faith. I therefore appeal to you[7] and to them, (and the office is properly yours, if the necessity should arise) to answer this attack upon me, and with a confirming word clear my name from so foul a stain of falsehood.

But to turn from you for a moment, O King, to my accusers, I venture to answer their charge briefly in my own name. I venture to say that, if the case were to be tried before a judge sitting in court, I have living witnesses, not cited from the dregs of the rabble either, but men of eminence, to show that, if I wished to decorate my work with a king's name, it was not necessary for me to go so far as Cyprus for so clumsy a pretense. There was a king nearby[8]—nay, right here, I am bold to say— who if he had thought that he could win the dedication of the book I had undertaken, would have asked for it in person—though, of course, the matter never entered my mind while Donino was with me. Being a prince of no particular culture he would have sought the inscription with little thought of adding to my glory through his name, but rather with the hope of giving his title eternal distinction through my book. This is not at all strange: the names and distinctions of all kings really depend upon

the suffrage of literary men. There was Alexander of
Macedon, who, in his great courage, made bold to invade
the whole earth with only a little band of soldiers. When
he marched into Persia he took along many writers qualified to record his exploits. When he came to Sigeum,
where he saw the tomb of Achilles, he could not help
declaring how great he thought the glory which kings
derive from literary men, and said that that hero was most
fortunate in having Homer for his herald. So Pompey
the Great, whose fortune equalled his valor, conferred
citizenship on Theophanes of Mitylene in the presence of
the army, as a man likely to eternize his fame. In the same
way the Scipios, Fulvius, Cato the Censor, Quintus
Metellus Pino, Gaius Marius, Cicero, and many other
famous men were generous and familiar with authors,[9]
in hopes of becoming the subjects of their writings. What
inducement have I, then, to couple fictitiously the name
of a renowned king with my book, as if I would bestow
glory upon another without his consent, and thereby stain
and disgrace my own reputation. Besides, if I were really
so anxious to increase my glory by deceitful means, there
are other works of mine, none of which is distinguished
in this manner except the eclogues.[10] The dedication of
this work was requested by Donato Appennino,[11] a poor,
but upright man, and my particular friend. But why do
I not label all these works with kings' names? And is it
unprecedented that kings should call upon their literary
friends to write such books as they think desirable? Not
at all. I recall a contemporary instance in King Robert[12]
of Jerusalem and Sicily—a man splendidly adorned with
many honors. He asked the distinguished Francis Petrarch
to inscribe his recent poem *Africa* to him, if it were not
already dedicated. Now, was this likely to add more
lustre to Petrarch or himself? To himself, of course.
Obviously then, it is not the names of great leaders that

make authors famous; rather, kings are known to posterity with the help of authors. Besides, if the work is really praiseworthy, what increase of authority can a king's name give it, or what reputation add to an author who rests on his own merits? And if it is undeserving, how can the dedication rightly make it otherwise, or purge the blot on the author's reputation? It is the approval of great men that brings honor and glory to the performer, not the inscription of a royal name. But, to repeat, I am too proud and obstinate to dedicate even one poem to anybody unrequested, except to God, to whose glory all works should be ascribed; and in this I should persist though Caesar the Dictator were to rise again, or Scipio Africanus; only a request, or friendship, would move me. I hope, my King, you will kindly pardon such words as these; and finally I entreat you, if you should ever happen to hear anyone making such objections, in your consciousness of the truth to silence them with a king's disapproval, and in your royal goodness, defend the work written at your command and inscribed to you at your request.

There was much more to say, but, as I deem this enough, I have decided to omit the rest, and entrust the fortune of this book to God, the Giver of all gifts, and to you. Provided it please you when it comes to you, I hope it may reach the public under the auspices of your protection and command.

XIV. CONCLUSION

Lo, AT length, merciful King, I have, by the goodness of God, reached the end of my task. I have employed such skill as I have in recounting the traditionary genealogy of the Gentile gods and their posterity; these I have ascertained with wide research and set down in order. In obedience to your command, I have according to my ability added interpretations to the myths, both derived from the

ancients and from my own slender intellect. I have also
performed what I considered in some directions a most
urgent duty, and shown that the poets, contrary to the
notion of my opponents, are, I will not say all just men,
but at least not absurd nor mere story-tellers—nay,
they are marked with secular learning, genius, character,
and high distinction.

I have also fastened my little craft[1] to the shore with
anchors and cables of my own invention, yet ever trusting more in God's favor than in the strength of my own
contrivances. I have warded off such darts as seemed likely
to hurt the mariner, though doubtless I have missed a
great number against which I could hardly expect to be
forearmed. No soldier, be he the best of fighters, is so
wary that he is not at some point exposed to his enemy's
sword. Wherefore God be my Protector, who alone
knoweth the wiles of the wicked, and, if He will, can bring
them to nought. But I am only human, and I have found
no man so circumspect that, without the protecting hand
of God, he will not slip and fall time and time again. By
the same token I have very likely both omitted what I
ought to have written, or again written what I ought to
have omitted; or my words have gone uncorroborated by
sufficient proof, or I have disappointed your desires, or
failed in a hundred other ways. For all this I am heartily
sorry. But conscious as I am that my errors are matters of
negligence, I meekly crave your pardon, and humbly beseech your distinguished Eminence to supply these defects
out of your own lofty genius, making necessary excisions.
emendations, corrections of style, and all, such as your fair
judgment may suggest. Perhaps, as usual with kings, you
are too busy with more important matters to find leisure
for this work. If so, then, in the name of Christ's most
precious blood, I beseech all honest, holy, and devout
Catholics, into whose hands this book falls, and par-

ticularly my eminent teacher, the far-famed Francis
Petrarch, piously and kindly to remove any errors which
I may have made unawares, and alter them to sacred truth.
To their criticism and revision I gladly submit this work.

Further, if it contain anything good, O famous King,
any virtue of style, any gratification of your wish, I am
indeed most delighted and happy; for thence I derive the
real satisfaction of my labor. I seek no credit for my
learning, nor ask for it laurels or other distinctions; but
unto God, from whom cometh every good and every perfect gift,[2] render honor and thanksgiving.

For myself, it is my habit, at the conclusion of any
honest labor, to utter with all devotion of which I am
capable, that prayer of David's[3]—"Not unto us, O Lord,
not unto us, but unto Thy name be the glory."

Here endeth the Fifteenth and Last Book of the
Genealogy of the Gentile Gods, *by*
John Boccaccio of Certaldo
Inscribed to the Illustrious
Prince, Hugo, King
of Jerusalem
and Cyprus.

NOTES

1 I cannot help thinking that B. wrote his Preface, and perhaps conceived his whole work, having in mind Gregory's Proem to his *Moralia on the Book of Job*. As Gregory addresses Leander, Bishop of Seville, so B. addresses King Hugo; as Gregory undertook the work at the importunity of the brethren, seconded by Leander, so B. acted at the request of Hugo through Donino; as Gregory employs the nautical figure of himself, tossed on the stormy sea of secular affairs until he finds a safe port in the monastery, so B. is exposed to the rough weather of literary vicissitude; Gregory's brothers request "that I would not only unravel the words of the history in allegorical senses, but that I would go on to give to the allegorical senses the turn of moral exercise, with the addition of somewhat yet harder, that I would crown the several meanings with testimonies, and that the testimonies . . . should they chance to appear involved, should be disentangled by the aid of additional explanation" (Proem 1; cf. 3); which is exactly B.'s intention and practice at Hugo's request. As Gregory sinks under his huge task, but trusts God to help him (Pr. 2), so B. As Gregory rehearses his difficulties, apologizes for them, and shows at length his concern for the articulation and proportions of his work, so B. (15.3, 4, 12). B.'s interest in the Proem is evident in his quotation from it at *Com.* 5 (12.163) of a passage showing the twofold meaning of Holy Writ—the external, which "nurses the simple-minded," and the secret, "whereby men of loftier range may be held in suspense of admiration" (Pr. 4). He glances at it again, probably at this passage, in *Life of Dante* 22 (12.39), cf. *G. D.* 9.33, end. See Gregory, *Morals on the Book of Job*, vol. 18 of *Library of Fathers*, Oxf., 1844.

2 Hugo IV was King of Cyprus and Jerusalem from 1324 to 1358. He was one of the Lusignans, who had ruled the island since 1141. His reign falls in the golden period of the island's history, when it was one of the richest, busiest, and most beautiful spots in Europe (de Mas Latrie, M. L., *Histoire de l'Ile de Chipre*, etc. 1. xiii). B.'s praise of his piety and enlightenment is echoed by others. Jacopo di Verona, an Augustinian monk, visited Hugo for three weeks in 1335, and found him "virtuous, gracious, and devout." "Every Sunday and Feast day he hears sermons from clergy in his own chapel—I too preached before him—and he has ten chaplains who celebrate daily, and himself is always present at the service." Another bears witness to the unprecedented luxury of the nobles in Hugo's court, "the

noblest, best, and richest in the world" (Cobham, C. D., *Excerpta Cypria,* Cambr., 1908, pp. 16-19). He was strict and severe, and rapped sharply for silence if anyone talked or made a noise at service. "Il regna grandement et puissament" (de Mas Latrie, p. 207, n. 1). B. never met Hugo. How the king knew of the young man's qualifications for the great work, there is nothing to show. Hugo had some business correspondence about the dowry of his prospective daughter-in-law, Marie de Bourbon, with the Paris branch of the bank of the Bardi (de Mas Latrie 3.149, 164), and one letter (1332) addresses B.'s father by name. It implies only formal relation. Andalò di Negro, who taught B. astronomy, had been associated with Hugo in his youthful studies in that subject (15.6), but that, at the latest, must have been in B.'s early boyhood. If he, at a later date, mentioned B. to Hugo, B. would have been likely, though not certain, to speak of it. Andalò died about 1340, and shortly after this B. began his work. Another common acquaintance—at least so implied in 15.13—was Paul the Geometrician, who brought sealed letters from Hugo, encouraging B. However, B. implies a possibility that the letters were not genuine, and in 15.6 intimates that Paul was known to Hugo only by reputation. B. once speaks to Donino of Hugo as "your king, who, by the grace of God, will soon be ours too," and a bit later calls him "our king" (p. 2). Hecker suggests (p. 163, n. 8.) that the phrase may indicate B.'s expectation to enter the service of Hugo in some capacity. Hauvette (pp. 420-1) observes that Donino may have been charged by Hugo merely to find some suitable young scholar for his service, and that Donino, on inquiry in Italy, heard of B. and approached him. But B.'s words in the passage before us, whether in conformity with fact or not, assume Hugo's personal and explicit request for this work to B. himself, though at p. 5 Donino seems to have discretion in the choice.

³ *Cyclades.* The genesis of this sketch of the euhemeristic rise and progress of paganism may be in Lactantius (cf. *D. I.* 1.15; *22, 23*). He says that pagan worship began in Crete, and shows something of its propagation throughout the world. It sprang from the pride of eminent men who deified themselves. B.'s elaborate geography may owe much to Paul of Perugia (15.6).

⁴ *Sourceless Nile.* At 7.30 and 50 B. refers us to his discussion in *De Montibus,* where he cites many curious theories of the Nile's source, all of which are doubtful, since an expedition sent out by Nero could find no source more definite than a vast and trackless swamp.

⁵ *Small Corner.* Probably Britain. See 15.6 and n. 15.

⁶ *Abraham . . . a youth.* B. here turns to the chronology of Eusebius (*Chronicon,* tr. Jerome 2, Pref. 6: *Patr. Lat.* 27.233). Abraham lived in the time of Ninus of the Assyrians, when the Sicyonians flourished in Greece. According to Augustine (*C. D.* 16, 17), Abraham was born after Ninus had reigned 43 years. Isidore (*Etym.* 8; cf. Vincent of Beauvais, *S. D.* 8.15) says that Ninus was the first

idolater. For he made and worshipped an image of his father Belus. This was long before Cecrops, a contemporary of Moses, founded Athens (Jerome, *Chron.* 2 Pref. 2, 4) and the worship of Jove.

7 *Sons of the gods.* Ovid, *Met.* 13.140-7; Hecuba, Ov. *Met.* 13.565. Polydorus, Verg. *Aen.* 3.19-68; cf. Ov. *Met.* 13.534-75. The story of Polydorus B. tells in *G. D.* 6.30, citing Vergil and Euripides; cf. Hortis, p. 387.

8 *Foolish faith.* At *G. D.* 13.71 this foolishness kept B. from recording Alexander's and Scipio's claims that they were sons of Jove. See also 11.1.

9 *Paul . . . Barlaam.* See 15.6 and nn. 6, 7.

10 *Argeiphontes.* This epithet of Mercury B. could hardly have found in Latin literature, unless at Macrobius, *Sat.* 1.19.12. More likely he learned it from Leontius' version of the *Odyssey.* Cf. A. S. Cook, *Petrarch's Odyssey,* in *Philological Quarterly* 4.33, l. 137. B. does not use the epithet in his other allusions to Mercury.

11 *Varro.* See 15.8 and n. 2.

12 *Petrarch.* See 15.6 and n. 11. If B. means that he has long known Petr., these words must have been written some time after 1350 when they met. But he had long admired him and studied his works before that.

13 *Young man.* Cf. 15.6 n. 8; Introd. p. xiii, n. 2.

14 *Reputation.* See 15.13 and n. 2.

15 *Alexandrian Library.* B. may have read Aulus Gellius, *Noct. Atticae* 7.17.3: "A prodigious number of books were in succeeding times collected by the Ptolemies in Egypt, to the amount of near seven hundred thousand volumes. But in the first Alexandrine war the whole library, during the plunder of the city, was destroyed by fire, not by any concerted design, but accidentally by the auxiliary soldiers" (tr. Beloe, Lond., 1795, 2.43). B. cites this author at *Com.* 15 (13.63; cf. Hortis, p. 455); he is Richard de Bury's authority for the same fact, *Philobiblon* 7.106.

16 *Christ's . . . name.* B. loses no chance to protest his Christianity in this treatise by way of disarming his opponents' charge of pagan infidelity.

17 *Avarice.* See 14.4 and n. 3.

18 *Indolence.* Indirect self-reproach. Cf. 15.13.

19 *Mountain snails.* Snails still abound on these mountainsides, as a midsummer traveller along the road up to San Gimignano may observe. Hecker, citing *Filocolo* 5, p. 240, and "Elsa" in *De Montibus* (*De Flum.*), thinks B. refers to blanched shells in well-bottom and river-bed near Certaldo, which were left by Noah's flood. But B.'s phrase, "montanis Certaldi cocleis et sterili solo derelictis" favor the other meaning.

20 *Craft.* See 14. Pr. n. 6.

21 *Proportion.* See 15.12 and n. 1.

BOCCACCIO ON POETRY

[22] *Penetrate the hearts.*

> "What's in the scroll," quoth he, "thou keepest furled?
> Show me their shaping,
> Theirs who most studied man, bard and sage—
> Give!"

> Browning, *Grammarian's Funeral.*

[23] *Veiled.* See 14.7 and n. 8.

[24] *Freedom.* See Introd. pp. xv, xxix, xlviii.

[25] *Exquisite language.* See 14.7.

[26] *Tree.* See E. H. Wilkins, *The Genealogical Trees in Boccaccio's Genealogia De rum,* Chicago, 1923; also Chap. 3, of same author's *The University of Chicago Manuscript,* etc. 1927.

[27] I have omitted an appended paragraph, discussing the choice of Demogorgon as ancestor of all the gods.

[28] *Plato.* In *Com.* I (12.111) B. quotes Chalcidius' Prol. to his Latin version of the *Timæus* to this effect.

PROEM

[1] The course here traced is roughly that of Books 1 to 13. The infernal deities, with many others, are described in the earlier books; the descendants of Oceanus in Book 7; and of Neptune in Book 10; of Olympian Jove in Books 11-13. With this rhetorical passage one may read Milton's fine lines in *Vacation Exercise* 29-47, expressing in inverted order his love of the ancient myth which had inspired creative power in him.

[2] *Sounded.* "Gurgites adeo perspicaci quadam indagatione sulcavimus." B. sometimes mixes his figures. I have tried to harmonize his discords, which would offend the modern ear. Cf. 14.9, close.

[3] *Golden throne.* Verg. *Aen.* 7.210. House of the Sun. Ov. *Met.* 2.1-4.

[4] *Demogorgon . . . Athamas.* B., in 1.1 (cf. Pref., end) makes Demogorgon first and father of the gods on the authority of "Theodontius," with citation of Lucan, *Phars.* 6.744; Statius, *Theb.* 4.516, especially with Lactantius' comment on the lines in Statius. B. owned both Lucan and Statius (Hecker, pp. 31, 33). He ends with Athamas and his sons in 13.67-71. Cf. 15.3.

[5] *Jove the Third.* "They who are called theologists say that there are three Jupiters: the first and second of whom were born in Arcadia; . . . the third one born of Saturn in the isle of Crete" (Cicero, *De Natura Deorum* 3.23). Cicero's distinction helped B. bring order into his subject-matter. The descendants of Jove I are enumerated in Book 2; of Jove II in Book 5; of Jove III in Books 10-13.

[6] *Leap ashore.* This figure of the literary voyage is common in all literature, though B. may here have assumed it at the suggestion of Gregory; see Pref. n. 1. He first uses it as Pref., p. 13, and continues it at Proems of Books 2, 5, 11, 15 (see p. 102). Hauvette notes that B.

abandons it in his latest emendations. Cf. *Life of Dante,* end. It occurs at Plato, *Rep.* 4.441; Aristophanes, *Knights* 543, 756. It is almost a commonplace in Vergil, Ovid, and Propertius; see G. Riedner, *Typische Äusserungen der Römischer Dichter* 57-9. Jortin, on Spenser, *F. Q.* 1.12.1, cites many instances from Latin poetry. See also Quintilian, *Inst.* 12.1.2; Jerome, *Epist.* 14.10; Dante, *Par.* 2.1-18; Milton, beg. of *Tetrachordon;* Keats, sonnet on Chapman's Homer; Whitman, *In Cabin'd Ships.*

⁷ *Objections.* See Introd., p. x.

⁸ *Envy.* A traditional enemy of poetry; cf. *Com.* 3, beginning (12.14).

14.2

¹ *None too articulate.* See 15.12 n. 1.

² See Introd., p. xxx.

³ *Gnathos.* The proverbial parasite in the *Eunuchus* of Terence, who describes himself at 2.2.25-33, concluding: "If one says no, I say no; if one says yes, I say yes. In fact, I have given orders to myself to agree with them in everything. . . . As schools of philosophers have their names from their masters, so hangers-on (parasiti) may be called Gnathonists" (tr. Sargeaunt, *Loeb Library*). There are Gnathonici at Jerome, *Ep.,* 50.4; Gnatho at Sidonius, *Ep.,* 3.13; John of Salisbury, *Policr.* 6.27.

⁴ *Grave of an unhappy soul.* Perhaps a reminiscence of Macrobius, *Som. Scip.* 1.11.3: ". . . nuncupatur, et σῶμα quasi quoddam σῆμα, id est animae sepulcrum."

14.3

¹ *Second class.* See Introd., p. xxx. Cf. Sidney's philosophers, *Defence,* p. 13.

² *Popular books.* Such as epitomes and *specula* of the Liberal Arts much in use throughout mediaeval times. Cf. Rashdall, *Universities of Europe* 1.441 and n. 2; Introd., p. xi.

³ *The corner.* So Petr., *De Vita Solitaria* Pref. (tr. Zeitlin, pp. 100-1). He will not address the half-educated crowd. "It would have been much better if they had never seen the schools, since the only thing they learned there was, with the overweening arrogance of their education, to become vainer than all other men. They go about airing their Aristotle at street-crossings, while the common people crowd gaping about them. . . . What gives the last touch to their madness is the pleasure they take in crowds and in noise. These are the men who carry their educated folly over the entire city like a vulgar and purchasable commodity." All day they are abroad. Jerome's language is similar, *Ep.* 53, *Patr. Lat.* 22. 544, about unqualified expounders of Holy Writ, garrulous, sophistical, verbose, supercilious, grandiloquent; "inter mulierculas de sacris litteris philosophantur." Cf. John of Salisbury, *Met.* 1.3. B.'s language may be

traditional, but the persons he describes are doubtless actual: the sciolist is perennial.

⁴ *Jumping*. See 15.2, 3, 12 and n. 1.

⁵ *Priscian, etc.* These names stand for certain of the Liberal Arts, esp. in the Trivium: Priscian and Aristarchus for grammar; Cicero for rhetoric; Aristotle, logic; Euclid, geometry; Ptolemy, astronomy. Cf. Rashdall, *Universities*, etc. 1.240, 249; B.'s letter, *Lett.*, 454, where he praises one as an Aristarchus in grammar, an Occam in logic, a Cicero and Ulysses in rhetoric, a Jordanus in arithmetic, a Euclid or Archimedes in geometry, a Boethius in music, a Ptolemy in astronomy.

⁶ *Legislators*. That is, they contemn the study of philosophy (ethics), history, and law, both canon and civil.

⁷ *Five years*. Aulus Gellius (*Noct. Att.* 1.9) says that the pupils of Pythagoras were required to listen for at least two years, but before that they underwent probation. When they had learned the two most difficult things, *tacere* and *audire*, "tum verba facere et quaerere quaeque audissent scribere et quae ipsi opinarentur expromere potestas erat."

14.4

¹ This chapter is one of the most interesting for its comment on lawyers by one who had studied law; for its distinctions between liberal and "useful" arts; for its praise of plain living and high thinking; for its insistence upon the perennial and eternal quality of great poetry. Its burden is the impossibility of appraising poetry by material standards, since Liberal Arts are in essence higher and more constant than mechanical or useful arts. The poet's measure of value is not that of the money-getter.

² *These men*. B. here has first in mind practitioners of civil law, though at 15.10 he clearly implies that canon lawyers are liable to the same charges. For his early study of canon law see 15.10. Naturally he draws illustrations from the law, as at 14.13, 19.

³ *Love of money*. Avarice, particularly of lawyers and physicians, is a well-worn mediaeval theme, with abundant precedent even from Alexandrian times (cf. Theocritus, *Id.* 16, close); naturally it recurs more frequently with the increase of private wealth toward the Renaissance. In *De Cas.* 3.10 B. indicts lawyers for prostituting the law, and starting litigation for gain; for luxury of living, for indifference to poetry and philosophy. In *Com.* 57 (14.199) he remarks that Florentines are most avaricious in their litigation. He inclines to wring from the myths a homily against avarice where he can: cf. *G. D.* 1.15; 8.6; 9 Pr.; 14. Pr.; 14.6 and n. 12; 15.6 near end. Hauvette, p. 29, remarks B.'s contempt for money-getters as a result of youthful experience. The avarice of lawyers is noted by Petr. (*Fam.* 12.24, to Homer, Frac. 5.191); Vincent of Beauvais devotes a chapter to it (*S. M.* 7.13) citing Bernard, Jacques de Vitry, Augus-

tine, Ambrose, and a "certain tragedy" of Seneca, showing Nero and the advocates in Hell. Petr. indicts the physician (*Inv.* 1, p. 1087) as "mercenarius et infamis artifex," and deplores the general prostitution of culture and poetry to gain (*Fam.* 12.24; 13.7; 17.1; *Sen.* 5.2, p. 270; *De Vita Sol.* 1.4.1. Cf. *G. D.* Pref., p. 59). The intellectual pride of lawyers, asserted also by Petr. and Vincent, is mentioned by B. in a ms. note cited by Zenatti (p. 212 n.).

⁴ *I readily grant.* From this point to p. 32, "I therefore . . .", B. has revised his original draft, as overwritten and marginal additions show.

⁵ *Wisest of men.* Especially Dante and Petr.

⁶ *Mistress.* So at 14.19.

⁷ *She dwells.* On such personification see 14.5 n. 1.

⁸ *Elsewhere,* 14.11.

⁹ *Science.* Here, and at 14.6, B.'s argument rests on the mediaeval distinction between "scientia" and "facultas." See n. 12 below. The terms are clear, but present various difficulties in translation. I have had to render "scientia" as "science" in spite of its narrower meaning today; and "facultas" variously as "practice," "technique," "art."

¹⁰ *Excellent style.* That much of the Bible is poetry, since it is both metrical, and "veils the truth" beneath literal statement, hence is allegory, B. often alleges: 11.2; 14.8; 9; 13; 16; 18; 22; see notes on these passages. Jerome is the customary authority for the literary quality of Holy Writ (cf. 14.22; *Com.* 13 (13.29); *Life* 22 (12.39); Petr. *Fam.* 10.4; Mussato, cited by Zenatti, p. 231, n. 3), though of course it is often asserted by others. In *Ep.* 53 (*Patr. Lat.* 22.540 ff.) Jerome reviews the Books of the Bible, distinguishing between literal and allegorical meaning. Job and the Prophets, both major and minor, are poetical. "David, Simonides noster, Pindarus et Alcaeus, Flaccus quoque, Catullus et Serenus, Christum lyra personat," and Solomon sings the sweet epithalamy of Christ and the Church. In his Preface to the Book of Job he asserts that Job 3.3 to 42.6 is hexameter verse relieved at times by a pleasant rhythm of "numeris lege solutis," but more metrical than a simple reader would realize. If he cannot believe that the Hebrews employed metre, and that the Psalter, Lamentations, and nearly all the *cantica* of the Bible are metrical after the manner of Horace, Pindar, Alcaeus, and Sappho, let him consult Philo, Josephus, Origen, and Eusebius on the subject. But the passage which B. has most in mind is one which he quotes in 11.2 from the Prefatory Letter (not the Proem, as he says) of Book 2 of Jerome's translation of Eusebius' *Chronicon*: "Denique quid Psalterio canorius, quod in morem nostri Flacci, et Graeci Pindari, nunc iambo currit, nunc Alcaico personat, nunc Sapphico tumet, nunc semipede ingreditur? Quid Deuteronomii et Isaiae cantico pulchrius? Quid Salamone gravius? Quid perfectius Job? Quae omnia hexametris et pentametris versibus, ut Josephus et Origenes scribunt, apud suos composita decurrunt."

[11] *Proclaimed adjournment.* "Indictum justitium"; the phrase is in Livy 9.7.8.

[12] *Science . . . practice.* "Scientia . . . facultas." B. contends that poetry, like philosophy and theology, despises wealth. Like philosophy, it reveals the secrets of Nature; like theology, it aspires to a knowledge of God and permanent truth. The law, however, is literal, technical, limited, and variable. The difference is that between a "scientia" and a "facultas." B.'s argument runs close to that of de Bury's *Philobiblon,* chap. 11 (cited by Hortis, p. 178), showing that the Law is not a scientia, but a facultas: "The lucrative practice of positive law . . . the more useful it is found by the children of this world, so much less does it aid the children of light." "Law indeed, encourages rather than extinguishes the contentions of mankind, which are the result of unbounded greed." Law is a mere facultas, but science opens "its very vitals to display the heart of its principles, that the roots of its growth may be disclosed, and the flowing of its springs be clearly seen; for thus from the harmonious and blended light of the truth of conclusions drawn from principles, the whole body of science itself becomes lucid." But the laws "refuse to be reduced to *synteresis,* or the first principles of justice." The author alleges the law's mutability, citing Aristotle (*Pol.* 2.8.35), and concludes that "as laws are neither arts or sciences, so the books of law cannot properly be called books of art or science; nor is this faculty . . . to be reckoned among the sciences" (tr. A. F. West). Petr. employs similar reasoning against Medicine in *Inv.* 1, p. 1089; cf. 3, p. 1101. See 14.6 and n. 2; 15.1 and n. 7. B., in *Com.* 12 (13.21) cites Albertus' commentary on Aristotle's *Ethics* (doubtless on *Eth.* 6.3-7) in distinguishing between science and art, and between speculative arts and mechanical arts. See below 14.6, n. 5. John of Salisbury distinguishes nature, science, art, and faculty at *Met.* 1.11, and at 4.8 from accumulated experience comes "Scientiae aut artis, ratio"; from art, "quae usu et exercitatione firmata est," comes faculty. On these various distinctions see also Arist. *Met.* 1.1 (end); *Pol.* 2.8.1268-9; Quintilian 2.13-18; Isidore, *Etym.* 1.1; Vincent of Beauvais, *S. D.* 1.9; Brunetto Latini, *Tes.* 6.1; Petr. *Lett. Fam.* 1.6, Frac. 1.292; Caxton, *Mirour of the World,* 1490, 1.2; Toynbee, *Dante Dict.* s. v. Paradiso; H. O. Taylor, *Mediaeval Mind* 2.350 f. Spingarn, *Lit. Criticism of the Renaissance,* p. 25. The source of the discussion seems to have been Aristotle, *Eth.* 6.3-7, where he distinguishes science from art as being eternal, and 10.9, where it is concerned with the universal. Doctors and painters both teach and practise, but politicians ignore science and theory, and get along "by dint of a certain skill and experience rather than of thought." On the relation of poetry to philosophy and theology Petr. discourses in *Sen.* 15.11, where, citing Martianus Capella's *Marriage of Mercury and Philology* he avers that poetry is not one of

the Liberal Arts, but embraces them all, and thus ranks with philosophy and theology.

[13] *Immortal.* B. follows the same reasoning at *Com.* 57. (14.207). Mechanical arts, trade, the law, both civil and canon, may fill the purse, but they do not prolong life. But poetry rewards the poet with the life of fame prolonged for ages, even for ever. He cites many instances from Musaeus to Petr., and seems to be combating the same active criticism as he does here. See 15.13 and n. 2.

[14] So Petr. *De Vita Sol.* 1.1.3, p. 108, pictures the lawyer roused early by his clients, and wretchedly devoting his day to falsehood. "On treachery his heart is bent—whether he meditates driving a corrupt bargain . . . spreading the veil of justice over a litigious quarrel, or whatever other mischief of a public or private character he intends."

[15] *Choice.* B. himself declined more than one invitation to share the home and wealth of another, including Petr.; he preferred the independence of his humbler mode of life at Certaldo: see *Lett.*, pp. 96, 315; Petr. *Sen.* 1.5. In *Ecl.* 13 B. embodies a dispute between himself and a Genoese merchant on the comparative value of the study of poetry and a mercantile career. *Am. Vis.* 32 shows the worries of the rich man. Petr. *De Rem.* 2.9 cites Plautus, Horace, Pacuvius, Statius, and Vergil, as poets at once famous and poor. Zenatti cites Dante, *Conv.* 4.13; *Par.* 2.67-9; Salutato, *Epistolario* 1.255; 3.228.

[16] *Homer.* See 14.19 and n. 4. In *Com.* 12 (13.26-8) B. again tells this story of Alexander and refers it to Quintus Curtius.

[17] *Plautus.* Aulus Gellius tells this story after Varro (*Noct. Att.* 3.3).

[18] *Ennius of Brundisium.* Rather of Rudiae, nearby. The first sentence may be from Jerome's version of Eusebius' *Chronicon* (2 Olymp. 135). The rest may derive from Ovid, *Ars. Am.* 3.409, or Cicero, *Pro Arch.* 22.9, though B. may have uppermost in his mind Book 9 of Petr.'s *Africa.* He refers to the story of the burial at 14.4; 11; 15.13; *Lett.*, p. 192, where is a similar list of great poets who found patrons.

[19] *Vergil.* On B.'s biographical details concerning Vergil, see 14.19 n. 5. Of Vergil's father's occupation and the burdened homestead, B. may have read in the *Life* by Donatus, or probably in some version of the so-called *Donatus Auctus* (Diehl, *Vitae Vergilianae,* pp. 8, 26). Andes was identified with Pietola by Dante and his contemporaries (*Purg.* 18.82, 3); see below 14.19. The "elegant verses," some forty odd, may be read in *Anth. Lat.*, ed. Riehl, 1.2.145, no. 672. The incident of Augustus' suspension of the law and his edict in verse is told, among the Lives of Vergil, only in the *Donatus Auctus* (Diehl, p. 33), which quotes eight of the verses. But B.'s concluding words seem to suggest knowledge also of the closing lines, not quoted in *Donatus Auctus*:

Immo sit aeternum tota resonante Camena
Carmen, et in populo divi sub numine nomen
Laudetur vigeat placeat relegatur ametur!

The whole poem B. might have seen in some group of selections now embodied in the *Anthology*. His word here, "carmine" for "versibus," and his phrase, "in tempus usque nostrum leguntur" (14.19), imply that he had seen it entire. See D. R. Stuart, *Petr.'s Knowledge of the Life of Vergil*, in *Class. Phil.* 12.378, 9; Osgood, *Boccaccio's Knowledge of the Life of Vergil, Class. Phil.* 25. 27-36.

[20] B. distinguishes the two kinds of poverty at *G. D.* 1.23. "Egestas" is not poverty in the vulgar sense, mere want of conveniences which brave men overcome by endurance. It is rather the weakness of rich men. *Am. Vis.* 32 portrays the fears and worries of the rich man whose wealth makes him really poor.

[21] *Aglaus.* B. may have read the story in Pliny, *N. H.* 7.47.1, or more likely in Valerius Maximus 7.1.2. He cites it again at 15.2.

[22] *Diogenes.* The story of his renunciation of his wealth may come from Macrobius, *Sat.* 7.3.21; of the encounter with Alexander from Valerius Maximus 4.3.4. B. owned a copy of John of Wales' *Compendiloquium, De Vitis Philosophorum* (Hecker, p. 32), but in a hurried examination of the copy in the Huntington Library I could not find that he had made special use of it in the present work; he mentions it at *Com.* 15 (13.61).

[23] *Xenocrates.* Cicero, *Tusc. Disp.* 5.91; Valerius Maximus 4.3, end, which is closer to B. in phrase.

[24] *Democritus, Anaxagoras.* Val. Max. 8.7. ext. 4, 6. Petr. notes the story of Democritus in *Rer. Mem.* 1, and cites all four philosophers for different anecdotes in *De Vita Sol.* 2.7.1; 8.4. B. mentions Diogenes and Xenocrates in praise of poverty in *De Cas.* 1.16. Such citation is conventional; see John of Salisbury, *Pol.* 5.17; Jerome, *Adv. Jov.* 2.14 (*Patr. Lat.* 23. 316f.). Cf. 14.19.

[25] *Amyclas.* Lucan, *Phar.* 5,519-31.

[26] *Aruns.* Lucan, *Phar.* 1.584ff.: "Arruns incoluit desertae moenia Lucae (*var.* Lunae)." He took the omens which pointed to civil war; his interpretation ends "Non fanda timemus." But his skill as an astrologer B. has added, confusing him perhaps with Figulus (1.639), "quem non stellarum Aegyptia Memphis Aequaret visu." Luca and Luna (Spezia) were often confused. The "marble mountains" are those of Carrara close by.

[27] *Body . . . mind.* Matt. 6.25.

[28] *Homer.* Cf. 14.19. B. probably infers Hesiod's poverty from Ovid, *Ex. Ponto* 4.14.31; Euripides' from Val. Max. 3.4. ext. 2 (cf. below 14.11), or Aulus Gellius 15.20; Horace's from *Sat.* 1.6.6. Terence was a manumitted slave (Jerome, *Chron. Euseb.* 1859: *Patr. Lat.* 27. 417, 18; Suetonius, *Life of Terence* 1); for Ennius, see 14.4, n. 18; for Homer, Vergil, 14.19, n. 4, 5.

²⁹ *Camilli*, etc. Such stereotyped lists of illustrious, but unpretentious Romans occur in old poets: Verg. *Aen.* 6.843; *Georg.* 2.169; *Culex*, 362; Propertius 3.11.61-8; Juvenal 2.154; Lucan 1.168. They furnish occasional illustration in Valerius Maximus. B. cites them in *Life* 18 (13.29). Camillus delivered Rome from the Gauls in 390 B.C.; Quintii refers to Cincinnatus; Curtii to young Marcus Curtius, who, in 365 B.C., rode full-armed into a fissure in the Forum, when the state's safety demanded the sacrifice of her bravest citizen; the incorruptible Fabricius triumphed over Pyrrhus and other enemies of Rome. For Cato and Scipio, see 15.13.

³⁰ *Tantalus.* In *G. D.* 12.1 B., citing Fulgentius, points the same moral of Tantalus: "His punishment clearly exhibits the detestable life of a miser," who suffers want amid plenty.

³¹ *Solon.* Also at 14.19; *Com.* 3 (12.145). Reminiscent of Cicero, *De Senec.* 8.26; more likely of Val. Max. 8.7. ext. 14; cf. 5.3. ext. 3. Petr. notes the story, *Rer. Mem.* 1; *Inv.* 3 (p. 1103), to prove the affinity of poetry with philosophy; *De Vita Sol.* 2.8.4, where Solon takes to travel in Egypt instead of poetry; *Fam.* 3.18; 20.4 (Frac. 4.262); *Sen.* 1.5. Petr. cites Plato, *Timaeus* 21 D.

14.5

¹ *Philosophy.* The same lady appears in *Am. Vis.* 4.5. as the central figure of a fresco in a great hall of an allegorical castle. As here, she holds in her left hand a small book, in her right a sceptre, and is clothed in purple. About her are grouped the Seven Liberal Arts and the philosophers and poets of antiquity, with Dante, bearing themselves much as here, but described at greater length. She is apotheosized as Truth by Petr. *De Cont. Mund.* Pref.; as Nature by Alanus de Insulis, *De Planctu Nat.* Prose 1 ff.; as Calliope by Fulgentius, *Myth.* 1, Pref.; as Philosophy by Boethius, *De Cons. Phil.* Prose 1.3, and by Macrobius, *Som. Scip.* 1.2.3ff.; Cf. Lucian, *The Fisher;* as Wisdom by Prudentius, *Psychomachia* 823-915; cf. Spenser's Sapience, *Hymn of Heavenly Beauty* 183ff. Her ancestress is Wisdom in Prov. 9; Book of Wisdom 7 ff. Cf. B.'s words: "Ex dei missa gremio Philosophia rerum magistra" with Wisdom 7.25: "Vapor est enim virtutis Dei, et emanatio quaedam"; with 8.1, 4: "Attingit ergo a fine usque ad finem fortiter, et disponit omnia suaviter. . . . Doctrix enim est Disciplinae Dei." Cf. Wisdom 9.2, 3, 9, 11. B.'s debt to Boethius is obvious: "Her clothing was wrought of the finest thread. . . . Yet the hands of rough men had torn this garment and snatched such morsels as they could therefrom. In her right hand she carried books, in her left was a sceptre brandished. . . . I recognized my nurse Philosophy" (Prose 1, tr. Cooper); in Prose 3 Epicureans, Stoics, and others, contending for the legacy of Socrates, "tore my robe which I had woven with my own hands, and snatched away the fragments thereof." Skelton may have B. in mind at his *Replycacion, Wks.* ed. Dyce 1.208, 221. This mediaeval set

piece of the "House of Philosophy" derives in part at least from Ovid; see K. Francke, *Gesch. der Lat. Schulpoesie,* etc., 1878, p. 27.

² *Ideals . . . forces . . . secrets.* The threefold division of theology; see 15.8 n. 2.

³ *Another group.* For the differences of these from the critics in 14.3, see Introd. p. xxxii. Petr. also contrasts the few real philosophers with the "cathedrarii," *De Vita Sol.* 1.7.1. An early and lively satire on these sciolists occurs in Lucian, *Icaromenippus* 29-32. Hortis and Zenatti think that B. had in mind John of Salisbury's chapter *De Hypocritis, Pol.* 7.21, but the few resemblant details would occur independently to observant writers. Langland indicts the friars for superficial learning (*Piers Plowm.* B. 20.271; C. 23.273 ff.) ; cf. Chadwick, *Social Life in the Days of Piers Plowman,* pp. 34, 5. They still invite such criticism in the 16th Cent.; see G. Buchanan, *Franciscanus,* esp. ll. 98-171.

⁴ *Prophet.* David (Ps. 69.9; John 2.17). "David propheta," Isidore, *Etym.* 1.39.

⁵ *Attack.* This indictment is read again in terms even more scathing at 14.11 ; 14.16; cf. 14.18; 22.

⁶ *They say.* B. here lists the objections to poetry which he refutes in the remaining chapters of this book: (1) that poetry is naught, or at most a futile art (14.6-8) ; (2) that poets are tellers of untrue stories (14.9,10; cf. 13) ; (3) that they are rustics (14.11) ; (4) that they are full of false (14.13), obscure (14.12), and absurd (14.14) statements about the gods; (5) that they are seducers to evil (14.15, 16) ; (6) that they are apes of the philosophers (in 14.17) ; (7) that it is a crime to read them (14.18) ; (8) that Plato banished them from the state (14.19) ; and (9) that Boethius called the Muses drabs (14.20). Of these charges nos. 2, 4, 5, 8 are derived from Augustine and Lactantius; no. 6 may be inferred from Boethius and John of Salisbury; no. 9 from Boethius. The rejoinders, as Hortis points out (p. 208), are all essentially those of Petr. in the last of Book 1 and the first part of Book 3 of his *Inv.,* and in his letters, *Fam.* 10.4; *Sen.* 1.5 (to B.).

⁷ *Tale-mongers* (fabulosi) *. . . liars* (fabulones). See 14.9 and n. 1.

⁸ *Jove.* In his chapter on Jove of Crete (11.1; cf. 9.1) B. draws heavily upon Lactantius, who shows (*D. I.* 1.2) that Jove was originally a great man exalted by poets and theologians to be "patrem dominumque deorum, et caeli regem." Under stories of adulteries they veiled the operations of nature. Thus Servius (on *Aen.* 6.727) makes him fire and air; Ovid makes him a man (*Met.* 8.616) ; a bull (*Met.* 2.848, cited by B. at 2.62) : "Ille pater rectorque deum . . . Induitur faciem tauri"; an eagle (*Met.* 10.156-8; cf. *G. D.* 6.4). See 14.14, n. 8.

⁹ *Lions.* Like the Devil: 1 Pet. 5.8.

¹ *Mare's nest.* "In scirpo quesisse nodum," Plautus, *Menaech.*
2.1.247.

² *Poetry is naught.* A stock objection. Petr. rebuts it at *Inv.* 3, p.
1101, where he recalls having rebutted it years before to a Sicilian
dialectician. If necessity argues true nobility, then the farmer,
cobbler, miller, are the true nobles, and the ass and the cock are
nobler than the lion and the eagle. But the Liberal Arts are not
"mechanical." If it be argued that a science is "firma et impermuta-
bilis," while poetry is a matter of variable words and metres, therefore *not* a science, then remember that only words change, but
things remain, "in quibus scientiae fundatae sunt." The argument is
from Aristotle. See 14.4, n. 12.

³ *Later.* 14.8.

⁴ *Science . . . technique.* "Scientia . . . facultas"; cf. 14.4 nn. 9, 12.

⁵ *Elsewhere.* 14.4; see n. 12. There poetry was rather a *scientia*
than a *facultas.* In *Com.* 12 (13.21) B., following Albertus on
Aristotle (*Eth.* 6.3-7), distinguishes "sapience," as knowledge of
things divine, from "science," as knowledge of lower things, and
from "art" as pertaining to things performed—usually "mechanical."
But when Vergil in his poetry combines science with the devices of
the Liberal Arts, that art is not mechanical but speculative.

⁶ *Beguile the reader.* Almost Augustine's words. *C. D.* 8.4, 5.

⁷ *Filled with adulteries.* Macrobius, *Somn. Scip.* 1.2.8, characterizes
bad poetry as "argumenta fictis casibus amatorum referta."

⁸ *Iole.* No such story. B. probably means Ovid's obscene tale of
Priapus and Lotis, *Fasti* 1.415-40. He owned the *Fasti* (Hecker,
p. 33). See 14.15, n. 6. Statues and paintings here mentioned are
imaginary.

⁹ *Apelles.* B. may have read of the ancient painters in Pliny, *Natural History,* or in Petr. *Inv.,* 3, p. 1108, who cites Pliny at *De Rem.*
1.40, 41. This appeal from literature to the fine arts reflects some
ingenuity of argument for B.'s time; it was no doubt the more convincing to his readers for the reviving interest in fine arts, especially
as represented by Giotto. In Petr. *De Rem.* 1.40 Reason enters a
Platonic protest against the revival of painting as a sort of impedi-
ment between us and the works of God. Besides, this age boasts itself
the discoverer of painting, or at least the "eleganti sima consumma-
trix, limatrixque," and asserts its superiority to the ancients in both
painting and sculpture.

¹⁰ *Giotto.* In *Am. Vis.* 4, B., dreaming, saw a painting beyond the
achievement of any human hand except Giotto's, from whom fair
Nature hid no secret. Giotto appears also at *Decam.* 6.5. B. probably
knew him at Naples 1330-2 (Hauvette, p. 40). On B.'s interest in
painting see Schöningh, pp. 40-2. If by "the enthroned Jove" B. has
even remotely in mind any picture, it may be Giotto's Last Judg-

ment in the Arena Chapel at Padua. He passed through Padua in 1368 (Petr. *Sen.* 10.4; Hauvette, p. 443). See also 14.18 and n. 9.

[11] *Venus . . . Mars.* Homer, *Od.* 8.266-366.

[12] *Money or popularity.* This crowd is described at length by Petr. in *Fam.* 13.7; *Sen.* 5.3, tr. in Robinson and Rolfe, pp. 198 f., where Petr. cites Juvenal, *Sat.* 7.87 taking the same exception. B. is probably not unaware that the precedent occurs more than once in the Roman poets. In his mind they seem to include the "comic" poets; see below 14.19, n. 25.

[13] *Later.* 14.19.

[14] *Things of heaven.* Like phrases in Macrobius, *Sat.* 1.17.2: "Nam quod omnes paene deos," quoted 14.17, n. 1; *Somn. Scip.* 1.2.3.: "si rerum caelestium notionem."

[15] *Art.* See n. 4 above.

14.7

[1] Perhaps the most significant chapter; it embodies most of B.'s ideas about poetry: definition, etymology, elements and conditions of creations, effects and function, and the superiority of poetry to mere rhetoric. In setting these down, B. has consulted his own experiences as a poet, as well as traditional criticism, especially as recorded by Petr., Dante, Isidore, Macrobius, Augustine, and Cicero. He uses much the same material in *Life* 21, 22; *Com.* 1, 3, 5; *De Cas.* 5. 1. 3. Corresponding passages in Petr. are *Inv.* Bk. 1 (end), Bk. 3 (beginning); *Africa* 9.1-315; *Fam.* 10.4; *Sen.* 12.1.

[2] *Invented.* "Poesis . . . est fervor quidam exquisite inveniendi atque dicendi, seu scribendi, quod inveneris." See Introd., p. xxxv. *Invenire, inventio* are stock technical terms in mediaeval rhetoric, deriving from Cicero, *De Inventione* and the similar *Ad Herennium* once ascribed to him. *Inventio* was originally "excogitatio rerum verarum aut veri similium, quae causam probabilem reddant" (*De Inv.* 1, 7; *Ad Her.* 1.2), one of the five "parts" of rhetoric. See references to Faral and Clark in n. 25 below. But in mediaeval rhetoric and poetic it degenerates almost beyond a vestigial trace (Baldwin, *Med. Rhet. and Poet.*, 1928, index, s. v. *inventio*). B. endeavors to release the word from the bonds of rote and bring it to life by an appeal to fact.

[3] *Bosom of God.* Like Philosophy, on which Poetry feeds: see 14.5 and n.1; 14.7; 17; 18.

[4] *Rarest of men.* No wonder, says Petr. (*Inv.* 3, p. 1104), there are few poets, though many doctors, since poetry does not admit mediocrity, as Cicero says in his *De Oratore*—doubtless at 1.3: "A smaller number of eminent poets have arisen than of men distinguished in any other branch of literature" (tr. Watson). Cf. *Inv.* 1, p. 1092, where Homer, Euripides, and Vergil are cited as greatest poets; *Fam.* 13.7, Robinson and Rolfe, p. 167.

[5] *Unheard of creations.* This conception of the poet as a free cre-

ator of a world of his own, and wielder of power over the minds and
acts of men seems to derive ultimately from Horace and Aristotle,
though it is not explicit in them. It is basic in Sidney's *Defence*
(esp. Cook's ed., pp. 22-6), who owes it to Minturno (Spingarn, *Lit.
Crit. in the Renaissance*, pp. 272-3) ; but by what course it develops
before B.'s use I cannot say. Cf. 14.9; 17 and n. 1. It is implied in
Cicero's *Tusc. Disp.* 5. 39.114: "There is the tradition also that Homer
was blind: but it is his painting not his poetry that we see; what
district, what shore, what spot in Greece, what aspect or form of
combat, what marshalling of battle, what tugging at the oar, what
movements of men, of animals, has he not depicted so vividly that
he has made us see, as we read, the things which he himself did not
see?" Cf. Hor. *Ep.* 2.1.250-7.

⁶ *Fixed order.* Perhaps reminiscent of Isidore: "Vates . . . a viendis
carminibus, id est flectendis, hoc est modulandis . . . quodmodis verba
connectarent, viere antiquiis pro vincire ponentibus" (*Etym.* 7.3). Cf.
15.12, n. 1.

⁷ *Adorns the whole.* The sentence contains traces perhaps of mediaeval directions for the poetic elaboration of a theme, such as those
of Geoffroi de Vinsauf's *Poetria*; *see* Faral, pp. 194-262.

⁸ *Veils truth.* Same phrase at *G. D.* 1.3; 14.9; 10; 12; 13; 18; *Life 22*
(12.39) ; *Com.* 1, 5. It is a stock expression of the mediaeval idea of
allegory: Petr. *Sen.* 4.5 (Frac. 1.240, 2) ; *Africa* 9.90-107; Dante
Inf. 9.63; *Purg.* 8.20. It occurs as early as Macrobius, *Somn. Scip.* 1.2.
11 : "Aut sacrarum rerum notio sub pio figmentorum velamine honestis
et tecta rebus et vestita nominibus." B. quotes from this passage, *G. D.*
1.3; *Com.* 5 (12.160). It is even in Augustine: see 14.12, n. 6; cf. *De
Mend.* 1.5.5 quoted 14.9, n. 18. Lactantius implies the figure at *D. I.*
1.1 (cf. 1.11) ; he is quoted by Isidore, *Etym.* 8.7.2 (cf. 8.7.10) ;
Vincent of Beauvais, *S. D.* 4.110; Petr. *Inv.* 1, p. 1092; *Sen.* 12.1;
Campidoglio Address, Hortis, *Scritt. Ined.*, p. 320. It survives as late
as Milton, *Prose Works*, ed. Symmons, 6. 153.

⁹ *Instruments.* A significant list of studies considered necessary for
the poet. B. mentions, of the Trivium, grammar and rhetoric; the
omission of logic may be an oversight, though it never flourished in
Italy as in the North. Of other mediaeval studies he includes ethics
and "natural philosophy," but emphasizes more than the mediaeval
cursus is wont to do, history, archaeology, and geography. Within
the list here sketched B. includes the subjects of his various humanistic compilations. His interpretation of myths in *G. D.* draw upon
all of them. *De Casibus Virorum Illustrium, De Claris Mulieribus*
are historical; *De Montibus, Silvis*, etc., is geographical and historical. See p. xv. Cf. also Shelley's Preface to his *Revolt of Islam*
beginning: "There is an education peculiarly fitted for a poet" and
the ensuing enumeration, ending: "The poetry of ancient Greece and

Rome, and modern Italy, and our own country, has been to me, like external nature, a passion and an enjoyment."

[10] *Mother tongue.* B. at one time resolved to burn his compositions in Italian (Petr. *Sen.* 5.2, p. *272*). In *Com.* I (12.114, 15) he says that Italian is effeminate compared with Latin, and yet Dante's great poem is none the less "ornato e leggiadro e sublime," though it might have been "piu artificioso e piu sublime" in Latin, since Latin admits "piu d'arte e di gravitá." In *Life* 26 (12.53, 4) he replies to the criticism of the learned that Dante, though a scholar, had written in Italian. His reasons were many, but chiefly that he wished to communicate its beauty and meaning both to learned and to common people, who had been too much neglected; then, too, in the present decline of learning, he could reach his patrons only in Italian. But B. does not heartily subscribe to this fashionable opinion of the *savants* on the relative value of Latin and Italian. See 14.22. Doubtless Dante's poetry and opinions (*Volg. Eloquio; Conv.* I), with his own experience in poetry, qualified his opinion. See Zenatti's long note for references, esp. to various defenders of the mother tongue.

[11] *Liberal Arts.* So of Homer, *Com.* 12 (13.25); Vergil, *Com.* 2 (12.139); Dante, *Com.* I: *Life* 3 (12.8-10; 117); cf. Petr. *Africa* 9.1ff

[12] *Moral and natural.* See 15.8 and n. 6.

[13] *Monuments and relics.* Their presence in Italy was of course a powerful stimulus to the first revival of humanism on that ground. See Burckhardt, *Renaissance in Italy,* Pt. 3, chap. 2; Petr. *Africa* 3.262ff. (bas-reliefs in Syphax' palace); 8.862-951 (glories of Rome); cf. *De Rem.* 1.118. B. often refers to them in *G. D.;* see Proems of Books 4, 6, 9; cf. 12.2 (Niobe); he cites the gigantic image at Drepanum at 4.68; 10.14 (end). Often in his geographical works he records his own observation of ruins and sites, or inserts a local legend. See his notes on Baiae, Baianus, Vesuvius ("Hodie nec fumus nec ignis emittitur"), Sorge, Avernus, Arno, Elsa, Mintius, Padua, Septem maria, and the fine conclusion of *De Maribus; Fiammetta* 5.

[14] *Retirement . . . glory.* See 14.11; 15.13 and nn.

[15] *Ardent period.* His own experience; cf. *Lett.,* p. 198. He must be thinking too of Petr. and Dante; cf. *Life* 3-6; *Com.* I (12.70-75; 117), where study, solitude, and love unite in the making of the poet.

[16] *Art.* Conscious skill, technique, indispensable to poetic creation; cf. 14.4; 14.6 and nn.

[17] *Poetes.* B.'s limitations in Greek have allowed him to follow Isidore of Seville (*Etym.* 8.7.2, De poeta)—bad etymology and all—in this whole passage, as did writers before him who knew no Greek. He seems to recall the sentence in which Isidore, having shown that primitive worship uttered itself in a combination of fit words and pleasing numbers, this combination, "quia forma quadam efficitur,

quae ποιότης dicitur, poema vocitatum est, ejusque fictores poetae." B. cites this passage at *G. D.* 11.2. But his peculiar wording, esp. the Ciceronian word "exquisita," reflects also Petr.'s words in *Fam.* 104 (which he cites at *Com.* 3 (12.141) on the same point) ; Id [language of primitive poetic ritual] sane non vulgari forma sed artificiosa quadam et exquisita et nova fieri oportuit : quae quoniam graeco sermone *poetices* dicta est, eos quoque qui hac utebantur poetas dixerunt." Perhaps too he recalls Isidore's derivation of Muse from μᾶσαι "id est a quaerendo, quod per eas [Muses], sicut antiqui voluerunt, vis carminum et vocis modulatio quaereretur" (cited at 11.2). Petr. owned from youth a copy of Isidore's *Etymologies,* now in the Bibliothèque Nationale (de Nolhac, *Facsimilés de L'Écriture de Petr.*). On the etymology of "poet" and the origins of poetry in primitive worship Isidore cites the authority of Suetonius. Nothing to this effect occurs in the surviving texts of Suetonius. Traube, *Geschichte der tironischen Noten,* p. 18, suggests that Isidore had a manuscript of excerpts from various writings of Suetonius, of which there were two copies, one at Seville, one at Monte Cassino, derived from a common archetype of excerpts. Cf. Schanz, *Röm. Litt. geschichte* 8.3.66 of Müller's *Handbuch.* Isidore's passage is rehearsed twice almost literally by Rabanus Maurus (*De Universo* 15.2 : *Patr. Lat.* 111 :419; *Excerp. de Arte Gramm. Prisc: ibid.* 111.666) and by Vincent of Beauvais (*S. D.* 4.110).

[18] *Song.* In *De Ordine* 2 Augustine, in discussing education and human aspiration towards things divine, shows that in one stage it methodized sound into music and the modification of voice and number : (1) in syllables; (2) in feet conjoined; (3) verses of set length; (4) in rhythm and method; "sic ab ea poetae geniti sunt."

[19] *Poesy, but poem.* "Poesis dicitur Graeco nomine opus multorum librorum; poema unius" (Isidore, *Etym.* 1.39.21). The same distinction is made by the grammarians such as Marius Victorinus and Diomedes.

[20] *Bosom of God.* See 14.5 and n. 1.

[21] *Archias. Pro Arch.* 18, quoted by Petr. *Inv.* 1. p. 1091. Zenatti cites also Salutato, *De Fato et Fortuna.*

[22] *Practical art.* "Facultas."

[23] *Raise flights . . . go winding.* Dante's mountain of Purgatory, and perhaps the steps from circle to circle (*Purg.* 11.40; 13.1 ; 17.65, 77; 25.8; etc.) ; or the three steps in *Purg.* 9.76ff.; or the mystic stairway of the Seventh Heaven (*Par.* 21.8 ; 22.68).

[24] *Trees.* Like Pandarus and Bitias in *Aen.* 9.678-82 :

> While they within stand at the right and left
> Before the turrets, armed, their lofty heads
> Flashing with plumes. So by some river's bank,

Whether the Po or pleasant Athesis,
Two breezy oaks lift up their unshorn heads,
And nod their lofty tops.

[25] *Poetry alone.* The distinction between poetry and rhetoric is touched again at 14.12. The upshot of the two passages seems to be that, while the poet should know and employ the precepts, rules, and method of rhetoric, poetry transcends rhetoric in majesty of style and dignity, and particularly in the freedom and spontaneity of its invention, especially allegorical invention. Though mindful no doubt that the distinction between poetry and rhetoric had been a subject of wide variety of opinion and of much discussion, often heated, from Aristotle down, B. seems here as usual to consult his own experience as a poet, and to assert the fervid creative act of genius, as he does in his definition (14.6). According to Aristotle (*Rhet.* 3.2) poetry can create wonder by strange matter and expression, as rhetoric should not. Cicero (*De Or.* 1.16) says that the poet is more restricted than the orator by "numbers," but less in choice of words. Augustine (*De Ordine* 2.14.40) finds in the poet "non solum sonorum, sed etiam verborum rerumque magna momenta," as well as "rationabilium mendaciorum potestatem"; hence the grammarians rather than the rhetoricians are its proper judges. In the Middle Ages the academic conception of poetry became debased and subordinated to rhetoric or grammar. See D. L. Clark, *Rhetoric and Poetry in the Renaissance*, chaps. 3-5, esp. pp. 31-4; 43-55; E. Faral, *Les Arts Poétiques du XII. et du XIII. Siècle;* John of Salisbury, *Met.* 1.17; Vincent of Beauvais, *S. D.* 4.109; Dante, *De Volg. Eloq.* 2.4.18; Petr. *Inv.* 3, p. 1105, who cites Aristotle, *Rhet.* 3.1. B. obviously is protesting against the mediaeval opinion partly by appealing to the Ancients, but chiefly by consulting the fact of a poet's experience.

14.8

[1] *Came to light.* B. adopts, as the basis of this chapter, the theory that poetry sprang from the religious instinct. In *Com.* 3; *De Cas.* 9.9-11, he explains it very much as he here says he learned it from Leontius. In *Com.* 3 (17.142) he refers it to Petr. *Fam.* 10.4; but he must have read it also in Isidore, *Etym.* 8.7, quoted above at 14.7, n. 17, who refers it to Suetonius.

[2] *The Hebrews.* So Isidore, *Etym.* 1.39.11, says that heroic metre is older than all others. "Hoc primum Moyses in cantico Deuteronomii, longe ante Pherecydem et Homerum cecinisse probat. Unde et apparet antiquius fuisse apud Hebraeos, studium carminum quam apud gentiles." Again: "Hymnos primum David propheta in laudem Dei componuisse ac cecinisse manifestum est." Rabanus, *Excerp. de Arte Gramm. Prisc.: Patr. Lat.* 111.666, is a little closer to B.: "Primumque notandum quod sicut a disertissimis et veracissimis historiarum scrutatoribus exquisitum est, antiquiorum apud Hebraeos quam apud gentiles fuisse carminum curam; nam Moyses qui Exodi et Deuter-

onomii cantica exametro sicut Josephus et Origenes scribunt com-
posuit, ab omnibus quos Graeci antiquissimos putant senior depre-
henditur." Both passages derive from Jerome; see 14.4, n. 10.

[3] *First to offer.* Cain, Gen. 4.3, 4; Noah, Gen. 8.20-2; Abraham,
Gen. 14.13-20; Moses, Ex. 24-31.

[4] *Tabernacle.* Ezek. 41.1.

[5] *Marathius.* Jerome's version of Eusebius' *Chronicon* 1.25: *Patr.
Lat.* 27.121. According to the *Chron.* 2, s. v. Marathius, it was in the
first year of his reign that Moses led Israel out of Egypt, in the
17th that he brought the commandments down from Sinai, and in
the 20th and last that he built the tabernacle. By the reckoning of
the *Chron.*, Marathius died in the 3691st or 3692nd year of the world;
cf. *Chron.* 1.16, 18,19.

[6] *The Venetian.* Paolino, bishop of Pozzuoli, 1324-44. In the so-called
Zibaldone Magliabechiano, a miscellaneous notebook thought to be
B.'s, are several excerpts from Paolino's compilation, there described
as a "labyrinth of annals," full of error and citations from authors
of small account. Paolino is called "iste bestia," "bergolus," "insipi-
dus." B. seems to have met him, and, apart from his distrust of his
scholarship, to have disliked him. Cf. S. Ciampi, *Monumenti d'un
Manoscritto Autografo di Boccaccio,* Firenze, 1827; Hortis, p. 331,
n. 1; 485; H. Simonsfeld has identified him with a so-called Jordanus,
and as the probable author of a historical epitome, composed before
1327, from which was derived a chronological or synchronistic table
before 1329 (evidently the work which B. used), and the whole
was reworked in a *Satirica Jordani;* these are fully described by
Simonsfeld in his paper, *Handschriftliches zur Chronik des sogenann-
ten Jordanus* in *Forschungen zur deutschen Geschichte* 15 (1875).
145-52.

[7] *His authority.* Perhaps Paolino was elaborating a passage in
Isidore's *Chronicon* (9: *Patr. Lat.* 83.1023) which describes the tower
of Babel surrounded by incredibly splendid temples, the work of
Nimrod, who, after the confusion of tongues, went to live among
the Persians and taught them to worship fire.

[8] *Often enough.* I do not know where. Augustine, *C. D.* 4.6, quotes
Justinus, who quotes Trogus Pompeius, as saying that Ninus (Nimrod) first extended his kingdom by war. Isidore, *Chron.* 12, says
that he "primus bella instituit, et armorum instrumenta invenit."

[9] *Greeks also.* That is, Isidore, on the authority of Suetonius and
Varro, described the origin of poetry as does this paragraph; see
14.8, n. 23. He does not say that it began among the Greeks, though
his etymology and citation of authorities would so imply. Yet at
Etym. 1.39.11 he ascribes the invention to the Hebrews. B. in this
chapter claims it for the Hebrews, but in *Com.* 3 (12.142) for the
Greeks. See 14.7 and n. 17.

[10] *Leontius.* See 15.6 and n. 10.

[11] *Believe . . . in some Being.* Cicero attributes the idea to Epicurus: "For he alone first founded the idea of the existence of the Gods on the impression which nature herself hath made on the minds of all men. For what nation, what people are there who have not, without any learning, a natural idea, or prenotion of a Deity?" (*De Natura Deor.* 16). Cicero adds that the prenotion is universal, and common to philosophers and the vulgar.

[12] *Musaeus, Linus, and Orpheus.* B. here owes something to Augustine, *C. D.* 18.14: "During the same time arose the poets, who were also called theologues, because they made hymns about the gods; yet about such gods as, although great men, were yet but men, or the elements of this world which the true God made, or creatures who were ordained as principalities and powers according to the will of the Creator and their own merit. And if, among much that is vain and false, they sang anything of the one true God, yet, by worshipping Him along with others who are not gods, and showing them the service which is due to Him alone, they did not serve Him at all rightly; and even such poets as Orpheus, Musaeus, and Linus were unable to abstain from dishonoring their gods by fables. But yet these theologues worshipped the gods." Cf. Aristotle in n. 19.

[13] *Barlaam.* See 15.6 and n. 6.

[14] *Phoroneus.* In the *Chronicon* of Eusebius, tr. Jerome, he is assigned to the 210th year of Abraham (*Chron.* 2: *Patr. Lat.* 27.271), i.e. the 3394th year, according to the reckoning by the Septuagint, at *Chron.* 1.14. Isidore, in his *Chronicon* says that he was the first who established "leges judiciaque" in Greece (sec. 15, *Patr. Lat.* 83.1025).

[15] *Theologians.* See nn. 12,19.

[16] *Paul of Perugia.* See 15.6, n. 7.

[17] Orpheus. The matter of this paragraph is rehearsed by B. in *G. D.* 5.12, whence it is copied in *Com.* 16 (13.74, 5). Jerome's version of Eusebius' *Chronicon* says merely: Argonautorum navigatio (752); Orpheus Thrax clarus habetur, cujus discipulus fuit Musaeus filius Eumolpi" (year of Abraham 747; i.e. 3931st year of the world: *Patr. Lat.* 27.310). The rest of the paragraph is chiefly from Lactantius, who calls Orpheus "vetustissimus poetarum" (*D. I.* 1.5: *Patr. Lat.* 6.130) and ascribes to him the inauguration of the rites of Bacchus (*D. I.* 1.22). "The learned Greeks" cited by Leontius, may have been Suidas or Eustathius, whom he may well have used in his exposition of Homer to B. Suidas mentions several called Musaeus, two of them poets, of which one was "a pupil of Orpheus, though older." This may explain B.'s apparent inconsistency in making Orpheus at once the successor and teacher of Musaeus. But Suidas makes this Musaeus father of Eumolpus, while Eusebius makes him a son. Suidas distinguishes seven Orpheuses—among the rest the singer, a Thracian and pupil of Linus, from a king of Thrace. Eustathius, in his comment on *Il.* 2.847, p. 359.15, says that there were two, separated by eleven generations.

¹⁸ *Rape of Europa.* Variously assigned by Eusebius to the years of Abraham 587, 694, 732; Orpheus to 747 (*Patr. Lat.* 27.307 *ff.*). Linus, the musician, he says, flourished 150 years earlier (587-97).

¹⁹ *Aristotle.* This oft-cited sentence is in the *Metaphysics* (2.4.12): "Οἱ μὲν οὖν περὶ Ἡσίοδον καὶ πάντες ὅσοι Θεολόγοι." B. mentions it below, 15.8; again at *Com.* 3; *Life* 22 (12.142, 43). Petr. mentions it in *Fam.* 10.4; *Inv.* 3, p. 1106, where he refers it to the *Metaphysics,* but cites also Augustine, *C. D.* 18.14 (quoted above in n. 12), where he may have learned it. Aristotle, of course, means only authors of theogonies; but poet, mythographer, and pagan theologian were essentially one to B., especially in the interests of his argument.

²⁰ *Moses . . . Musaeus.* Cf. John of Salisbury, *Entheticus* 1187-96, De Musaeo, qui putatus est Moyses. Eusebius, *Praep. Evang.* 9.27; 9.8, states that the Greeks, notably Numenius, gave Moses the name Musaeus, and identified him with their poet.

²¹ *Beast Nimrod.* "Gigas diaboli typum expressit, qui superbo appetitu culmen divinae celsitudinis appetivit" (Isidore, *Allegoriae Quaedam,* etc.: *Patr. Lat.* 83.103). In his *Quaestiones in Vet. Test.,* on Gen. 9, the confusion of tongues is said to typify heretical schism.

²² *Moses.* See Isidore, quoted at 14.8 n. 2; and Jerome, at 14.4 n. 10.

²³ *Energy of mind . . . seer.* "Vi mentis . . . vates." From Isidore, *Etym.* 8.73: "Vates a vi mentis appellatos Varro auctor est." H. Kettner, *Varron. Stud.* Halle, 1965, p. 37, points out that this sentence in Isidore is quoted from Servius on *Aen.* 3.443, but thinks that it, and indeed the whole section, is from Suetonius. Schanz says (*Röm. Litt. Geschichte* 8.1.2, p. 449): "Schon der Bischof Isidor scheint von Varro nicht mehr gehabt zu haben als wir heutzutage." Cf. 14.7, n. 17; *Com.* 7 (12. 202, 3).

14.9

¹ *Tale-mongers (fabulosi) . . . liars (fabulones).* These words as used and distinguished here and at 14.5 are not classical. *Fabulosus* was not used of persons. *Fabulones* does not occur except in a rejected reading in Macrobius, *Sat.* 2.1.9, which Isidore glosses in a note that B. may have seen (cited in Forcellini)—"fabularum inventores." Probably some of the pejorative force of It. *one* has part in B.'s use of the word. He uses it again, near the end of his life, of the physicians whose advice, through four months' illness, does not retard his decline (*Lett.,* p. 378). In 14.13 he has "mentientes," "mendaces."

² *Fable.* "Fabulas poetae a fando nominaverunt, quia non sunt res factae sed tantum loquendo fictae" (Isidore, *Etym.* 1.40), with illustration from Aesop as below.

³ *Luke.* 24.14.15: "Et ipsi loquebantur ad invicem de his omnibus quae acciderant. Et factum est dum fabularentur," etc.

⁴ *Sin.* B. doubtless knows how flimsy this etymological argument is,

but its literalness is quite in the obscurantist manner of his opponents. Cf. 14.16.

[5] *Converse.* B. here alters the scriptural word *fabulari* to *colloqui.*

[6] *Superficial.* See 14.7 and n. 8.

[7] *Fiction.* This definition seems, like the rest of the paragraph, to be based on Macrobius (see next note), though Isidore defines the *fabula ad mores* as at least invented "ut ad rem quae intenditur, ficta quidem narratione, sed veraci significatione, veniatur" (*Etym.* 1.40.6). Isidore's phrasing is from Augustine (*Contra Mendacium* 28; cf. below 14.9 n.18.). Chapter 13 of de Bury's *Philobiblon*— "Why we have not wholly neglected the Fables of the Poets"—urges a two-fold defence: (1) that such study improves one's style; (2) that "where a fictitious but becoming subject is handled, natural or historical truth is pursued under the guise of allegorical fiction."

[8] *Four kinds.* B.'s distinctions seem to be based upon a favorite passage in Macrobius (*Somn. Scip.* 1.2), with some suggestion of Cicero's *De Inventione* 1.27. With B.'s first kind cf. Cicero's "fabula est, in qua nec verae nec veri similes res continentur." In Macrobius the question arises whether philosophers may properly resort to fables in their teaching. Macrobius then makes a distinction between good and bad poetry which B. observes throughout, and which is fundamental to his defence. Philosophy accepts some "fables" and rejects others, "velut profana a ipso vestibulo sacrae disputationis." "Fables"—their very name bewrays them as fiction—are of two main kinds: they serve merely to flatter the ear, or to bring forth good fruit. Of the first are the comedies of Menander and his imitators, or love stories such as Petronius and Apuleius tell. These Wisdom relegates to the nursery ("in nutricum cunas"—1.2.8; cf. B.'s fourth class and 14.10, end). Of good "fables" there are two kinds: (a) Aesop's, where both *argumentum* and *ordo* are fictitious; (b) the kind which is really not *narratio fabulosa,* whose argument is based on truth (B.'s second and third kinds). These are used in mystic sense by Orpheus and Hesiod. But even of (b) there are two kinds, one of which relates the crimes of the gods; and these Philosophy abjures. There follow the two passages more than once rehearsed by B.—the one about the veil of fable, quoted 14.7 n. 8; the other: "de diis autem, ut dixi, ceteris, et de anima non frustra se, nec ut oblectent, ad fabulosa convertunt, sed quia sciunt inimicam esse naturae apertam nudamque expositionem sui, quae sicut vulgaribus hominum sensibus intellectum sui vario rerum tegmine operimentoque subtraxit, ita a prudentibus arcana sua voluit per fabulosa tractari."

[9] *Aristotle. Rhet.* 2.20, where Aesop, in a counsel's plea, used his fable of the vixen, the ticks, and the hedgehog.

10 *Daughters of Minyas . . . Acestes.* Ovid, *Met.* 4.31-415; 3.582-686. Neither myth is recorded in *G.D.*

11 *Comic writers.* See 14.19 and n. 25.

12 *Vergil, Homer.* See 14.13.

13 *Terence and Plautus.* On B.'s knowledge of these poets see Hortis, pp.389-92; 14.4, n. 17; 18, n. 28. Cod. Laur. Plut. 38.17 is a MS. of Terence said to be in B.'s hand. Cf. facsimile, Hecker, Tafel xi.

14 *Or might.* "Et hec si defacto non fuerit, cum communia sint, esse potuere vel possint." So in *Com.* 1: "Sono ancora le cose che nelle commedie si raccontano, cose che per avventura mai non furono, quantunque non sieno sì strane dai costumi degli uomini, che essere state non possono." These passages are interesting especially as reflecting Aristotle's doctrine of universality in poetry, however faintly (cf. 14.7, n. 5; 17, n. 1), as set forth in chapter 9 of the *Poetics.* Of course B. had never seen the treatise. Cf. L. Cooper, *The Poetics of Aristotle,* p. 99. Petr. *Inv.* 3, pp. 1101, 2, cites it at second hand through *Rhet.* 3.1, and taunts his opponent with never having read it! B. may have learned what he knew through Leontius. But this sentence, and indeed B.'s whole classification of fables, may derive from Cicero's *De Inventione,* or the pseudo-Ciceronian *Ad Herennium,* where the author distinguishes three kinds of *narratio in negotiis*: *fabula, historia, argumentum.* A *fabula* is neither true nor probable, like those of tragedy; a *historia* is remote in time, but a fact; an *argumentum* is fiction, yet possible—"quae tamen fieri potuit"—as the stories of the comedies (*Ad Heren.* 1.8.13; cf. *De Inv.* 1.19.27).

15 *Old wives' tales.* Cf. Macrobius in 14.9 n. 8.

16 *Conference of the trees.* Judges 9.8-15. Isidore cites this story with Aesop's fables as "fabulae ad mores" (*Etym.* 1.40.6), after Augustine, *Contra Mend.* 1.13.28, who includes them in the same class of fables with the parable of the Prodigal Son.

17 *Keep step.* B. cites Holy Writ as documentary of myths at *G. D.* 7.20; 34; 10.1; and especially alleges agreement between pagan poets and the Bible concerning Hell; cf. *G. D.* 1.14; *Com.* 1: "Di questo inferno sentono i poeti co' santi." Petr. *Inv.* 1, p. 1092, claims for Orpheus and Amphion "allegoricus, sapidissimus, ac jucundissimus sensus . . . quo fere omnis sacrarum etiam scripturarum textus abundat." Cf. 14.13 n. 17. Zenatti quotes two passages from Mussato to the same effect (p. 231, n. 3). So Lactantius, *D. I.* 1.5, cites pagan poets and philosophers as confessing one God, together with prophets, Sibyl, and oracles. Cf. Augustine, *Contra Manich.* 13.1, 2, 15: *Patr. Lat.* 42.281, 282, 290.

18 *Our theologians.* In his *Enarr.* on Ps. 77.3: *Patr. Lat.* 36.985 Augustine quotes 1 Cor. 10.5-11, and speaks of the powerful reinforcement or emphasis in figures: "Quas autem figuras dixit Apostolus, eas

dicit iste psalmus, quantum existimare possumus, parabolas et propositiones; non in eo habentes finem, quod contigerunt; sed in eis rebus ad quas rationabili comparatione referuntur." In *Contra Mend.* 24.1. 10: *Patr. Lat.* 40.493, Augustine argues that Jacob's deceit of his father is not a lie but a "mystery." If "mysteries" are lies, then all parables and figures are lies, "quod absit omnino"; such are Christ as the rock, 1 Cor. 10.4, the stony heart of the Jews, Ezech. 36.26, the lion, Rev. 5.5, the devil as the lion, 1 Pet. 5.8; "and innumerable such"; these are not lies, he says in *De Mend.* 1.5.5: *Patr. Lat.* 40.491, but "locutiones actionesque propheticae ad ea quae vera sunt intelligenda referendae. Quae propterea figuratis velut amictibus abteguntur, ut sensum pie quaerentis exerceant, et ne nuda ac prompta vilescant." Cf. also *Sermones* 4.22: *Patr. Lat.* 38.45.

[19] *Literary semblance.* See 14.4 and n. 10.

[20] *Parable.* Cf. Petr. *Fam.* 10.4: "What indeed are the parables of our Savior in the Gospels, but words whose sound is foreign to their sense, or allegories? . . . But allegory is the very warp and woof of all poetry" (Robinson and Rolfe, *Petrarch*, pp. 261-2). Cf. quotations from Augustine in preceding note. Jerome, *Ep.* 58; *Patr. Lat.* 22.585, says that not only the face of Moses wore the veil of mystic meaning, but the Evangelists and Apostles; even Christ attested the allegorical meaning of His words, saying: "He that hath ears to hear, let him hear."

[21] *Quelling minds.* Cf. 14.7; 17.

[22] *Agrippa.* The fable of the belly and the other members, Livy 2.32. On B.'s fondness for Livy, and possible possession of a copy, see Hortis, pp. 317, 416, ff.

[23] *Apuleius. Met.* 4.21. B. has in mind the words: "Then the old woman, rendringe out like sighes, began to speake in this sorte: 'My daughter, take a good harte unto you, and be not afearde at feigned and straunge visions or dreames. . . . I will tell thee a pleasaunt tale to put away all thy sorowe and to revive thy Spirites': and so she beganne" (tr. Adlington). B.'s copy of Apuleius in his own hand still survives (Hecker, p. 34).

[24] *My own.* See Pref. p. 10; 15.13, p. 137.

[25] *Sanseverino.* Tricarico is more than half way from Naples to Brindisi. Nothing seems to be recorded of Jacopo, who may well have been a friend or acquaintance of B. in the Naples days.

[26] *Robert.* Son of Charles II of Anjou. On his learning, esp. in theology, see 14.22 and n. 1.

[27] *Edified and delighted.* According to Horace, *Ars Poet.* 333. B. owned a copy (Hecker, p. 29).

[28] *Christ's commandment.* John 8.7.

14.10

[1] *Quintilian's saying.* Not in the *Institutio* in so many words.

NOTES

F. H. Colson (M. Fabii Quintiliani *Institutionis Oratoriae*, Liber I, Cambr., 1924, p. lviii, n. 2) refers it to *Inst.* 5.12.17: "Declamationes . . . ab illa vera imagine orandi recesserunt, atque ad solam compositae voluptatem nervis carent." Quintilian is proving that effeminate style is not eloquence, since it bears no trace of manliness, purity, gravity, or sanctity in the speaker. Therefore *his* pupil shall devote himself to the imitation of truth. It is his reiterated opinion (cf. 12.1; 2.16, esp. 11). De Nolhac, *Pétr. et Humanisme* 2.83, thinks that B. did not know Quintilian at first hand. Colson, on careful review of the evidence, infers that he knew at least the mutilated text known to Petr. On the knowledge of Quintilian in the Middle Ages see Colson's learned chapter 3, pp. xliii-lxiii.

2 *Bucolics.* Song of Silenus, *Ecl.* 6.31-86:

How seas, and earth, and air, and active flame,
Fell through the mighty void, and in their fall,
Were blindly gathered in this goodly ball.
The tender soil then, stiffening by degrees,
Shut from the bounded earth the bounding seas. . . .
From thence the birth of man the song pursued,
And how the world was lost, and how renewed.

Servius makes a long note on the Lucretian tone of the lines, and cites other philosophers.

3 *Georgics.* 4.219-27:

For God the whole created mass inspires
Through heaven, and earth, and ocean's depth, He throws
His influence round, and kindles as He goes.

Servius points the Pythagorean complexion of the passage and comments at length on the familiar speech of Anchises, which B. cites (*Aen.* 6.724-51), and which continues:

And both the radiant lights one common soul
Inspires and feeds, and animates the whole.

4 *Aristeus. Georg.* 4.415 ff. "Climene" for "Cyrene," but given correctly at *G.D.* 5.13. Fulgentius, *Virg. Cont.* 161, avers that Anchises is a symbol for God Himself instructing the soul.

5 *Theologian.* Zenatti cites Giovanni del Virgilio's epitaph of Dante, quoted by B. in *Life* 17 (12.27):

Theologus Dantes, nullius dogmatis expers,
Quod foveat claro philosophia sinu: . . .

Life 22 (12.42) shows that theology is naught but the poetry of God. See 14.8 and n. 19; 14.22.

6 *Griffon. Purg.* 29.108 ff. Benvenuto da Imola, contemporary with B., gives the accepted allegorical meaning of the passage (*Com.* ed. Vernon, 4.197-9).

7 *Every crumb.* Petr. describes his studies and watches in his

Letter to Posterity (*Fam.* vol. I, pp. 204-8), especially his composition of his eclogues, his treatise *On the Solitary Life,* and his
Africa. The treatise *On the Remedies* was finished later. He
remarks: "Vana è la gloria che dalla sola eleganza delle parole si
procaccia."

[8] *Gallus begging Tyrrhenus. Ecl.* 4. Gallus admires Tyrrhenus'
harp, not reeds, and begs to know where he got it. Tyrrhenus explains
that in a remote and flowery woodland Daedalus appeared to him
one day and gave it to him to solace his own sorrows. For Daedalus
had happened to be present at his birth, and then promised the lyre.
So precious is it now that it is not to be bought with any price that
Gallus can offer. Thus rich in possessing it,

> mundi prementia vincla,
> Pauperiemque levo, rigidas hac saepe per alpes,
> Perque nemus vacuum, perque atra silentia noctis
> Fisus, eo: plaudunt volucres, et concava saxa
> Interea tristes fugiunt per nubila curae.

[9] *Pamphilus and Mitio. Ecl.* 6. For Petr.'s general explanation of
his eclogues see *Fam.* 10.4 in Robinson and Rolfe, pp. 266-74; *Varr.* 42.
In *Com.* 3 (12.143), in the same connection, B. cites them again, but
not his own. Cf. 14.22.

[10] *My own eclogues.* B. explains each of them in a letter to
Martino da Signa *Lett.,* pp. 367-74. The modesty of this passage is
wholly sincere and characteristic. Cf. *De Cas.* 3.14, where he insists
that he is not a poet.

[11] *Old woman.* Not quite consistent with 14.9, where B. says that
such tales contain no truth at all. Cf. 14.9 n. 8 and Macrobius'
phrase "in nutricum cunas."

14.11

[1] The theme of this chapter is a favorite with both B. and Petr.
Cf. 14.19; *Com.* 3 (12.145); *G.D.* 11.2, where he says that the
grove of Helicon is sacred to the Muses because the poet needs a
quiet, lonely place for composition. He cites Quintilian. (*Inst. Or.*
10.3.22 ff.; cf. above 14.10 n. 1), who mentions the notion as popular
in his day, but qualifies it. In his *Lett.,* p. 96, B. describes Certaldo
in much the same idyllic terms as he employs in this chapter. Of the
many instances in Petr. I may cite *Inv.* 4, beginning; Pref. to *Fam.,*
To Socrates, *Var.* 14: Frac. 5.242, translated in Robinson and Rolfe,
Petrarch, p. 135: *De Vita Sol.* 2.7.2, the chapter entitled De Poetis
Solitudinem eligentibus, where Petr. cites the same classic examples
as here. Cf. Voight, *Wiederbelebung* 1.107 ff.; Körting, *Petrarcas
Leben,* pp. 131 ff. The idea is partly a conscious imitation of classical
precedent: see Riedner, *Typische Aeusserungen der Röm. Dichter,*
pp. 39-44, with ref. to Lucretius, Tacitus, Vergil, Horace, and Ovid.

But B. and Petr. both experienced sincere, if periodic, revulsion from the haunts of men to rural quiet, one at Certaldo, the other at Vaucluse.

2 *Above.* 14.5.

3 *Already.* 14.4.

4 *Euripides.* Aulus Gellius 15.20; Valerius Maximus 9.12. ext. 4; cf. above 14.4 n. 28.

5 *Ennius . . . Vergil.* 14.4 and n. 28; 14.19 and nn. 5, 15.

6 B., in *Life* 26 (12.54), records that Dante inscribed his *Paradise* to Frederick, or, as some maintain, to Can Grande della Scala.

7 Petrarch. He looked to Charles to restore the Roman Empire, and more than a dozen letters to him from Petr. survive, who often mentions him in others. Of John Petr. writes that he has invited him to Paris, and loves him dearly though he has never seen him (*Fam.* 15.8, vol. 3, p. 377). In 1360-1 Petr. went as a special ambassador to his court from Milan, and was warmly received (*Fam.* 23.2, p. 10).

8 *Robert.* See 14.22 and n. 1; 15.6, 13; Petr. To Posterity, *Fam.* 1.209 ff.

9 *Horace's words.* Ep. 2.2.65, 6; 76; 79, 80; 84-6. Petr. cites just these lines to the same point, *De Vit. Sol.* 2.7.2.

10 *Paul . . . Arsenius.* All these are mentioned in close connection by Petr. in his *De Vit. Sol.* 2.1.1. There are two Macharii. Petr. cites many exempla from patriarchs, popes, saints, philosophers, and poets—B.'s "many other reverend and holy men"—discussed at greater length than these, whom B. seems to have selected at a careless glance. B. especially valued Petr.'s *De Vit. Sol.* He distinguishes it among his other works as "tam exquisito atque sublimi stylo, ut divino potius quam humano editus videatur ingenio" (*De Fontibus,* s. v. Sorgia). B. may have thought also of Fulgentius, who represents himself as retiring from confusion to his country-seat, and there in quiet beholding the vision of the truth veiled in ancient poetic myth. See *Mythologicon,* beginning.

11 *Contemplation . . . expression.* The experience of Milton *Par. Lost* 3.37-40; cf. below, 14.17. This idyll may have been prompted by recollection of Verg. *Ecl.* 2, which Petr. quotes, *De Vit. Sol.* 1.5.2. But it is much like B.'s description of Certaldo, *Lett.,* p. 96, and Petr.'s of Vaucluse, *Lett. Fam.* 16.6, 7.

12 *Contributions.* Cf. indictments at 14.5; 16.

14.12

1 This chapter embodies material from Petr.'s *Inv.* 3, p. 1105—the obscurity of Aristotle and Plato, the corresponding obscurity of the Holy Ghost, creator of the World, the imminent risk of blasphemy, Augustine's testimony; cf. B.'s acknowledgment below.

He dwells upon the same theme in *Life* 8; *Com.* 3, 5 (12.39, 144, 160 ff.). If there and here B. uses Petr.'s material, he expands it and adds confirmatory citations, especially from Macrobius; and withal he imparts to it a certain enthusiastic momentum not in Petr.

[2] *Simple and clear.* Aristotle, *Rhet.* 3.2, Cicero, *De Inventione* 1.19.20, and the pseudo-Ciceronian *Ad Herennium* 1.8.9, insist that *narratio* of any kind must be short, "dilucida" or "aperta," and probable. Cf. Cicero, *Top.* 26; *De Or.* 2.80, where other parts of a speech as well must be clear; Quintilian, *Inst. Or.* 8.2.22; 4.2.35. Cf. 15.1, n. 9.

[3] *Intrude.* Above 14.5.

[4] *Expounders.* Above 14.5.

[5] *Augustine. Conf.* 4.16: "And what did it profit me that, when scarcely twenty years old, a book of Aristotle's entitled The Ten Predicaments [Categories] fell into my hands? . . . I read it alone and understood it. . . . And what did it profit me that I . . . read unaided, and understood, all the books that I could get of the so-called liberal arts? . . . Whatever was written either on rhetoric or logic, geometry, music, or arithmetic, did I, without any great difficulty, and without the teaching of any man, understand." Cited by Petr. *Inv.* 3, p. 1105.

[6] *Isaiah.* Augustine. *Enarr.* in Ps. 126.11, cites Is. 1.3 and ventures allegorical explanations, since "Propheta nescio quid illis velaminibus nominum texit." He adds: "Sed numquid ista exirent, nisi saccus excuteretur? Nisi prophetia involuta accedente diligentia discuteretur, numquid operta exirent ad nos?" Cited by Petr.

[7] *Artificer.* Wisd. 7.21, 22.

[8] *Punishment.* Mark 3.29.

[9] *Repelled.* Perhaps a reminiscence of Dante, *Par.* 1.54 ff. A favorite figure with Dante: cf. *Purg.* 32.11; *Par.* 25.118; etc.

[10] *More precious.* The threefold advantage of obscurity in poetry, then, is (1) to insure truth against becoming cheap and vulgar; (2) to challenge the reader to utmost effort; (3) to render the truth, once ascertained, more precious for the effort it cost. B. presents the same ideas thrice elsewhere—*Life* 8, near end; *Com.* 5 (12.162); *G. D.* 1.3. In the first he cites Gregory's *Moralia* as his authority (cf. Pref. n. 1); In *Com.* and *G. D.* he cites Macrobius, *Somn. Scip.* 1.2; cf. above 14.9 n. 8. The thought is common in Petr., e.g. *Africa* 9, beginning; *Inv.* 1, p. 1092, etc. Cf. Zenatti's note.

[11] *Book Eleven.* Chap. 19.

[12] *Psalm 126.* Enarr. on v. 11: *Patr. Lat.* 37.1675. B.'s quotation immediately precedes the passage on the obscurity of Isaiah cited above.

[13] *Psalm 146.* Enarr. on v. 12: *Patr. Lat.* 37.1907. The preceding words are: "Honor God's Scripture, honor God's Word, though it be not plain; in reverence wait for understanding. Be not wanton to

accuse either the obscurity or seeming contradiction of Scripture" (tr. Coke).

[14] *Grammar Schools.* The study of poetry was subject either to grammar or to rhetoric in the mediaeval scheme. See 14.7 and n. 1. Though B. does not mention Rhetoric in this passage, it is, like 14.7, a stroke in behalf of the liberation of poetry from technical bondage. His phrase, "figuras dictionum, orationum colores" have a technical sound. Just what he means is not clear. To the mediaeval rhetorician "figurae dictionum" might mean figures in the arrangement of words rather than of sentences. The very phrase occurs in Priscian (*Inst.* 5.11.56: Keil, *Gramm. Lat.* 2.177) as pertaining to simple and compound words. "Colores" are strictly the figures, often of mere arrangement of words, included under the "ornata facilitas" or "ornatus facilis" as distinguished from the "ornata difficultas" or "ornatus difficilis" (cf. Faral, *Les Arts Poétiques,* etc., pp. 91, 321); but the term is often loose as here in B. See C. S. Baldwin, *Cicero on Parnassus,* in *PMLA.* 42.106 ff. Perhaps B. is again merely flourishing in the face of his opponents technical terms of their scholastic armory, which they themselves, with their shallow training, do not understand too well; cf. 14.3; 5. The "ancient authority" seems to be Aristotle, *Rhet.* 3.2; cf. 14.12 n. 2; Horace, *Ars Poet.* 48-59, where he advises on the proper use of alien terms.

[15] *The old mind.* Eph. 4.22; Col. 3.9.

[16] *Petrarch. Inv.,* p. 1105. Petr. has just been comparing the obscurity of poets with that of Holy Writ, not citing the difference between oratory and poetry. B.'s quotation, either through his carelessness or corruption of his text, differs slightly from Petr. I have rendered "those who wish to understand" from Petr.'s "capere volentibus," not from B.'s "carpere nequentibus," which might mean "who cannot (readily?) understand."

[17] *Divine command.* Matt. 7.6.

14.13

[1] *Liars.* "Mendaces"; at 14.5; 9 they are "fabulones"; cf. 14.9 n. 1.

[2] *This position.* Petr. *Inv.* 1, p. 1092, calls this a vulgar objection. He replies by pointing out the "studiose abditus, allegoricus sapidissimus ac jucundissimus sensus" in poetry, like that of Holy Writ, and cites the eminent Christian Lactantius as one deeply versed in poets and philosophers, and skilful in Ciceronian expression. He quotes from *D. I.* 1: "Nesciunt quid Poeticae licentiae" etc.

[3] *Stone.* Perhaps Niobe, for whose legend B. gives explanations both archaeological and natural in *G. D.* 12.2.

[4] *Many gods.* The oft-reiterated argument of early apologists, particularly Tertullian, Arnobius, Lactantius, and Augustine.

[5] *Untrue story.* Cf. Augustine, *Conf.* quoted at 14.13 n. 25.

[6] *Above.* 14.9.

[7] *Augustine. De Mendacio* 14 (*Patr. Lat.* 40.505). The eight are lies (1) in doctrine; (2) to injure another unjustly; (3) of advantage to one, disadvantage to another, though not making for physical unchastity; (4) for mere lying's sake; (5) flattery; (6) to help one without injuring others; (7) in defence of the innocent; (8) in defence of personal chastity.

[8] *As I said.* 14.9 and n. 2, esp. quotation from Isidore.

[9] *Office.* As in Isidore's formula, *Etym.* 8.7: "Officium poetae in eo est, ut ea, quae vere gesta sunt, in alias species obliquis figurationibus cum decore aliquo conversa transducat." Copied by Rabanus, *De Universo* 15.2; Vincent of Beauvais, *S. D.* 4.410.

[10] *Duty.* So Petr. *Inv.* 1, p. 1092

[11] *Lawyer.* See 14.4, n. 2; 15.10.

[12] *St. John.* Jerome, *Ep.* 53: *Patr. Lat.* 22.548, 9: "Apocalypsis Joannis tot habet sacramenta, quot verba. Parum dixi pro merito voluminis. Laus omnis inferior est: in verbis singulis multiplices latent intelligentiae."

[13] *Other writers.* B. mentions Isaiah, Ezechiel, and Daniel at 14.9. Augustine, *De Mendac.* 7: *Patr. Lat.* 40. 492, shows that the figures of the Old Testament, especially the prophetic ones, are not lies— "ut aut indole proficientium et spe approbentur, aut significationis alicujus causa, non sint omnino mendacia."

[14] *Prophets.* Jerome reckons John the Evangelist as a prophet because of the prophetic mysteries in Revelation (*Ad Jovin.* 1. 26: *Patr. Lat.* 23. 259).

[15] *Figures.* 14.4, n. 10.

[16] *Poets.* Cf. 14.9 and n. 18. Augustine, *De Ord.* 2. 14: *Patr. Lat.* 32.1014 grants poets "rationabilium mendaciorum potestatem," wherein reason favors the poets.

[17] *One God.* In 2.2 (cf. 11.1) B. shows that certain more serious ancients understood the one true God when they named Jupiter (=juvans pater, which is God; in Greek, Zephs, Zeus, "quod latine vita sonat"—"I am the way, the truth, and the life"!). In 7.34 he praises Hermes Trismegistus and his book *De Idolo ad Asclepium* ("which I have seen," 5.21), which Hortis identifies with Apuleius' *Aesculapius* (p. 456, n. 6), and which B. may have owned (Hecker, p. 34). B. remarks that the author, for all he is a pagan, has "a wonderfully accurate idea of the true God." Cf. 14.18. Petr. *Inv.* 3, pp. 1101, 1106, contends that pagan poets, by the intuition of genius, outstripped the philosophers in their notion of God, and that both secretly rejected popular polytheism. He probably recalls Lactantius, *D. I.* 1. 5, who shows that both pagan poets and philosophers "touched upon the truth, and almost grasped it." He mentions Orpheus, Vergil (*Aen.* 6. 724; *Georg.* 4. 221), Ovid (*Met.* 1.1 ff.),

and a dozen philosophers, including Aristotle, Plato, Cicero, and Seneca.

[18] *Vergil. Aen.* 2.689. In *Com.* 1 B. girds himself for his task, "poetically" invoking God's help in these words.

[19] *Plato's opinion.* Derived from the *De Dogmate Platonis* of Apuleius. Whether B.'s copy of Apuleius included this treatise is not certainly known; cf. Hecker, p. 34. B. might also have read the theory in Dante, *Conv.* 2.5, or in Petr. *De Sui Ipsius et Al. Ignor.*, p. 1151. See Introd., pp. xx, xxi.

[20] *Liars . . . wilful deceivers.* "Mendaces . . . mentientes."

[21] *A further distinction.* A legal distinction which B. elaborates in *Com.* 17 (12.92,3). Both civil and canon law rightly distinguish between "ignorantia *Facti*" and "ignorantia *Juris.*" It is the difference between the transgression of a secret papal law, and of one promulgated. He then shows, as here, that the ignorance of the Gentiles and Jews before Christ was "ignorantia Facti," and was therefore not guilty. See 14.4 n. 2; 15.10.

[22] *Liberal Arts.* See 14.7 and n. 11.

[23] *Every man.* John 1. 9; Matt. 22.2 ff.; Rev. 19.9.

[24] *Be damned.* So Petr. *Inv.* 3, p. 1104, who adds that even great Catholics erred *after* the Revelation. But the real test of the poets is the truth, sacred or profane, which their works contain; on this score no one can condemn the great Ancients. Cf. p. 1106.

[25] *Dido.* Augustine, *Conf.* 1.13, bewails once having wept at the death of Dido, and having preferred "those poetic figments" to the duller disciplines.

[26] *Rather die.* She is praised for this in almost the same terms by Jerome, *Adv. Jov.* 1.43: *Patr. Lat.* 23.286.

[27] *Historic Dido.* In *G.D.* 2.60; 6.53 B. points the difference between the Dido of history and of Vergil. In *Sen.* 4.5, ed. Frac. 1.252, Petr., with some display of authorities sacred and profane, does likewise. He shows, as does B., that by her situation, her beauty, her chastity, and her widowhood, she was adapted to the use which Vergil made of her. Cf. below n. 32. The distinction becomes traditional; see Ronsard, Pref. to the *Franciade*. Cf. Ausonius 118; Macrob. *Sat.* 5.17; Boccaccio, *De Clar. Mul.* 40.

[28] *Fourfold.* Of the four, the first corresponds roughly to the historical or literal interpretation; the second to the moral or allegorical (cf. Introd.). They also represent B.'s usual twofold interpretations—euhemeristic and moral. But the first includes interesting comment on Vergil's skill. For the first two B. seems to lean on Petr.

[29] *Metrical historian.* In *Com.* 13 (13.33) B. makes the same observation. Servius, on *Aen.* 1. 382, remarks that Lucan belongs not among the poets because he seems rather to have composed a history than a poem. The remark is repeated by Isidore, *Etym.* 8.7, and Rabanus, *De Univ.* 15.2: *Patr. Lat.* 111.419. John of Salisbury calls him a most

learned and grave poet, unless, by his "true narration" he belongs rather to the historians (*Pol.* 2.19; 8.23; cf. Webb's ed. I. xxxii), or, as Quintilian prefers, to the orators (Quint. *Inst.* 10.1.90). Servius and the others miss in Lucan that disguise of fiction, whereas B. points out his unepic, chronological order of events.

³⁰ *Midst of the events.* Horace, *A.P.* 148, who refers to Homer. But B.'s illustration may come from Leontius' instruction in the *Odyssey.* Cf. *G.D.* 11.40 and 15.6.

³¹ *Later.* Petr. says possibly 300 years (*Sen.* 4.5). His authority, though he does not cite it, was Jerome's version of Eusebius' *Chronicon* (*Liber Temporum*) where Aeneas' journey is dated in the 838th year of Abraham, but the founding of Carthage by Dido, according to various authorities, in 971, 1011, 1167, any of which would support B.'s statement, and the last of them, Petr.'s.

³² *Second purpose.* Here B. employs the prescribed moral-allegorical explanation of the *Aeneid* set forth in Fulgentius' *Virgiliana Continentia,* and in a lost commentary by Bernard Silvester, which is perhaps essentially embodied in John of Salisbury's *Policraticus* 8.24. But B.'s phrasing seems to point to Petr. *Sen.* 4.5 (ed. Frac. 4.4; ed. of 1581, pp. 785 ff.), who remarks Dido's beauty and widowhood, from the first of which comes "libidinis incentivum," from the second, "libertas oritur." Both B. and Petr. are interested in the Fourth Book as an allegory of the triumph of the soul over concupiscence. Of Mercury's warning Petr. says that when one is fast bound in the toils of sin, "aliquando tamen Dei instinctu tacito vel alicujus monitu, Dei placitum nunciantis assurgit, neglectaque qua tenebatur voluptate, ad virtutis, et gloriae rectum iter redit. Hic Mercurius eloquii dux, a Iove missus" (p. 787). In Bernard Mercury is "ratio," in Fulgentius, "ingenium."

³³ *Third . . . fourth purpose.* "In quo [*Aeneid*] quod studebat, Romanae simul urbis et Augusti origo contineretur" (Donatus, ed. Brummer, p. 6). "Ut celebret Romanos et praecipue Augustum" (Serv. on *Aen.* 6.752).

³⁴ *Dido's execrations. Aen.* 4.622-9, obvious reference to the Punic Wars, and so explained by Servius.

14.14

¹ *Above.* 14.13; cf. 14.9, 10.

² *Revealed.* Books 1-13; see Introd. pp. xvii-xxv.

³ *Comic poets.* See 14.19 and n. 25.

⁴ *Cicero.* B. refers to a fragment of the *Republic* (4.10) which he found quoted in Augustine, *C.D.* 2.13: "Cum artem ludicram scaenamque totam in probro ducerent, genus id hominum non modo honore civium reliquorum carere, sed etiam tribu moveri notatione censoria voluerunt." Cf. 8.15; Hecker cites also 2.9.

⁵ *Sylvester.* Sylvester I, Pope 314-35, in Constantine's reign. The *Liber Pontificalis* (ed. Duchesne, pp. 170-201; Introd., p. cix) speaks

of moral reforms in his time, though it does not mention the stage.

⁶ *Plato.* See 14.19.

⁷ *Whatever.* See 14.5 and n. 8.

⁸ *Time and again.* These types are nearly all listed by Rabanus Maurus in his *Allegoriae in Sacram Scripturam, Patr. Lat.* 112.850 ff. He refers them to the Bible: God as the Sun, Wisd. 5.6; fire, Lk. 12.50; lion, Amos 3.8; Rev. 5.5; serpent, Num. 21.8; lamb, Exod. 7.5; worm, Ps. 21.7; stone, Zech. 3.9; cf. Petr. *Inv.* 3, p. 1103, bottom; Zenatti adds *Lett.* 10.4. As types of the Church Rabanus mentions a ship, Matt. 8.24; Lk. 5.3; ark, Ps. 131.8; house, Ps. 92.5; temple, Ps. 28.9. The woman clothed with the sun is the Church in Rev. 12.1, according to Bede, *Explan. Apoc.* 2.12: *Patr. Lat.* 93. 165. A chariot typifies the Church, Dante, *Purg.* 29.108 ff.; cf. above 14.9, n. 17. Rabanus cites many types of the Virgin; see Salzer, *Sinnbilder u. Beiworte Mariens.* Of Satan he mentions the serpent as a type from Is. 65.25; the lion, I Pet. 5.8.

14.15

¹ *Comic poets.* See 14.19 and n. 25.

² *Art of Love.* Petr. condemns it as "an unwholesome work and in my opinion justifiably the cause of his exile" (*De Vita Sol.* 2.7.2), and considers Ovid "a man of great genius, but of a lascivious, unsteady, and extremely effeminate temper." For his opinion of ancient erotic poetry see *De Rem.* 1.69, cited by DeNolhac 1.165, n. 4.

³ *Read . . . Hesiod.* Neither had B. (Hortis, p. 384). On Homer see 15.7 and n. 10. Horace and Juvenal he owned (Hecker, pp. 29, 30).

⁴ *Venerable man.* Hecker, p. 237, n. 3, thinks that this may have been Fra Francesco di Biancozzo de' Nerli, the first to be promoted Doctor of Theology (1359) in the University. Hauvette doubts it (p. 424. n.). Pietro di Monteforti congratulated B. especially on this passage, *Lett.* ed. Corazzini, p. 350.

⁵ *Our University.* "Generali studio nostro." See Rashdall, *Universities of Europe* 1.7 ff.; 2. 3-5. The Studium Generale at Florence was finally established in 1349.

⁶ *St. John.* A slip. The only possible passage is Acts 17.28. His citation of Scripture is faulty at 15.9; see n. 9. B. often deplores his treacherous memory: see Pref. pp. 56-7; 15.4; and four passages cited by Hecker, p. 153, n. 1. In *G.D.* 9.37 and 2.25, 63, he tells the story of Cadmus with discrepancies of name and interpretation of which he is apparently unconscious. Cf. 14.6, n. 8.

⁷ *Practice.* Ironical, of course. In *G.D.* 7.23 Phoroneus is an Argive judge of such fame as to create the name "forum." Minos, 11.26, and Eacus, 12.45, were such just judges that they euhemeristically became judges in Hell. Of Lycurgus, Valerius says that Lacedemon produced no greater man. The Delphic oracle knew not whether to reckon him a man or a god (5.3. ext. 2; cf. 1.2. ext. 3)

⁸ *Aeneid.* His friends, 1.198-207; his ardor, 2.657-70, esp. 668-70;

his father, 2.707 ff.; Archimedes, 3.590; passion, 4.279 ff.; games, 5.104 ff.; his descent, 6.236; Pallas, 11.29.

⁹ *Vergil.* Cf. 14.13 and n. 17.

¹⁰ *Horace . . . Juvenal.* Also at 14.19; *Com.* 13 (13.29); see 14.15 and n. 3. Persius he quotes at 11.2.

14.16

¹ *David . . . Job.* See 14.4 and n. 10.

² *Maevius.* Verg. *Ecl.* 3:90: "Qui Bavium non odit, amet tua carmina, Maevi." Servius says: "Nam Maevius et Bavius pessimi fuerunt poetae, inimici Horatio quam Vergilio." Cf. Hor. *Epod.* 10.2.

³ *Accusation.* Like Johnson to the ladies who commended the omission of all naughty words from his *Dictionary, Misc.* ed. Hill, 2.390.

⁴ *Zealots.* See 14.5; 11.

⁵ *Catullus, Propertius, Ovid.* In the apotheosis of Philosophy, *Am. Vis.* 5, Ovid is mentioned only as the poet of love, the others not at all. Nothing shows that B. read the first two. See 14.15, n. 2. Petr. did; see Ellis, *Catullus in the XIVth Century,* pp. 16-23; 29, 30; De Nolhac 1.89, 170. B. may have had in his eye Petr. *De Rem.* 1.69: "Quid ex vestris Ovidio, Catullo, Propertio, Tibullo, quorum nullum ferme nisi amatorium est poema." Cf. 14.19 and n. 25.

⁶ *Allurer.* The word here and at the beginning of the chapter is "seductor" ("seducunt") from Matt. 27.63, translated "deceiver," as elsewhere in the Bible. It is difficult to find an English word which will admit of B.'s literal argument. See 14.9 and n. 4.

14.17

¹ *Apes of the philosophers.* The whole chapter perhaps has something to do with Macrobius. "Cave aestimes, mi Aviene, poetarum gregem, cum de diis fabulantur, non ab adytis plerumque philosophiae semina mutuari. Nam quod omnes paene deos, dumtaxat qui sub coelo sunt, ad solem referunt, non vana superstitio sed ratio divina commendat." *Sat.* 1.17.2. Cf. *Somn. Scip.* 1.2.6 ff. cited at 14.9, n. 8. The contrast between poetry and philosophy which B. develops in this chapter, while in some respects unlike that in the later Renaissance critics, which derives from Aristotle's *Poetics* (cf. Spingarn, pp. 271-2), contains, however, the same point of difference between the abstraction of philosophy and the concreteness of poetry, between the baldness of the one and the charm of the other. It adds another intimation of indirect influence from the *Poetics.* See 14.9 and n. 14; Introd. pp. xlv-xlvi. On the relation of poetry and philosophy, see further 14.13; 18; 19; and Petr. cited below n. 4: Zenatti cites Mussato, col. 442; 41.b-c.

² *Elsewhere.* Hecker cites *G.D.* 4.43: "Sunt simiae animalia inter alia hoc a natura infixum habentia, ut quidquid viderint quenquam agentem, et ipsae facere velint, et aliquando faciant."

³ *Noble arts.* Cf. 14.19.

⁴ *Of the very number.* So Petr. calls Homer not only a sacred philosopher, but even greater and more sublime, "Siccome quegli che le più esquisite bellezze della filosofia orni ed adombri di sottilissimo velo." In *Inv.* 3, p. 1103, he maintains that philosophers claim poets as their own, or Aristotle would not have written his *Poetics* (cf. 14.9, n. 14). The philosophers Cicero, Seneca, and Solon, also cherished poetry. In *Sen.* 15.11 he says that, if poetry is not among the Liberal Arts, neither is theology nor philosophy, nor is a prince counted among his lords. The Liberal Arts make for knowledge, but others there are which render the mind fair and perfect.

⁵ *Poet conceives.* As described in 14.7.

⁶ *Contemplation.* Cf. 14.11 and n. 11.

⁷ *Mountains . . . rivers.* See 14.7 and nn. 9, 13; Introd., pp. xiii, xiv.

⁸ *Vividly set forth.* Also 14.7 and n. 5; 14.9.

14.18

¹ This chapter is practically reproduced, citations and all, at *Com.* 3 (12.145-8). The gist of the argument is contained in Vincent of Beauvais *S.D.* 1.8; 2.35. He summarizes early and mediaeval opinion with citations of authorities from Ambrose to Bede, and defends his own citation of pagan poets and philosophers, on the basis of Jerome, *Ep.* 70, by Paul's three precedents, and by the instance of the captive woman. See below n. 16.

² *Damasus.* See below n. 16.

³ *Doctors.* From Socrates; see 15.3 and n. 3.

⁴ *Gentiles.* Cf. 14.13; below pp. 83-4.

⁵ *Just above.* 14.16.

⁶ *Glass houses.* Reinsberg-v. Düringsfeld, *Sprichwörter* 1.310, records this proverb or its equivalent in 12 modern European languages, including Italian. I do not find it in mediaeval or ancient Latin collections.

⁷ *So incline.* See 15.10.

⁸ *Recognize them.* Ambrose, *Exposition on Luke* 1.2: *Patr. Lat.* 15.1613: "Legimus aliqua ne ignoremus . . . et ut sciamus qualia sint"; cited by Vincent (see above n. 1).

⁹ *Pictures.* Schöningh, p. 41, suggests that by "holy precincts of the church" ("etiam in sacris aedibus") B. may point to Giotto's *Inferno* in the Bargello, though certain details do not correspond; or possibly Orcagna's Heaven and Hell in his *Last Judgment* in S. Maria Novella; or an unknown artist's *Triumph of Death* and *Hell* in the Campo Santo at Pisa. For the "crimes" which decorate the palaces, Schöningh mentions Lorenzetti's allegorical pictures of Tyranny, Treachery, Fury, War, etc., in the Palazzo Publico, Siena; or possibly Giotto's allegorical figures of Envy, Anger, etc., in Scrovegni Chapel of S. Maria dell' Arena, Padua. B. probably knew Giotto in Naples, when the painter was executing a commission for Robert in two

chapels and the sala maggiore of the Castelnuovo. See 14.6 n. 10. These pictures have perished, but they are known to have been single figures of famous men and women including such mythological ones as Hector, Aeneas, Achilles, Paris, Hercules, Andromeda, Dido, Helen, Deianira. These, however, were mere figures not in action. See Paolo d'Ancona in *L'Arte* 8 (1905).102; I. B. Supino, *Giotto,* 1920, p. 319. But B. doubtless had in mind instances in or about Florence.

[10] *Vessel of Election.* See 14.18 and n. 23. Another slip—it is not from Paul. Cf. 14.15 n. 6.

[11] *Female admirers.* Cf. 14.5; 11.

[12] *Philosophy . . . Poetry.* Cf. 14.17 and n. 1.

[13] *The veil.* See 14.7.

[14] *Homer . . . Horace.* Cf. 14.15 and n. 3; 14.19.

[15] *Fragments.* See 14.5.

[16] *Damasus. Ep.* 21.13; *Patr. Lat.* 22.385: "Daemonum cibus est carmina Poetarum, saecularis sapientia, Rhetoricorum pompa verborum." Such learning, especially pagan philosophy, Jerome likens to the captive woman in Deut. 21.11-13. "Si quid in eis utile reperimus, ad nostrum dogma convertimus; siquid vero superfluum de idolis, de amore, de cura saecularium rerum, haec radimus, his calvitium inducimus, haec in unguium morem ferro acutissimo desecamus." See below n. 25.

[17] *Comic poets.* See 14.19 and n. 25.

[18] *Other works.* There is a strong tendency to figurative style in Jerome. Perhaps B. has in mind the elaborate mystical interpretation of the vision of Isaiah (Chap. 6) and of the seraphim in *Ep.* 18: *Patr. Lat.* 22.362; but see also his review of the books of the Bible with respect to their figurative meaning, *Ep.* 53. Cf. 14.4 n. 10.

[19] *Fulgentius.* Bishop of Ruspe, identified in many mss. with Fulgentius the mythographer. The distinction, if any, has never been settled (Pauly-Wissowa, *Realencycl.* 7.1.222). The *Mythologicon* contains extravagant allegorical explanations of myths. "Mutatas itaque vanitates manifestare cupimus, non manifesta mutando fuscamus. . . . Certos itaque rerum praestolamur effectus quos repulsos mendacis Graeciae fabuloso commento, quid mysticum, in his sapere debeat cerebrum, agnoscamus." His style, affected and pedantic (*ecce signum*), is anything but finished. Though B. often cites him in *G.D.,* he disparages his extravagance. See Introd., p. xvii.

[20] *Augustine.* As a schoolboy he delighted in Vergil and Latin literature, but disliked Homer and Greek (*Conf.* 1.12-14). Besides Vergil he more frequently cites Terence, Lucan, Horace, and Ennius (*C.D.* 1.3; 2.6,7; 3.12; 10.1, 27; 21.6). Vergil is "poeta magnus omniumque praeclarissimus atque optimus teneris ebibitus animis" (1.3); "insignis" (5.12); "clarissimus" (8.19); "Latini eloquii magnus auctor" (10.1); "nobilissimus" (10.27); cf. 7.9; *On Romans* 1.3. But "almost

never" is stretching it. Petr., *Inv.* 3, p. 1107, cites *C.D.* Proem, to the effect that youngsters should be saturated with poetry.

[21] *Preface. Patr. Lat.* 23, 983. He must first answer his vilifiers, "Terentii quippiam sustinens, qui comoediarum prologos in defensionem sui scenis dabat." Besides Terence's answer to the charge of plagiarism, he mentions those of Vergil and Cicero. He also quotes Horace and Quintilian, but not Persius. In general he quotes the poets much oftener than Augustine, especially in his letters—Homer, Vergil, Horace, Ovid, Persius, Terence, Plautus, Juvenal.

[22] *Augustine.* Of the various letters to Augustine B. probably means 112: *Patr. Lat.* 22.916-31, and the passage concerning the title of Jerome's work, *De Illustribus Viris* on analogy of the pagan writers "De Illustribus Viris," including poets, "epic, tragic, and comic." But no poets are named.

[23] *Vessel of Election.* "Vas electionis est mihi iste," Acts 9.15. So above p. 137; *Com.* 3, 7, (12.147, 209); Dante, *Inf.* 2.28.

[24] *Caught up.* II Cor. 12.2, 4.

[25] *Poets.* On the Areopagus he cited Aratus, Acts 17.28; for Menander, see I Cor. 15.33; for Epimenides, Titus 1.12. These are all noted by Jerome; see his *Com. on Titus* 1.12-14: *Patr. Lat.* 26.606,7; cf. *Com. on Eph.* 3.5.14; *On Gal.* 2.4.24; and esp. *Ep.* 70.2: *Patr. Lat.* 22.665, in which is a host of instances of the proper use of pagan writings, from Moses down; including these and the symbol of the captive woman. Cf. n. 16 above.

[26] *Dionysius.* Acts 17-34. For the legend of his martyrdom, see Hilduin's *Passio Sanctissimi Dion.: Patr. Lat.* 106.23 ff. His authorship of the *Celestial Hierarchy* was disproved by Laurentius Valla and Grocyn. It is probably of the 6th century. B. quotes from chap. 2: *Patr. Lat.* 122. 1040.

[27] *Parable.* The third kind of fable, 14.9.

[28] *Terence.* Hauvette (*Notes sur des manuscrits autographes de B.,* etc., in *Mel. d' Archeol. et d' Hist.,* L'Ecole Franc. de Rome 14, 1894, p. 87) points to a Laurentian ms. of Terence, wherein, at 1.2.27, 8 of the *Phormio*: "Inscitast adversum stimulum calces," occurs, in B.'s hand, the note, "hinc paulus." The line is really an old proverb; cf. Pind. *Pyth.* 2.174; Aesch. *Prom.* 323; Eur. *Bacch.* 794. Hortis finds no other citation from Terence in B. (p. 392).

[29] *Measure.* Matt. 7.2; Mk. 4.24; Lk. 6.38.

14.19

[1] This chapter is reproduced in condensed form in *Com.* 3 (12.144, 5), with many of the examples here cited, including Petr. Plato's objection in *Rep.* 2.10B may have been learned from Augustine, *C.D.* 2.14, to whom it is referred by Petr. *Inv.* 3, p. 1103; it has been bandied about by many critics and apologists even down to the late Renaissance. Cf. Cicero, *Tusc. Disp.* 2.27; Tertullian, *Ad Nat.* 2.7.

[2] *Already.* See 14.14.

[3] *Have said.* 14.11; cf. n. 1.

[4] *Homer.* See also 14.4 B. records these and other "facts" about Homer in *Com.* 12:1.319-26. Most of them he learned, orally no doubt, from Leontius (see 15.6), who safely supported his statements by the authority of Callimachus, the grammarian, whom B. could not consult. Homer's poverty and blindness, and his death in Arcadia, are mentioned in the biographies. The more extraordinary details mentioned by B. Leontius may have invented. He could not have read them in anything from Callimachus that survives.

[5] *Vergil.* See 14.4 and n. 19. B. makes in his various works some nine or ten biographical allusions to Vergil, which I have considered in *Classical Philology* 25.27-36. A comparison of these allusions with all possible sources shows that among others B. consulted one of the expanded versions of the *Life* by Donatus, commonly called the *Donatus Auctus* (E. Diehl, *Die Vitae Vergilianae*, pp. 27-37; Heyne-Wagner ed. of Vergil, 1830, 1.lxxxi-cvi). The story of Vergil's modesty, of his composing the *Aeneid* near Naples, of Augustus rescuing the poem from burning, of the burial at Naples occur variously in one *Life* or another, but are all told in the *Donatus Auctus*. Furthermore a detailed comparison shows definite verbal relation to the *Donatus Auctus*. For the account of Mantua and Vergil's birthplace, and of Augustus' interference to save the *Aeneid,* see 14.4 n. 19. In *Com.* 2 (12.139) B. cites Macrobius' *Saturnalia* as authority for Vergil's composition of the *Aeneid* at his Neapolitan villa, but I do not find the statement in Macrobius. It is true that the dozen or so versions of the *Donatus Auctus* which we have are all of the fifteenth century. But K. L. Roth has shown that these expansions were progressive from the early twelfth century on (*Ueber den Zauberer Vergilius,* in Pfeiffer's *Germania* 4.285-7). B. evidently used a version either identical with, or very close to, that in Diehl or Heyne-Wagner.

[6] *Barillus.* A Neapolitan knight, seneschal of King Robert in Provence, lawyer, poet, friend of Petr., and doubtless of B. during his first sojourn in Naples. He was sent to accompany Petr. to his coronation with the laurel in Rome, but missed the occasion by falling among thieves (Petr. *Ep. Carm.* 2.1, p. 188 of Basel ed. See also Petr. *Ecl.* 2; *Fam.* 4.8; 5.4; 12.14; 13.10). See Zenatti's note, p. 251; N. Faraglia, *I Due Amici del Petrarca, Giovanni Barrili e Marco Barbato* in *Archiv. Stor. Napoletano* 9 (1884) 35-42; also *Archiv. Stor. Ital.* 5.3.313. Of Vergil's retirement to a spot near Naples, and his eventual burial there by the Puteolan Way, B. could, and perhaps did, learn without Barillus' help. Either he introduces the name here for the sake of compliment and old association, or Barillus may have pointed out to him the exact spot. Barillus seems to have been chosen by King Robert to guide Petr. in his excursion to Pozzuolo and Baiae on a happy day in 1341 (*Fam.* 5.4: Basel ed., p. 642). B. visited the tomb repeatedly in his first Neapolitan sojourn (*Filocopo* 4, p. 27, ed. Moutier), or perhaps lodged near by. He dates letters "apud busta

Maronis Vergilii" (*Lett.* 440, 452, 467). Villani (*Life of B.* in his
Liber de Civ. Florent. Famosis Civibus, ed. Galetti, 1847, p. 17) says
that it was contemplation of the tomb of Vergil that finally converted
B. from a mercantile to a literary career.

⁷ *Petrarch.* B. takes every occasion to praise him: Pref. pp. 7, 8;
14.11; 19 (below); 15.6, 13; 14. Avignon is usually "the Western
Babylon" in B., Petr., and others of the time. Petr. first lived at
Vaucluse, fifteen miles away, in 1337, and returned from time to
time till 1353 (aet. 49). The present passage is evidently of later date.
A closely similar one is in *De Fontibus* s.v. Sorgia. B. refers to Benedict XII (1335-42), Clement VI (1342-52), both of whom Petr. knew;
and perhaps to Petr.'s friends the Colonnas, cardinal and bishop. Cf.
14.11 n. 7. A glance at Petr.'s description of Vaucluse in *Fam.* 10.3
shows that B. has somewhat simplified the simplicity of Petr.'s *ménage,*
especially in the matter of servants and tilth.

⁸ *Homer.* B. overlooks Tertullian, *Ad Nat.* 2.7: "Plato censuit,
ipsum Homerum sane coronatum civitate pellendum."

⁹ *Pandects of Pisa.* Cf. 15.10. The oldest and best ms. of the Digest
of Justinian, dating from the sixth or seventh century, kept at Pisa
till 1406, when Florence took it away. It is now in the Laurentian. For
a description see H. J. Roby, *Introduction to the Study of Justinian's
Digest,* 1884, pp. ccxxxvi-viii; also Mommsen's Preface to his edition
of Books 1-10, 1866. The Proem, near the end, quotes Homer as
"patrem omnis virtutis." The chapter De Justitia does not refer to
Homer, but B. in a hasty glance may have mistaken a short Greek
quotation there for Homer. Or he may have trusted his untrustworthy
memory; cf. 14.15, n. 6. In De Contrahenda, etc. (*Digest* 18.1.1) *Il.*
6,234; 472 ff.; *Od.* 1.430 are quoted; In De Legatis, etc. (32.65), *Od.*
13.407; Hecker cites these and *Digest* 48.5.14 (*Il.* 9.340); 48.19.16(*Il.*
23.85); 50.16.236 (*Od.* 4.230), where Homer is "summus poetarum."

¹⁰ *Archias.* Chap. 19.

¹¹ *Greek verse.* The distich written in Greek in the ms. (see 15.7,
n. 1) is somewhat altered from the usual version, which B. might
have read in a late ms. of Aulus Gellius (3.11). It reappears at the end
of a Terence ms., written by B., in the Laurentian Library, with a
Latin interlinear gloss. Hauvette (*Notes sur des manuscrits autographes de Boccace,* etc. in *Melange d'Archéol. et d'Hist.* of L'Ecole
Franc. de Rome 14 (1894), pp. 11-16) and Hecker, pp. 153-7, find reasons for thinking that B. got this version from Leontius.

¹² *Very book.* Homer is quoted some half dozen times in *Rep.* 2.
Hecker asks if B. may have seen the *Rep.* The more likely source of
his information was the word of Leontius.

¹³ *Ennius.* See 14.4 and n. 18.

¹⁴ *Solon.* See 14.4 and n. 31.

¹⁵ *Vergil.* Cf. above n. 5. For "Parthenias" see *Donatus Auctus* in
Diehl's *Vitae Vergilianae,* p. 29; and the blush, p. 36. On Octavius and

the native Mantua, see 14.4 and n. 19. B. means that the Mantuans were disappointed when the ashes were brought from Brundisium, that they were not given to them rather than to Naples. He mentions the village Andes, "hodie Pietola," in his *De Fluminibus*, s.v. Mintius, as Vergil's birthplace, hardly two miles from Mantua, where the people proudly cherish the memory of the great "vates," and have named a little nearby hillock Vergil's Mount, as marking the location of his farm. See *Com.* 57 (14.208). Two centuries later Hoby observed: "Upon the hill there, there is a little brick house, which the inhabitants of the country call Casetta di Virgilio, holding opinion that was his house" (Ms. Egerton 2148, B.M., quoted in Einstein, *Ital. Ren. in England,* p. 135).

[16] *Horace . . . Juvenal.* Cf. 14.15; and n. 3.

[17] *Perfect model.* For the times perhaps. Though an ecclesiastic, he had two illegitimate children, son and daughter. The son was legitimized by Clement VI. Cf. 14.19, n. 7.

[18] *Prose . . . verse.* Cf. 15.6. B. here thinks of Petr.'s works in Latin. At *Com.* 57 (14.208) he remarks that Petr.'s powers were for some time concealed within the shadow "of our common mother tongue" (volgar materno), but now he has joined the ranks of the greatest men of literature, the famous poets of Greece and Rome. The reference to Petr.'s old age points to this as one of the late passages in *G.D.*

[19] *Claudian.* "Minuit praesentia famam," *De Bello Gildonico* 385.

[20] *Seneca.* "Platon et Aristoteles et omnis in diversum itura sapientium turba plus ex moribus quam ex verbis Socratis traxit," *Ep.* 1.6.6.

[21] *Philosophy, mistress.* See 14.5; 17. Petr. employs this same argument in *Inv.* 3, pp. 1103-4; cf. 2, p. 1092; *Sen.* 15.11. Theology as a whole is not to be condemned for the heretics; neither do false teachers discredit philosophy, nor unworthy poets poetry.

[22] *Dregs.* "In vino fex, et in oleo amurca, sic in rebus fere omnibus . . . . Itaque et Philosophiae quaedam species . . . infames," e.g. Epicurus, Aristippus, Hermacus, Metrodorus, and old Hieronymus (not the Father) (*Inv.* 3, p. 1103).

[23] *Socrates . . . Panetius.* See 14.4 and nn. 22-4.

[24] *Donatists . . . Fotini.* Heretics of the fourth century. Basil, Chrysostom, and Ambrose were all of the same time. Leo I (the Great) was of the fifth.

[25] *Comic poets.* See also 14.9; 15; 18; 20; 22; 15.8; B. has the same in mind at 14.6; 16. By "comic" poets B. seems roughly to mean money-seeking writers who cultivate a vogue by licentious themes and treatment, usually, but not necessarily on the stage. At 14.15 Ovid is the "comic" author of the *Ars Amatoria*. At *Com.* 3 (12.144, 5) B. describes these "comic" poets as actually reciting stories of adulteries from a little stage in the midst of the theatre, which were forthwith enacted by mimes and buffoons to the general corruption of morals. I find no authority for such a statement, though it might come from

one who had read such passages as Ovid, *Trist.* 2.497-520; 5.7.25; Hor. *Ep.* 1.19.40 Juv. *Sat.* 8.186-98 (cf. Mayor's n. on 8.188); and the account of Menander's contemporary, Philemon, reading his comedy in an open-air theatre to a large crowd, Apuleius, *Flor.* 16. B. had also seen Augustine's attack, *C.D.* 2.14, on both actors and playwrights, whom Plato would expel. B.'s exception of Plautus and Terence may have something to do with Isidore, who distinguishes them from the satirists (*Etym.* 8.7.7), and elsewhere says that comedians were those who "privatorum hominum acta dictis atque gestis cantabant, atque stupra virginum et amores meretricum in suis fabulis exprimebant" (*Etym.* 18.46). At 14-16 Catullus and Propertius are coupled with Ovid, as in *Com.* 3 (12.149) are "comici disonesti" and "elegiaci passionati." But B.'s distinctions, if loose, serve well enough the rough and ready purposes of his argument. The moral distinction between good and bad poets is drawn by Aristotle (*Met.* 1.2; 14.8). B. had read Macrobius' clear and urgent statement, *Somn. Scip.* 1.2.6. ff., who mentions Apuleius and Petronius as sometimes errant. Petr. fortifies the distinction with Cicero (perhaps thinking of *Arch.* and *Tusc. Dis.* 2.27) and the Fathers.

26 *Hesiod . . . Claudian.* See 14.4 and n. 28.

14.20

1 This chapter, like 18 and 19, is reproduced in substance in *Com.* 3 (12.148, 9). The same matter is presented by Petr. in *Inv.* 1, p. 1091; 3, p. 1103; *Sen.* 15.11. But B. does not depend upon Petr. He quotes Boethius at greater length and develops the whole point more fully. The passage in Boethius seems to have been a stock weapon of the enemies of humanism; cf. Abelard, *Introd.* 2.701; *Theol. Christ.* 2.418.

2 *Gorgonian cave.* Perhaps the cave of the spring Hippocrene, which rose beneath the hoof of Pegasus, offspring of the Gorgon. B. may recall Propertius, "Gorgoneo . . . lacu" for Hippocrene (3.3.32); but cf. 14.16 n. 5. In 11.2 B. remarks the sacredness of springs and groves to the Muses, as solitary and therefore fit the poetic meditation as the noise of cities and the beaten highways are not.

3 *Beginning. De Cons. Phil.* 1, Prose 1.

4 *Diminutive.* "Scenicas meretriculas."

5 *Eleventh Book.* Chapter 2, where the "great men" are chiefly Macrobius, Isidore, and Fulgentius, especially the last, whose fantastic etymologies of the Muses' names B. quotes at length. But cf. Introd., pp. xvii, xxvi.

6 *I said.* 14.19.

7 *Comic poets.* See 14.19 and n. 25.

8 *A little later.* "Sed abite potius, Sirenes, usque in exitum dulces meisque eum Musis curandum sanandumque relinquite."

9 *Later cites.* Boethius makes such use of mythology in *De Cons. Phil.* 3, Metre 12; 4, Metre 7. He most frequently cites Homer and Horace. Lucan is "Familiaris noster," 4, Prose 6.

[1] *King Robert.* B. knew him during the dozen years of his first visit to Naples. In the *Ameto* he is the avaricious Midas. The beloved Fiammetta may have been a natural daughter of Robert (Hauvette, p. 44). Robert's knowledge of medicine is mentioned by B. in *Lett.* p. 138, and of this and other sciences by a comment on Petr. *Ecl.* 3, and by Petr. himself in ed. Frac. 1.209. See also B.'s Third Eclogue; and Petr.'s praise cited in Körting's *Petrarca's Leben*, p. 148; also 14.9; 11; 15.6; 13; and nn. Opinions vary widely concerning Robert's learning and mind, but of his enthusiasm and willing patronage there is no doubt. See W. Goetz, *König Robert von Neapel*, Tübingen, 1910; N. F. Faraglia, *Barbato di Sulmona e gli Uomini di Lettere della Corte di Roberto d'Angio*, in *Archivio Storico Italiano* 5.3 (1889).313-60; St. C. Baddely, *Robert the Wise and his Heirs*, 1897, pp. 271-8. His library (Faraglia 357 ff.) contained a rich collection of Provençal poets, but otherwise ran to patristics and the traditional learning of the time. The conservative or prescriptive tendency appears also in his 289 sermons listed by Goetz (47-68); cf. Hauvette p. 41 and n. 1. It is not surprising if he accepted the cant ecclesiastical objection to humanism without giving the matter much thought; nor if the charm of Vergil reinforced by the charm of Petr. proved a revelation to him in his old age. Petr.'s method was only the allegorical method, familiar to Robert, applied to a new text. One must remember also that the crowd of lesser men who in their enthusiasm for antiquity were harbingers of Petr. and B., were welcome at the brilliant Neapolitan court, and could count upon Robert's encouragement. See Goetz, pp. 38-43.

[2] *Sixty-sixth year.* Originally "seventieth" in the ms., corrected by the scribe to "sixty-sixth." In fact it was really his sixty-fourth, as he was born in 1278 (Goetz, p. 7 and reff. in notes 1, 2). But the usual date given until recently is "about 1275."

[3] *Actually heard.* "Eo dicente, meis auribus." The words create an unsolved problem. The incident of Petr.'s exposition of Vergil to Robert must have occurred in March, 1341, during his visit in Naples. But B. had left Naples in January of that year at the latest (Hauvette, p. 106), not to return till years after the death of Robert in 1343; presumably he never saw him again. How could he, then, have heard Robert tell the story? Furthermore, if he had been in Naples when Petr. was there, they would certainly have met; but by the testimony of both, this did not happen till 1350. Various possibilities have been suggested; perhaps the best is that the antecedent of "eo" is Petr., not Robert (suggested by Hecker, p. 259, n. 4), which indeed strains B.'s Latin a little, but not more than its flexible habit will stand. Petr. himself seems to refer to the anecdote in *Rer. Mem.* 1.2. 26 (p. 405 f.) in a vivid account of a conversation with Robert about poetry—"una vox ejus . . . quam ego meis auribus audivi"—words

so close to B.'s phrase above quoted that they may have been carelessly transcribed.

4 *Philosophy.* See 14.5.

5 *Comic writers.* See 14.19 and n. 25.

6 *Jerome.* See 14.4 n. 10; 14.8 and nn. 2, 22.

7 *Christian writers.* So Petr. (*Fam.* 10.4) cites Ambrose, Augustine,
and Jerome as Christian Fathers who "employed poetic forms and
rhythms"; and Prudentius, Prosper, and Sedulius, and the rest, as
Christians whose poems are "numerous" and well known.

8 *Dante.* See 14.10; 15.6.

9 *Mother tongue.* See 14.7 and n. 10.

10 *Theology.* Cf. 14.19; 15.8; *Life* 19 (12.88 ff.).

11 *Bucolics.* Petr. *Ecl.* 6, 7; cf. 14.10.

12 *Prudentius.* Fourth century. Greatest of early Christian poets,
author of the famous and influential allegorical poem *Psychomachia*
(cf. Bergman's ed., p. xxx); his technique was developed by schooling
in ancient poetry and rhetoric.

13 *Sedulius.* Fifth cent. Composer of the *Paschale Carmen* in
hexameters, dealing in doctrinal and allegorical fashion with the life
of Christ, especially the miracles and the Passion.

14 *Arator.* Sixth cent. For his poem on the Acts see *Patr. Lat.* 68.
63-246. It was a popular mediaeval textbook, chiefly allegorical. See
Manitius, *Gesch. der Lat. Lit. des Mittelalters,* Müller's *Handbuch*
9.2.1, pp. 163-7.

15 *Juvencus.* Fourth cent. First poet known to have treated a
Christian subject with ancient epic technique. Saturated with Homer
and Vergil, he composed his *Evangelica Historica*—not an allegorical
poem. B. had probably glanced only at the Proem, where, in eight
lines, the types of the Evangelists are stated.

16 *Origen.* Epiphanius, *Adv. Haereses* 2.1.64. 63: *Patr. Gr.* 41.1177,
says that Origen himself put the number of his books at 6,000. The
statement is quoted from Rufinus in turn by Jerome, *Contra Ruf.*
3.23: *Patr. Lat.* 23.495. After centuries of controversy certain doc-
trines of Origen were condemned by Justinian in 545, and formally
anathematized by the Council of 553. These were chiefly in his
treatise *De Principiis,* heresies on the Trinity, the preexistence
of the soul, the resurrection of the body. See Mansi, *Conciliorum
Omnium Amplissima Collectio* 3.982-4; 9.487-534; 655 ff. Except that
Origen is often quoted by the orthodox I do not find that the Church
has formally distinguished his orthodox writings from the rest.
See H. R. Percival, *The Seven Ecumenical Councils,* vol. 14 of the
Second Series of *A Select Library of Nicene and Post Nicene Fathers,*
pp. 318-20, for the anathemas.

17 *Jeromes.* See 14.5.

18 *Archias.* Chaps. 16, 17.

15.Pr.

[1] *Little craft.* See 14.Pr. and n. 6.

[2] *Israelites.* Dan. 3.19 ff.

15.1

[1] *No use.* Cf. 14.4.

[2] *Mistake.* As he proves it in 14.6, 9.

[3] *House.* Similar figure at 15.2.

[4] *Samian.* Primitive, and, in more luxurious Roman days, humbler kind of pottery. Cf. Plautus, *Stichus* 5.4.11; Tibullus 2.3.49; Pliny, *N.H.* 35.46.

[5] *Caesar.* Suetonius, *Caesar* 45.

[6] *Beard.* Hecker somehow infers from this passage that B. in later life wore a beard. He cites *Corbaccio* (ed. Moutier, 5.183, 243), where B. twice refers to his white beard. But B. certainly means only "growth of beard." Cf. 9.33, end, where Hercules' rape of Cerberus' beard signifies the dog's loss of strength and fierceness. "For Nature gave men beards in proof of their virility, as Gregory says in his *Moralia.*"

[7] *Embellishment.* Possibly reminiscent of Augustine, *C.D.* 23.24, where he dwells at length on utility and beauty in God's creation: "There are some things, too, which have such a place in the body, that they obviously serve no useful purpose, but are solely for beauty, as e.g. . . . the beard on his [man's] face; for that is for ornament." "Shall I speak of the manifold and various loveliness of sky, and earth, and sea? . . . of the multitude of birds, all differing in plumage and in song . . .?" But the contrast between mere utilitarian and higher values, already touched upon at 14.4, 6 (see 14.4, n. 12), seems to derive, at least for the fourteenth century, from Aristotle. Cf. *Politics* 1.11.1258b.10; 1.7, to which passage Petr. may refer in *Inv.* 3, p. 1101 (bottom). On the general subject in Aristotle see W. L. Newman's ed. of the *Politics* 1.111-15.

[8] *Occasional story.* See Introd., p. xxix.

[9] *Cicero or Jerome.* B. may recall such instances as *Ep.* 43, 60, 79, 108, 123, *Adv. Jovin.* 1. 41-3; in Cicero perhaps the *Tusculan Disputations,* or the *Actions against Verres,* from the second of which (4.50) he cites a myth at *Com.* 29 (13.232). See *De Or.* 2.80: "A narration [in the course of a speech] . . . affords much gratification" (tr. Watson); cf. 2.66. The same passage may be in B.'s mind at 14.12; cf. n. 2. But the same idea he was as likely to find in *De Invent.* 1.19, or *Ad Herenn.* 1.8.

[10] *Some men.* Answered in 14.10, 14.

[11] *Brought back to life.* This fine passage not only utters B.'s patriotic purpose in his work as a scholar, but is a noble expression of the humanistic spirit which he shared with Petr. See Introd. pp. xv, xliii ff.; Pref., p. 11.

NOTES

¹² *I hope.* On the abundant fulfilment of this hope see Introd., pp. xliii ff.

15.2

¹ *I anticipated.* Pref. pp. 6, 11; 14.2.

² *Fortress.* Architectural figure at 15.1, and just below.

³ *Aglaus.* See 14.4 and n. 21.

⁴ *The Lord watches.* Ps. 127 (Vulg. 126). 1. The next sentences seem to echo Wisd. 8.8; Ps. 90 (89). 1-4; 33 (32). 11; 18; 62.7 (61.8 "Spes mea in Deo est"); I Pet. 1.21. Giveth grace, I Pet. 5.5.

15.3

¹ *Better order.* See 15.12, n. 1.

² *Chest.* Anatomical figure resumed from Pref. p. 11.

³ *Socrates.* See 14.18. Perhaps B. recalls the saying from Petr. *Inv.* 1.1089. I have not found the ancient source.

⁴ *Most ancient.* See 14. Pr. n. 4.

15.4

¹ *Near the beginning.* See Pref. pp. 8, 9.

² *Lapse of memory.* See 14.15, n. 6.

³ *God only.* Possible reminiscence of Deut. 32.4: "Dei perfecta sunt opera et omnes viae ejus judicia; Deus fidelis et absque ulla iniquitate, justus et rectus."

⁴ *Philosophy.* See 14.5.

⁵ *Horace.* A.P. 359.

⁶ *Argus.* B. tells the tale at *G.D.* 7. 27 (cf. 9.1) after Ovid, *Met.* 1.622 ff.

⁷ *Old age.* "Totis pedibus in senium tendam." B. died at 62. He may have been 58 when he wrote this. Cf. 15. 10. Dante, *Conv.* 4.24, says that "senettute" lies between 45 and 70, and "senio" begins at 70. In a letter written perhaps as early as 49 he mentions "canum caput meum et aetas provectior" (*Lett.*, p. 125). In his forties his hair grew gray; cf. Körting, *Boccaccio,* pp. 207, 277.

15.5

¹ *Commentaries.* See below 15.6 where B. is more explicit. But, though it there appears (near end) that his word "commentaries" may be taken literally, yet he cannot refer especially to the ancient commentators whom he ordinarily cites—Servius, Lactantius, Macrobius, Fulgentius—who could hardly be called unfamiliar in B.'s time. Possibly he has in mind elucidating comment at first or second hand which he cites from Cicero's *De Natura Deorum* and *Tusculan Disputations,* or such authors as Livy, Pomponius Mela, Varro, Quintilian, or the Greek philosophers of whose lives and opinions he learned chiefly from Valerius Maximus, or his copy of John of Wales (Hecker, p. 32).

² *Easy to read.* At 15.12 B. says that he has written more easily

and obviously for the sake of the less cultivated readers whom he wishes to include in his audience. He is generally easier than Petr., partly by nature, but often in his conscious desire to propagate the study of poetry and the Ancients.

³ The points of this chapter are a little confused. It answers in effect the charge that B. has been recondite, both in matter and style, for mere ostentation.

15.6

¹ *Approved by the great lapse of time.* Though B. ostensibly is speaking of the authority of various writers on this subject, mythology, the whole chapter reminds us that to him mythology and poetry are often synonymous, and that these opening words express his opinion on the duration of literature, and on novelty as an early evidence of its greatness.

² *Andalò di Negro.* B. cites him at least twelve times in the *G.D.* as an authority on points of astronomy, astrology, or chronology; also at *Com.* 20 (13.140), and in *De Cas.* 3.1. He is probably the Calmeta of *Filocolo* 5 (*Op. Volg.* ed. Moutier, 8.243 ff.), as shown by E. H. Wilkins in *M.L.N.* 21.212-6. He is usually "venerabilis" and "senex," but is "festivus" and "hilari vultu," and "placidi et flexibilis ingenii" in *De Cas.,* where B. gives a glimpse of Andalò in the act of teaching him and others. He came of noble Genoese family, born not later than 1260, was, in 1314, a successful ambassador to the Emperor of Trebisond. He may have known Marco Polo. Another pupil of his, some time Bishop of Isola, has left in ms. an astronomical treatise. Andalò died in 1334. If not quite first-rate in his time as an astronomer, he enjoyed high and long reputation, no doubt helped by B.'s citations. He is cited by E.K. in *S.C., Gen. Arg.* He also had some fame as a poet, but his surviving works are on astronomy or astrology. B. Boncampagni (*Bulletino di Bibliografia e di Storia delle Scienze Mathematiche e Fisiche* 7 (1874)) mentions fourteen works from his hand, of which only three have been printed. He adds thirteen others cited in various places, some of which may be identical with Andalò's surviving works. The best account of him is by De Simoni, *Intorno alla Vita,* etc. in the *Bulletino* 7(1874). 313-38. The Laurentian Library contains copies of two of his treatises which once belonged to B.

³ *Cicero.* See 14.3 and n. 5. In *De Cas.* 6 B. praises the eloquence of Cicero without qualification.

⁴ *Dante.* See 14.10, 11, 22. B. cites Dante also at *G.D.* 1.21; 3.5; 3.17; 8.

⁶ He is never tired of praising him. He gave Petr. a copy of the *Divine Comedy,* with verses gently remonstrating with Petr.'s indifference to Dante, to which Petr. protests (B.'s *Lett.* 53-65; Petr. *Fam.* 21.15). Besides his *Life of Dante* and his *Comento,* he praises Dante in his letter to Pizzinghe (*Lett.* 194), and includes him among the great philosophers in the *Amorosa Visione* (close of 5 and beginning of 6),

a poem in imitation of Dante. Cf. close of *Filocolo*. Of his importance in theology and of his learning B. speaks at length in *Life* 1; cf. 9. B. told Petr. that Dante had been the first light and guide of his juvenile studies (*Fam.* 21.15). See A. Dobelli, *Il Culto del B. per Dante* in *Giornale Dantesco* 5. 193-224.

⁵ *Francis of Barberino*. Cited only once in *G.D.* (9.4) for an allegorical description of Cupid. His poem, *Reggimento delle Donne* is quoted in *De Claris Mulieribus* 37. Villani calls him "semipoeta," and says that he understood poetry better than he wrote it. He wrote also *Documenti d'Amore*. His poems were intended ostensibly to castigate the loose morals of parvenus in Florence. He died in 1348 at 83; his epitaph in Santa Croce has been attributed to B. (Hortis 514-5; 83; 793; Villani, *Liber de Civ. Flor. Famosis Civibus,* ed. Galletti, 1847, pp. 31,2).

⁶ *Barlaam*. Cf. Pref. p. 5; 14. 8. B. cites him some twenty times in Books 1-11, chiefly as an authority for euhemeristic interpretation of myths. Though a Calabrian, born near Reggio at Seminara, he went to Constantinople, became a monk of St. Basil and Abbot of San Salvatore. He engaged in furious controversy over the orthodoxy of the monks at Mt. Athos. He was twice sent as ambassador to the Pope by the Emperor—in 1339 to Benedict XII, in 1342 to Clement VI. In 1342 Petr. met him at Avignon, and agreed to instruct him in Latin in return for much desired lessons in elementary Greek. But the lessons had not gone far when Barlaam was elevated, with Petr.'s support, to the bishopric of Geraci, Calabria, where he died in 1347 (*Fam.* 18.2: Frac. 4.90; 24.5: Frac. 5.193; *Var.* 25; *Sen.* 11.9; *De Contemptu Mundi* 2, p. 346; *De sui . . . Ignor.,* p. 1054). Petr. implies that Barlaam taught not merely the elements of Greek, but gave him some insight into the thought of Plato, whose works in Greek Petr. owned. In 1339 Barlaam spent some time at Naples, where he helped Paul, the King's librarian, as B. says; perhaps B. knew him then. He taught Leontius also (14.8). See Hortis, pp. 498-502; de Nolhac, *Pétrarque e l'Humanisme* 2.135-41; A. Mandalari, *Fra Barlaamo Calabrese,* Rome, 1888; who prints a list of 38 works, of which those in Latin rather obviate Petr.'s and B.'s disparagement of his Latin culture; F. LoParco, *Petrarca e Barlaam,* Reggio, 1905.

⁷ *Paul of Perugia*. B. cites him frequently, and, through him, the lost Theodontius, chiefly on genealogical details. From him or Theodontius B. seems to have taken the notion of Demogorgon as father of all the gods. Paul was no longer young when he came to Naples in or before 1332 when B. first knew him. The *Collections* may well have been in course of compilation through several years (see next note), and may, indeed, have suggested to B. his own more complete and literary work, the *G.D.* By 1348 Paul was dead. His last years were dark and miserable. Useful and important as he must have been in the learned group through which Robert created the high culture of his court, yet for some reason Paul left before Robert died, and

with his family fell into indigence, perhaps beggary. Robert and Joanna both granted him permission to practise as a notary in Terra di Lavoro. Poor Biella, much-tried wife and widow, doubtless had a bit of reason on her side. Life with this improvident scholar and his ill-nourished offspring had been no joy. It was all these useless books that were to blame. And now to get even! The surviving "works" are only some memoranda or genealogical notes chiefly from Ovid and Vergil, and a commentary on Persius. See Faraglia, *Barbato di Sulmone e gli Uomini di Lettere della Corte di Roberto d'Angio*, in *Archivio Stor. Ital.* 5.3 (1889). 320-6; Baddeley, *Robert the Wise and his Heirs*, 1897; below 15.13 and n. 6.

[8] *Youngster.* "Juvenculus"; B. was about 16 when he went to Naples in 1328 (Hauvette, pp. 26, 7); Paul was there by 1332 (Faraglia, p. 321), when B. was 19. If a copy of his *Collections* was then available for B., it must have undergone later revision, since B. says that Paul had Barlaam's help, and Barlaam did not come until 1339.

[9] *Theodontius.* An unidentified writer whose works are lost, and whom some have thought fictitious. Servius (on *Aen.* 1.28) speaks of "Theodotius, qui Iliacas res perscripsit"; and Domenico Bandini, contemporary with B., who made an index of *G.D.*, refers to "Teodontius Campanus diligens investigator poetici figmenti" (Sabbadini, *Stud. Ital. di Filologia Classica* 5 (1897).377). Otherwise he survives only in B.'s citations in *G.D.* B. says he is *not* "novus homo" (Pref. to *G.D.* in an appended paragraph, which I have omitted). Hortis gives the best account of him (pp. 464-8). B. held his authority in high esteem, sometimes above Paul's, and even above Servius, Lactantius, Eusebius, Pliny, Ovid, and Cicero. Yet he discredits him at times. Theodontius wrote in Latin, but cites more obscure Greek authors. B. cites him particularly for euhemeristic and naturalistic interpretations, on chronology, etymology, and genealogy. Hortis collected all B.'s citations of Theodontius with a view to restoration of his work, but never published the results. He concludes, but upon insufficient evidence, I think, that B. actually had a copy of Theodontius' work, besides the citations in Paul's *Collections* (p. 466).

[10] *Leontius.* See also 15.7 and n. 10. The strange Greek scholar whom Petr. met at Padua in 1358-9, and employed to make a Latin version of *Iliad* 1-5, or parts thereof (De Nolhac 2. 172-4); and whom B., within a year or so, dissuaded from his intention to go to Avignon, and brought to Florence to translate Homer. Petr. is even stronger than B. in his personal dislike of Leontius (*Sen.* 3.6; 5.3). Leontius was really a Calabrian, Petr. says, though he tells the Latins that he was born at Thessalonica, as he doubtless tells the Greeks that he is a Latin. He is a "magna bellua" in manners, restless, hypochondriac, affecting singularity to advertise himself, disparaging Italy, praising the East, till Petr. gladly speeds him on his way with a copy of Terence, and wishes him back in the miseries of his Constantinople, where he belongs! In 1367 (*Sen.* 6.1) it is a different tune,

when he hears how the poor fellow died by lightning at sea on his way back to Italy. Leontius is cited by B. in *G.D.* perhaps 50 times, as authority on etymologies, genealogy ("talium abundantissimus," 2.2) chronology, details of myths, and various interpretations, particularly euhemeristic. Heavily as he leans upon him, B. does not always approve, and even calls his theory "frivola" at 3.20. See Hortis, pp. 502-8, for résumé of Leontius' service to B. Cf. Pref. n. 10; 14.13, n. 30; 14.19, nn. 4, 12. For nearly three years Leontius lived in B.'s house in Florence, translating Homer, and B. seems to have made much of this opportunity to get information for the *G.D.* On Leontius' scholarship see G. Finsler, *Homer in der Neuzeit*, p. 16.

¹¹ *Paul the Geometrician.* Otherwise Paolo dell' Abaco, or Paolo di ser Piero Dagomari da Prato. Mentioned again at 15.13 as an intermediary between King Hugo and B. He died in 1367 on or just before Feb. 27. Salutato laments him as an eloquent, amiable, and successful astrologer, in a letter of this date, which is therefore the latest possible date of at least this passage in B. See Salutato, *Epistolario*, ed. Novati, 1.15, 345. B. apparently cites Paolo only once—at *G.D.* 8.2. B.'s eulogy here, so in excess of his debt, is clearly a proof of his sincere admiration.

¹² *Petrarch.* In the first thirteen books B. cites Petr. hardly more than half a dozen times; in the part here translated, however, he lays him under heavy contribution and often mentions him. See Introd., p. xli; Pref., pp. 57, 8; 14.10; 11; 19 (twice); 22 (twice); 15.13, 14. B. praises him always in unqualified terms, and here and elsewhere exalts him as a Latin poet of course, and a man of letters. See *Ecl.* 12, 15, 16; *De Cas.* 3.14; 9.27; *Lett.*, 243 (verses on *Africa*); 267; 355; 369; *Com.* 56 (2.428); *De Fontibus*, s.v. Sorgia. B. here mentions not all the Latin works of Petr. he knew (Hortis, p. 513), but those he has cited in *G.D.*: *Africa*, written 1339-52, not published in Petr.'s lifetime (cited 6.53); *Eclogues*, finished before 1356, cited 11.1; metrical *Epistles*, written "in his youth"—*Sen.* 3.4, cited 7.29; letters— *De Rebus Familiaribus*, collected 1359-61; *Variae*, collected 1361, both most important to B.'s defense of poetry, esp. *Fam.* 10.4; *Invective against the Physician*, 1352; cited 7.36; *On the Solitary Life*, 1347-54?, cited 4.44; 14.10; *On the Remedies of Fortune*, 1358-66, cited 14.10. Of unfinished work perhaps B. has in mind the *De Sui Ipsius et Multorum Ignorantia*, 1367-70.

¹³ *Not many years.* "Nuper"—twenty-five in fact. The *De Remediis*, here mentioned as "about to see the light in a few days," was finished in 1366. Petr. was crowned in 1341. Thus "nuper" is stretching— or contracting—twenty-five years, and my translation stretches "nuper." Curiously enough, in *G.D.* 6.53 B. uses "nuper" of this same event, and in 7.29 "jam pridem"—"long since"! If, as Hauvette maintains (he overlooks this last point), Books 14, 15 were an afterthought written not earlier than 1366, how explain these inconsistencies? I cannot, unless we are to suppose that, with the dedication to

Hugo and other details that date the work, B. found it impracticable to revise the whole to conform with the date of his later changes and additions, and gratuitously dropped in this "nuper" for consistency with the earlier and first-intended date of the book, as in 15.13 he has maintained and defended the dedication to Hugo as if he were alive, though he had been dead now these seven years at least.

[14] *Robert.* In his letter to Posterity (*Fam.* I. 209-10) Petr. tells how King Robert, after three days' examination of his learning, and inspection of his poem *Africa,* of which Robert requested the dedication, sent him on to Rome with the recommendation to the honor of the laurel crown. This was in 1341. See also *Fam.* 4.7; *Res Mem.* I, end, pp. 405, 6.

[15] *England.* It is customary for B.'s contemporaries to refer to England after the precedent of Verg. *Ecl.* 66; Hor. *Od.* 1.35.29; 4.14. 47; Catull. 11.11. Cf. Pref., p. 55; *Com.* 6 (12.190). At *G.D.* 6.57 B. mentions the barbarism of the English; at *De Cas.* 9.27 they are cowards and cravens.

[16] *A little above.* "Paulo ante," referring to earlier passages in this work (see n. 2), as it does twice at 14.18, and elsewhere. Hecker is mistaken in his attempt to refer it to a lost *Apologia* mentioned by Petr. *Sen.* 15.4, in 1373, and written between 1368 and 1371, and hence to date this passage later than the *Apologia.*

[17] *Stripped of the aids.* The reading in Hecker, "a se narrata non habet," to which he supplies "commentata," is, as he admits, less intelligible than M.'s: "his caret subsidiis." I follow M.

15.7

[1] *Greek poetry.* Hortis (pp. 384 ff.) enumerates, besides Homer, of whom B. knew something at first hand, Hesiod, of whom he learned from Pliny, Servius, Macrobius, and Leontius; the *Orphic Hymns,* from Lactantius; Phanocles, from Eusebius; Callimachus, Lycophron, from Leontius; Alcman, from Macrobius; Archilochus, from Eusebius; Euripides, Aeschylus from Macrobius and others; Sappho, from Ovid, Eusebius, and others. *G.D.* contains 46 quotations in Greek, all from Homer but one (14.19 and n. 11). These are said to be the first Greek quotations in any work of modern humanism. See Wilkins, *The University of Chicago Manuscript,* etc., pp. 9-12; Hecker, pp. 137-57.

[2] *Homer's Works.* Doubtless the copy from which Leontius made his Latin version (15.6). In 1360 B. wrote to Petr. asking him to purchase a copy of Homer which had been reported for sale in Padua. But Petr. on inspection found it an inferior example (*Var.* 25, Frac. 5.303). Nevertheless he promised his best efforts to procure it, and offered, if it was no longer available, to send his own fine copy procured for him by Sigeros in 1364 (*Fam.* 4.88) to be used in Leontius' translation. This proved unnecessary (deNolhac, 2.159, n.), for, it would seem, B. bought the Padua copy.

[3] *Drew . . . much.* Besides the quotations just mentioned, B. often cites a name or epithet in Greek. Cf. Introd., p. xxvi; Pref., p. 6 and n. 10. Second-hand citation occurs at 6.39 (Servius); 6.45 (Paul); 11.7 (Cicero); but he makes some endeavor to test these references by consulting the original.

[4] *Apuleius.* B. owned a copy which he had made (Hecker, p. 34).

[5] *Opuscula.* The name for the complete works of Ausonius. But B. has in mind his *Epistles,* particularly *Ep.* 12, a macaronic not only of Greek and Latin words, but of Latin words with Greek endings and *vice versa.*

[6] *Nobody now knows Greek.* In *Fam.* 18.2: Frac. 4.90, and 24.12: 5.186 Petr. bewails the decadent ignorance of Greek in his day. He says that in 1360 there were, or have been, in Florence five who knew Homer; at Bologna one; at Verona two; at Solmona one; and at Mantua one. Others of whom he has heard are now dead or have abandoned their studies (5.192 f.).

[7] *Sufficient unto itself.* B. is not so unequivocal as Petr. in claiming the superiority of Latin to Greek literature. See Petr. *Sen.* 12.2: Frac. 2.262.

[8] *Again.* "De hoc alias." But B. may refer back to such a passage as Pref., pp. 7, 8.

[9] *Erudite monarch.* Hecker points out what appears to be at least an inaccuracy in this passage. Hugo IV died Oct. 10, 1359. Nay, more, he ceased to be king Nov. 24, 1358 (Mas Latrie 2.225; Hecker overlooks this). Now the translation of Homer could not have begun before Sept. 1360 (Petr. *Var.* 25), and it is improbable that it would take two years or more for B. to learn that Hugo was no longer king. But the point is not important. His vast compilation was oft interrupted and resumed. Very likely B. was disappointed not to have it finished by 1358, when Hugo abdicated; but he may not have thought it worth the trouble, in his hope of early completion, to revise the dedication. Then, as completion was longer and longer deferred, he may have found it easier to resort to the expedient of 15.13. In the present passage it is possible that the sentences from "Was it not I" to "embodied in this work" are a later insertion.

[10] *Leontius.* See 15.6 and n. 10. B. intercepted Leontius probably by letter, not in person (Hecker, p. 372, n. 10; Voigt, *Wiederbelebung* 2.110 n.). Leontius was in Florence probably from April, 1360, to October, 1362, living at least some of the time in B.'s house. The consent of the Florentine burghers to pay his salary was not so purely humanistic as might appear. Would it not help trade with the East to know a bit of Greek (de Nolhac 2. 158; cf. revival of Spanish in the United States)? The expression "at my own expense" has given rise to much discussion, as opposed to Petr.'s statement (*Lett. Sen.* 16.1) that the translation of Homer was made "mea opera et impensa." Partisans of either of the two humanists have contended for the credit of each for reintroducing Homer to the modern world by a transla-

tion. A prolix and not wholly impartial *résumé* of the discussion may be found in Zenatti, pp. 282-326. DeNolhac may be right in saying that Petr. means that he paid Leontius for his work, and that B. had "called back" to Tuscany various writers by purchasing their works, particularly the Padua *Homer,* from which the translation was made (2.162, 3). The documentary evidence shows not the slightest rivalry between the two friends in this matter. But, if Petr. paid Leontius for his translation of Homer, one wonders that a copy did not come into his possession for seven years (deNolhac 2.165), and that Petr. showed no impatience, but refers to it in writing to thank B. for the copy as "Homerum *tuum* latinum mittentis amorem renovantem." One may conclude that the first impelling suggestion that Leontius translate Homer came from Petr. Indeed he seems as early as 1358-9 to have employed him in a Latin version of all, or parts, of *Il.* 1-5 (deNolhac 2.172-4). Petr. may have advanced some money for the complete translation, but it was left to the care and energy of B. to see the thing through, with considerable expense to himself for a copy of Homer, and for the entertainment of a very inconvenient guest. Petr.'s pride of achievement, and B.'s ever generous acknowledgment of his friend's superiority, and his characteristic modesty and deference must be taken into account. Leontius' version is now found in Cod. 7880.2 in the Bibliothèque Nationale. *Il.* 1 and *Od.* 1 are printed by Hortis, pp. 543-76; *Od.* 7 by Professor Albert S. Cook in *Philological Quarterly* 4.25-38; *Il.* 21.74-96 in Baldelli, *Vita di B.* 264 n.; and in Bernays, *Pentas Versionum Homericarum* 1,2; the passage is quoted by B. at *G.D.* 6.31. Cf. C. C. Coulter, *B.'s Acquaintance with Homer* in *Philological Quarterly* 5.44-53.

[11] *Marius . . . Duellius.* B. doubtless drew the stories from Valerius Maximus (3-6). Valerius' tone is not commendatory, but B. here, as elsewhere, is counting on his opponents' ignorance. Valerius mentions Marius' birthplace at 6.9.14. B. gives the life of Marius in *De Cas.* 6.

[12] *Valerius' words.* 8.14.5: "Nulla est ergo tanta humilitas, quae dulcedine gloriae non tangatur."

15.8

[1] *Theologians.* See 14.8 and n. 19.

[2] *City of God.* 6.5: "Now what are we to say of this proposition of his [Varro's], namely, that there are three kinds of theology, that is, of the account which is given of the gods; and of these, the one is called mythical, the other physical, and the third civil? Did the Latin usage permit, we should call the kind which he has placed first in order *fabular* (*fabulare*), but let us call it *fabulous* (*fabulosum*), for mythical is derived from the Greek μῦθος, a fable; but that the second should be called *natural,* the usage of speech now admits; the third he himself has designated in Latin, calling it *civil.* Then he says, 'they call that kind *mythical* which the poets chiefly use; *physical*

that which the philosophers use; *civil,* that which the people use.'"
Augustine condemns the first and third forthwith. For the second,
embodying as it does profound if erroneous doctrine about nature and
God, he has more respect (*C.D.* 7.5 ff.). On this B. leans, though one
suspects his citation of Augustine as a flourish for effect upon his
opponents. The same citation of Varro is quoted by Tertullian,
Ad Nat. 2.1.

[3] *Already said.* Pp. 6, 38.

[4] *Comic stage.* 14.19 and n. 25.

[5] *Aristotle.* 14.8, n. 19.

[6] *Physiology or ethology.* According as the myths are seen to express the facts of nature, or to embody "history" of moral truth.

[7] In the vulgate text follows the sentence: "Did not our Dante weave
the veil of his poetry about the truth that lies in the bosom of sacred
theology?"

[8] *The trees.* 14.9 and n. 16.

15.9

[1] This chapter, with its recital of the Creed, its abundant commentary, its citations from the Gospels and the very Fathers who
furnished B. opponents with arguments, its anxious display of
orthodoxy, is by no means irrelevant. It is aimed at the instinctive and
in some measure reasonable fear of the classics on the part of many
devout men who suspected the charm of the Ancients and their power
to divert the interest of cultivated men from Christianity. See Introd.,
p. xxxiv. B. displays his Christian zeal again in a fierce exhortation to
a Crusade in the Proem of Bk. 9. Salutato meets the same objection in
replies to Giuliano Zonarini in 1378, 9, in *Ep.* 1.302; 323, 4 (quoted
by Zenatti, p. 328, n.). Hortis, p. 203, quotes Petr. *Fam.* 10.4; and a
letter of Salutato to Brother Giovanni of San Miniato.

[2] *Sacred source.* Esp. Augustine, Jerome, Lactantius; see below
p. 128.

[3] *Dog.* Prov. 26.11.

[4] *Slightest danger.* B. could not, of course, foresee the excesses in
paganism of the sixteenth century.

[5] *Creed.* In *Ecl.* 11 B. again rehearses the mysteries of the faith,
beginning with the Creation, and ingeniously veiling all in the names
and incidents of pagan myth. Cf. "Pluto" below. He there, as here,
especially mentions Christ's teaching among the doctors, the miracle
at Cana, and the portents at the Crucifixion. Cf. Hortis, pp. 46-8. The
following passage, though it traces the outline of the Creed, is filled
with details from all four Gospels—the Magi (Matt. 2), "his thirtieth
year" (Lk. 3.23), the miracle at Cana (Jno. 2), vinegar and *myrrh*
(Mk. 15-23), the sun turned to darkness (Lk. 23.45), the spearman
(Jno. 19.34). It seems to rest upon the *Catena Aurea* of Thomas
Aquinas, or some compilation deriving therefrom.

[6] *Sabean kings.* Is. 45.14.

[7] *God saying.* B. has confused the words of the Father at the

Baptism of Jesus with those at the Transfiguration (Matt. 3.17; 17.5);
cf. 14.15, n. 6.

[8] *Aquinas.* Another flourish of orthodoxy. Various patristic commentators cited in the *Catena Aurea* make it a point that Christ died voluntarily. Cf. also Aquinas, *Summa Theol.* Pt. 3, qu. 47, art. 1, 3, esp.: "sic etiam quando voluit, subito cessit nocumento illato."

[9] *The moon.* The sun is mentioned only by Luke (23.45), and the moon in none of the Gospel accounts. B. may have read in the *Catena* Augustine's comment that the darkening was not an eclipse because the moon is full at Passover, and an eclipse of the full moon is impossible. The *Catena* quotes also the pseudo-Dionysius' letter to Polycarp (*Ep.* 7), testifying that he and another man were at Heliopolis at the time of the Crucifixion, and saw a miraculous conjunction of the sun and moon. No eclipse was due, and the moon was by miracle moved out of its place. The point of difference is petty, as B. knows, but it will impress scrupulous opponents.

[10] *Sacraments.* In the *Catena,* on Jno. 19.34, Augustine is quoted: "Whereby was opened the gate of life, from whence the sacraments of the Church flowed, without which we cannot enter into that life which is the true life."

[11] *Jonah.* A traditional interpretation set forth at length by Augustine, *Ep.* 102.30: *Patr. Lat.* 33.382. See Matt. 12.40.

[12] *Seed.* Alluding to the famous and oft misquoted words of Tertullian: "semen est sanguis Christianorum" (*Apol. adv. Gentes* 50, end: *Patr. Lat.* 1.603).

[13] *Fathers.* Another flourish. I Cor. 15 and the Creed are enough.

[14] *Terence. Eunuchus* 3.5.35-43. B. may have recalled Augustine's citation of the same instance, *Conf.* 1.16.

[15] *Snares and nets.* In the context apparently a reminiscence of Eccl. 7.26, though B.'s words "decipulis, retibus" are closer to Job 18.8-10. Lion; see I Pet. 5.8.

[16] *Mithridates.* Pliny, *N.H.* 25.2.3, or Aulus Gellius 17.16.

[17] *Armed my breast.* Eph. 6.11, 13, 16.

[18] Hecker cites Ovid, *Met.* 5.416, 7.

[19] *Saintly men.* So Petr. cites the precedent of Ambrose, Augustine, Jerome, Cyprian, Victorinus, Lactantius, whose works abound in evidence of study of the poets (*Inv.* 3, p. 1101). See 14.18 and nn. 16-19. B. may have in mind also Jerome's *Ep.* 70, *Patr. Lat.* 22,664, where Jerome defends the proper use of secular literature by the precedents of Moses, Solomon, the prophets, Paul, the implication of the captive woman, of David seizing the sword of Goliath. He gives a long list of Christian writers who have profited by the classics, including Lactantius, pupil of Arnobius, and his debt to Cicero's dialogues.

[20] *Psalmist's testimony.* Ps. 96 (Vulg. 95). 5. See Introd., p. xxii, n. 19.

[21] *Praised . . . defended.* Above, 14.13, 15.

22 *Toucheth pitch.* Ecclus. 31.1.

23 *Moloch.* I Kings 11.7 (Vulg. III Reg.). Cf. II Kings 23.13 (IV Reg.): "Excelsa [altaria] quoque quae erant in Jerusalem ad dexteram partem montis Offensionis, quae aedificaverat Salomon."

24 *The sex.* Hecker cites *De Cas.* 1.18. The notion is fixed in B.'s mind.

25 *From my youth.* His so-called conversion occurred in 1361, when B. was about 48. This he would not have called youth (cf. 15.4 and n. 7). Hecker (p. 300) cites evidence to show that B. was essentially religious throughout his life. It is easy, of course, to weigh against this his irregularities of living, his pornography, his criticism of the clergy, and a certain ostentation or convention of religious utterance. But it is correspondingly difficult for a man of the present thus to judge a man of the fourteenth century on this point. Everything considered, one cannot doubt that from his earliest recollection B.'s sentiments, inclinations, and beliefs had been essentially religious.

15.10

1 *Laws.* See 14.4 and nn. 1, 3. "Medicine" alludes to Petr.'s *Inv.* which B. has laid under heavy contribution in this treatise.

2 *Philosophy.* A glance at two of the three parts of Philosophy as distinguished by Plato and set forth by Augustine, *C.D.* 8.4—the first, moral; the second, natural, "quae contemplationi deputata est; tertiam rationalem, qua verum disterminatur a falso."

3 *Sacred books.* Holy Writ and the Fathers.

4 *Harp.* The figure is suggested perhaps by Augustine's quotation in *C.D.* 2.21 from Cicero's *Dream of Scipio,* wherein the harmony resulting from combinations of high tones and low, whether in stringed or wind instruments, is made analogous with the harmonious combinations of high and lowly ranks and functions necessary to the successful state. A slightly different use of the figure of the harp by Augustine (*C.D.* 16.2, end) is quoted by B. at *Com.* 6, end (12.194).

5 *Different pursuits.* In *G.D.* 1.3 B. reasons: As men differ in feature, so they differ in choice. Achilles preferred arms to inaction, Aegistheus inaction to arms. Plato renounced all for the pursuit of philosophy. The Celts carved statues, Phidias (!) and Apelles painted pictures. The poet preferred to veil the truth in fiction. Petr. touches on such variation at *Inv.* 3, p. 1105, bottom, mentioning farmers, sailors, physicians. But a passage far closer in argument and detail to this in B. is Petr. *Fam.* 20.4: Frac. 4.261; cf. *Fam.* 4.15, end. Zenatti cites also Dante, *Par.* 8.118-26; 139-48.

6 *Mother's womb.* Hauvette would read this as a warm acknowledgment that B. owed to his unknown French mother his talent for poetry (p. 22).

7 *Six years.* The chronology of B.'s early years has given no little difficulty. Hauvette's conclusions, since none can be final, are perhaps the most reasonable: that B. from 12 to 17 (1325-30) was an appren-

tice in business; that at 15 or 16 he went to Naples; that from 18 to 23 (1331-36) he studied canon law; that in 1336 he fell in love with Fiammetta and abandoned all else for poetry (Hauvette, pp. 23-8).

[8] *Teacher.* Possibly Dante's friend, Cino da Pistoia, professor of civil law at Naples, 1330-31 (cf. Hauvette, p. 32).

[9] *Canon-lawyer.* During the residence of the Papacy at Avignon, canon law offered a larger career than civil law. "Distinction in Canon Law at the Universities and practice at the Bar of the Ecclesiastical Courts constituted the great avenue to fame and preferments" (Rashdall, *Universities of Europe* 1.261).

[10] *Old man.* He commends Solon (14.19) and Robert (14.22) for turning to poetry late in life. But here he is speaking of taking up a new subject with professional seriousness.

[11] *Cultivate the poets.* This fascinating bit of autobiography was penned no doubt in full consciousness of its parallel to Petr.'s experience, as narrated in *Fam.* 20.4; *Inv.* 3, p. 1107, top; *Sen.* 16.1. As a mere child, before he could understand what he read, he was charmed with the music of Cicero and the poets. At first his father approved; but when he was sent to study civil law at Montpelier and Bologna, Cicero and the poets, which he kept in hiding, were hunted out and burned. Seven years he wasted at the study of law before his genius for poetry freed itself. In *Fam.* 20.4, he employs the same defensive argument—to each member of society his proper function—as does B. B. reviews his own case at *Corbaccio, Opere Volgare,* ed. Moutier, 5. 185.

15.11

[1] *Ancient kings.* On the euhemeristic theory. See Introd. p. xix.

[2] *Aristotle's Ethics.* "One who is excessively confident in facing fearful things is called foolhardy" (3.10, p. 49, tr. Welldon). Cf. Hortis, p. 380, n. 1.

[3] *Historians.* Livy is the only one much cited. B. appeals to him some half-dozen times, usually on a euhemeristic point. See Hortis, p. 417, n. 3. But B. quite as likely is thinking of Jerome's version of Eusebius' *Chronicon* and perhaps of euhemeristic passages in Lactantius and Augustine, or in Cicero's *De Natura Deorum.*

15.12

[1] B. is ever concerned, as in this chapter, for the articulate order and good proportions of his vast work. See Pref., pp. 6, 11; 14.2, 3, 7; 15.2, 3. Such care is the natural fruit of mediaeval scholastic training and its practice of viewing each detail as a part of one system. Cf. Pref., n.1 on B's relation to Gregory.

[2] *Prolix.* The chapters in *G.D.* vary widely in length. Many contain but two or three lines. Others run to two folio pages or more in Mycellus' edition (1532). These are on Pan, 1.4; the Fates, 1.6; Somnus, 1.31; Dies, 1.34; Venus, 3.22; Prometheus, 4.44; the Giants, 4.68; Orpheus, 5.11; Psyche, 5.22; Bacchus, 5.25; Aeneas, 6.53;

Saturn, 8.1; Ceres, 8.4; Pluto, 8.6; Juno, 9.1; Mars, 9.3; Jupiter III, 11.1; the Muses, 11.2; Ulysses, 11.11; Vulcan, 12.70.

[3] *So huge a tome.* Cf. Pref., pp. 5, 6.

[4] *Labor.* See 14.12.

[5] *Pure delectation.* Doubtless those on Pan, Venus, Prometheus, Orpheus, Psyche, the Muses. Cf. Introd., p. xxix.

[6] *Less educated.* The words leave no doubt that B.'s object was in part the propagation of classical culture, and must qualify the opinion of various critics that his theory is altogether aristocratic and exclusive. See Introd., p. xxxix.

15.13

[1] *Tully*: "Trahimur omnes studio laudis et optimus quisque maxime gloria ducitur" (*Arch.* 26).

[2] *Fame.* B. confesses the same longing in his letter to Pizzinghe (*Lett.* p. 198), and to Pietro di Monteforte (*Lett.* p. 350, where he quotes the passage here cited from Cicero). In 7.59 B. interprets Echo, in the Narcissus myth, as Fame, who "loves each mortal . . . Yet many think little of her, and flee from her, while in the waters of worldly pleasures . . . they behold themselves, that is, their own vainglory." And if any recollection of them survive, it is turned to a flower, which fades after a day into oblivion. But the longing for true fame is that which scorns delights and lives laborious days. Petr. inspired by Cicero, set the humanistic fashion of the hunger for fame. See Voigt, *Wiederbelebung des Class. Alt.* (3rd ed.) 1.123 ff.; Burckhardt, *Renaissance in Italy* 139-53; Riedner, *Typische Aeusserungen der Röm. Dichter*, 71-6.

[3] *Donino.* See Pref.

[4] *Bellincioni . . . met me.* Probably in 1350; see Introd. p. xiii, n. 2. Zenatti cites Manni, *Istoria del Decam.* 1742, for one or two irrelevant details. He finds a stone bearing the name in the cloister of Santa Croce. Bellincioni may have been alive as late as 1367. Cf. n. 6.

[5] *Paul.* See 15.6 and n. 7.

[6] *Alive.* Paul died Feb. 27, 1367. See Hecker, p. 111, n. 3.

[7] *Appeal to you.* Zenatti thinks that the tone of this passage implies with some force that it was written before Hugo died, 1359. Perhaps the first draft was. We know, however, that B. was revising the work as late as 1373; and the closing pages of this chapter somewhat disparaging the dedication to Hugo may very well have been written later.

[8] *A king near by.* Zenatti suggests Jacopo, king of Minorca, who invited B. to spend his old age in that court. Hauvette (p. 426n.) dates the passage ca. 1360, and proposes Louis of Tarentum. But B. preferred impecunious liberty (*Lett.*, pp. 319, 20). In 1363 Jacopo became the third husband of the notorious Queen Joanna, whom B. knew in Naples. Hecker suggests that it was his restless desire for war that drew B.'s comment, "of no particular culture."

⁹ *Familiar with authors.* This whole passage on the necessary alliance of military and political eminence with poetry is based upon the close of Cicero's oration for Archias, which B. has often laid under contribution (14.4, 7, 19, 22; 15.13). The instances of Alexander, etc., here cited are all used by Cicero. From the earliest Renaissance the idea is commonplace. It is elaborated by Petr. in *Africa* 9, in a conversation between Ennius and Scipio:

> Quisquis enim se magna videt gessisse, necesse est,
> Diligat aeternos vates, et carmina sacra.

Zenatti cites also *Inv.* 1, p. 1092; Dante, *Inf.* 31.124-31; 32.91. A *locus classicus* is Tibullus 1.4.65; see K. F. Smith's fine note in his ed., p. 283.The instance of Alexander became a commonplace in critics of the Renaissance; cf. Villey, *Les Sources Italiennes de la Défence de du Bellay,* p. 11.

¹⁰ *Eclogues.* B. refers to his Latin works, as Hecker observes (p. 295, n. 11), pointing out, however, an exception in the *De Claris Mulieribus,* dedicated to Andrea, the sister of Niccolò Acciaiuoli, the great seneschal of Naples, at whom B. later took strong offence. If, as Hauvette suggests, the dedication was made near the end of 1362, with some intention of pleasing Niccolò in anticipation of B.'s joining his household in Naples, what more natural than that B., offended with Niccolò's entertainment, should, when he wrote this passage soon after, deliberately ignore this dedication?

¹¹ *Appenino.* Donato di Lorenzo degli Albanzani, a grammarian, several years younger than Petr. and B., was their enthusiastic and devoted friend. He emended B.'s eclogues and wrote arguments for them (*Ecl.* 16). He translated into Italian B.'s *De Claris Mulieribus* and Petr.'s *De Viris Illustr.* Petr. dedicated to him his *De Ipsius Ignorantia.* In spite of Petr.'s protests, Donato embarrassed him with gifts, but also contracted debts to him, and was poor, for all his grammar. Petr. was devoted to Donato's two sons, and Donato stood godfather to Petr.'s grandson. Petr. describes him as "sweet, *schietto,* lovable, learned" (*Sen.* 3.1, Frac. 1.156), and "good, erudite, and wise, such as Horace would call perfect" (*Sen.* 13.5). See *Sen.* 5.4, 5, 6; 8.6; 10.5, 5; 11.7; 15.9. In later years he served the d'Estes at Ferrara as tutor and chancellor. See Hortis, pp. 600-3; 727-30; F. Novati, *Donato . . . alla Corte Estense* in *Archivio Stor. Ital.* ser. 5, vol. 6 (1890), pp. 365-85.

¹² *Robert.* See 14.9, 11, 22; 15.6. Petr. records the request in his letter to Posterity (Frac. 1.209). B. mentions it in *Lett.* 249.

15.14

¹ *Little craft.* See 14. Pr. n. 6.

² *Perfect gift.* Jas. 1.17.

³ *David's.* Ps. 113.1. Hecker cites the similar close with the same appeal to Petr. in *De Cas.*

INDEX

INDEX

INDEX